Mastering phpMyAdmin 2.11 for Effective MySQL Management

Increase your MySQL productivity and control by discovering the real power of phpMyAdmin 2.11

Marc Delisle

PUBLISHING

BIRMINGHAM - MUMBAI

Mastering phpMyAdmin 2.11 for Effective MySQL Management

First published: March 2008

Production Reference: 1110308

Published by Packt Publishing Ltd.
32 Lincoln Road
Olton
Birmingham, B27 6PA, UK.

ISBN 978-1-847194-18-3

www.packtpub.com

Cover Image by Bruno Abarca (bruno.granada@gmail.com)

Credits

Author

Marc Delisle

Reviewers

Alexander Marcus Turek

Garvin Hicking

Kai "Oswald" Seidler

Acquisition Editor

Rashmi Phadnis

Technical Editor

Ajay Shanker

Editorial Manager

Mithil Kulkarni

Project Manager

Abhijeet Deobhakta

Project Coordinators

Aboli Mendhe

Lata Basantani

Indexer

Monica Ajmera

Proofreader

Cathy Cumberlidge

Production Coordinator

Aparna Bhagat

Cover Work

Aparna Bhagat

About the Author

Marc Delisle is a member of the MySQL Developers Guild—which regroups community developers—because of his involvement with phpMyAdmin. He started to contribute to this popular MySQL web interface in December 1998, when he made the first multi-language version. He has been actively involved with this software project since May 2001 as a developer and project administrator.

Marc has worked since 1980 at Collège de Sherbrooke, Québec, Canada, as an application programmer and network manager. He has also been teaching networking, security, and PHP/MySQL application development. In one of his classes, he was pleased to meet a phpMyAdmin user from Argentina.

Marc lives in Sherbrooke with his wife and they enjoy spending time with their four children.

This book is Marc's first one, and was followed by "Creating your MySQL Database: Practical Design Tips and Techniques", also with Packt Publishing.

I am truly grateful to Louay Fatoohi who approached me for this book project, and to the Packt team whose sound comments were greatly appreciated during the production. My thanks also go to Garvin Hicking, Alexander Marcus Turek, and Kai 'Oswald' Seidler, the reviewers for the successive editions of this book. Their sharp eyes helped in making this book clearer and more complete.

Finally, I wish to thank all contributors to phpMyAdmin's source code, translations, and documentation; the time they gave to this project still inspires me and continues to push me forward.

To Carole, André, Corinne, Annie, and Guillaume, with all my love.

About the Reviewers

Garvin Hicking is a German webdeveloper working for Faktor E GmbH. He creates web applications using PHP, MySQL, and in his free time enjoys to work on OpenSource-projects like phpMyAdmin or Serendipity. At times when he's away from the computer, he likes going to the movies with his girlfriend and friends, or taking pictures.

Alexander Marcus Turek was born on June 2nd, 1984 in Düsseldorf, the capital of the German province Northrhine-Westphalia. Currently, he's studying Information Engineering and Management at the University of Karlsruhe, but his origin is Mülheim an der Ruhr, the home of his family. He first got in touch with the Web in 1998, when he won a 28.8k modem at the CeBit Home in Hannover, Germany. A few months later, he learned HTML and started his first Web project, a German game patch archive called Rabus' Update Site, which he renamed to bugfixes.info, when the .info domains became available. In the meantime, he switched from static HTML to PHP in order to be able to manage the growing archive more efficiently. He kept on learning PHP when trying to extend the portal.

Because the flatfile-based database system became too slow when searching the still growing archive, he also switched to MySQL in 2001. This is when he got in touch with phpMyAdmin and the project. He started with revising its language files because they were a bit outdated and inconsistent. He had fun doing so, and continued with grabbing some bug reports and submitting patches for them. Loïc Chapeaux, one of the two co-maintainers at that time, added him to the developers list and gave him a CVS account in March 2002, so he could merge his patches by himself. Since then, he has mainly worked on the compatibility with MySQL 4.0, reworked the server administration area, developed a simple abstraction layer in order to support MySQLi, and continued with compatibility fixing—this time for MySQL 4.1 and 5.0. Unfortunately, his studies and phpMyAdmin became too time consuming, and he had to stop working on bugfixes.info in 2003.

Kai "Oswald" Seidler was born in Hamburg in 1970. He graduated from Technical University of Berlin with a Diplom Informatiker degree (Master of Science equivalent) in Computer Science. In the 90's he created and managed Germany's biggest IRCnet server irc.fu-berlin.de, and co-managed one of the world's largest anonymous FTP server ftp.cs.tu-berlin.de.

He professionally set up his first public web server in 1993. From 1993 until 1998 he was member of Projektgruppe Kulturraum Internet, a research project on net culture and network organization. 2002, he co-founded Apache Friends and created the multi-platform Apache web server bundle XAMPP. Around 2005 XAMPP became the most popular Apache stack worldwide.

In 2006, his third book, Das XAMPP-Handbuch, was published by Addison Wesley.

Table of Contents

Preface

Providing a powerful graphical interface for managing MySQL, phpMyAdmin is one of the most popular open source applications. While most MySQL developers use routine features of phpMyAdmin every day, few are aware of the power and potential of its advanced features. This book builds a solid understanding of the core capabilities of phpMyAdmin before walking you through every facet of this legendary tool.

Used by millions of developers, MySQL is the most popular open source database, supporting numerous large dynamic websites and applications. MySQL has acquired this wide popularity by virtue of its open source nature, performance, reliability, robustness, and support for various platforms. However, this popularity has also been helped by the existence of phpMyAdmin, the industry standard administration tool that makes database management easy for both the experienced developer and their novice.

The powerful graphical interface that it provides to MySQL has made phpMyAdmin an indispensable tool for MySQL and web developers. Every phpMyAdmin user can benefit from unlocking the full potential of this powerful application.

What This Book Covers

Chapter 1 will take a look at how the Web has evolved as a means to deliver applications and why we should use PHP/MySQL to develop these applications. We'll also take a look at how phpMyAdmin is recognized as a leading application to interface MySQL from the Web, the history of phpMyAdmin, and a brief list of its features.

Chapter 2 will take a look at the common reasons for installing phpMyAdmin, the steps for downloading it from the main site, the basic configuration, and uploading it to our web server. We will also learn how to use a single copy of phpMyAdmin to manage multiple servers, and the usage of authentication types to fulfill the needs of a users' group while protecting authentication credentials.

Chapter 3 will take a look at the phpMyAdmin interface in detail.

Chapter 4 will cover how to create a database and tables, and how to enter data, manually, in the tables. We'll also see how to confirm the presence of data by using the browse mode; including the SQL query links, navigation bar, sorting options, and row marking.

Chapter 5 will examine concepts like editing data, including the null field and using the *Tab* key, applying a function to a value, duplicating rows of data, and deleting data, tables, and databases.

Chapter 6 will cover how to add fields, including special field types like TEXT, BLOB, ENUM, and SET, how to use a calendar popup for DATE, DATETIME, and TIMESTAMP fields, and how to upload binary data into a BLOB field. We'll also see how to manage indexes (multi-field and full-text) and get feedback from MySQL about which indexes are used in a specific query.

Chapter 7 will examine the various ways to trigger an export: from the Database view, the Table view, or a results page. We'll also take a look at the various available export formats, their options, the possibility of compressing the export file, and the various places where it might be sent.

Chapter 8 will look at the various options in phpMyAdmin that allow us to import data, the different mechanisms involved in importing SQL and CSV files, the limits that we might hit when trying a transfer, and ways to bypass these limits.

Chapter 9 will cover single-table searches with query by example criteria and additional criteria specification, selecting displayed values, and ordering results. We'll also look at wildcard searches and full database search.

Chapter 10 will cover the operations we can perform on whole tables or databases. We'll take a look at table maintenance operations for table repair and optimization, changing various table attributes, table movements, including renaming and moving to another database, and multi-table operations.

Chapter 11 will take a look at the installation of the necessary infrastructure for keeping special metadata (data about tables), and we'll learn how to define relations between both InnoDB and non-InnoDB tables. We'll also examine the modified behavior of phpMyAdmin when relations are present, foreign keys, getting information from the table, the Designer feature, and column-commenting.

Chapter 12 will take a look at the purpose of query boxes and where they can be found. We'll also look at query window options, multi-statement queries, how to use the field selector, how to use the SQL Validator, and how to get a history of the typed commands.

Chapter 13 will cover various aspects such as opening the query generator, choosing tables, entering column criteria, sorting and showing columns, and altering the number of criteria rows or columns. We'll also see how to use the AND and OR operators to define relations between rows and columns, and how to use automatic joins between tables.

Chapter 14 will take a look at how to record bookmarks (after or before sending a query), how to manipulate them, and how some bookmarks can be made public. We'll learn about the default initial query for **Browse** mode. We'll also see passing parameters to bookmarks and executing bookmarks directly from the **pma_bookmark** table.

Chapter 15 will cover the documentation features offered by phpMyAdmin—the print view for a database or a table, and the data dictionary for a complete column list. We'll also see PDF relational schemas.

Chapter 16 will examine how we can improve the browsing experience by transforming data using various methods. We'll see thumbnail and full-size images of .jpeg and .png **BLOB** fields, generate links, format dates, display only parts of texts, and execute external programs to reformat each cell's contents.

Chapter 17 will cover the use of language files in phpMyAdmin. We'll look at UTF-8 and the impact of switching from one character set to another. We also see how phpMyAdmin has to recode data when the version of MySQL is earlier than 4.1.x, and take a look at the character set and collation features of MySQL version 4.1.x and later.

Chapter 18 will cover how phpMyAdmin permits to manage the main features of MySQL 5.0.

Chapter 19 will discuss how a system administrator can use the phpMyAdmin server management features for day-to-day user account maintenance, server verification, and server protection.

Chapter 20 proposes guidelines for solving some common problems, and gives hints on how to avoid them. It also explains how to interact with the development team for support, bug reports, and contributions.

What You Need for This Book

You need to have access to a server or workstation that has the following installed:

- My SQL
- PHP
- Apache or IIS.

Conventions

In this book, you will find a number of styles of text that distinguish between different kinds of information. Here are some examples of these styles, and an explanation of their meaning.

There are three styles for code. Code words in text are shown as follows: "We can include other contexts through the use of the `include` directive."

A block of code will be set as follows:

```
$cfg['RestrictColumnTypes'] = array(
      'VARCHAR'        => 'FUNC_CHAR',   [...]
$cfg['RestrictFunctions'] = array(
      'FUNC_CHAR'     => array(
```

When we wish to draw your attention to a particular part of a code block, the relevant lines or items will be made bold:

```
'alpha_columnType'   => '#FF9900',
'alpha_columnAttrib' => '#0000FF',
'alpha_reservedWord' => '#990099',
'alpha_functionName' => '#FF0000',
```

New terms and **important words** are introduced in a bold-type font. Words that you see on the screen, in menus or dialog boxes for example, appear in our text like this: "clicking the **Next** button moves you to the next screen".

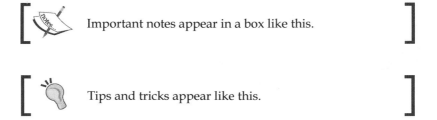

Important notes appear in a box like this.

Tips and tricks appear like this.

Reader Feedback

Feedback from our readers is always welcome. Let us know what you think about this book, what you liked or may have disliked. Reader feedback is important for us to develop titles that you really get the most out of.

To send us general feedback, simply drop an email to `feedback@packtpub.com`, making sure you mention the book title in the subject of your message.

If there is a book that you need and would like to see us publish, please send us a note in the **SUGGEST A TITLE** form on www.packtpub.com or email suggest@packtpub.com.

If there is a topic that you have expertise in and you are interested in either writing or contributing to a book, see our author guide on www.packtpub.com/authors.

Customer Support

Now that you are the proud owner of a Packt book, we have a number of things to help you to get the most from your purchase.

Downloading the Example Code for the Book

Visit http://www.packtpub.com/files/code/4183_Code.zip, to directly downlad the example code.

The downloadable files contain instructions on how to use them.

Errata

Although we have taken every care to ensure the accuracy of our contents, mistakes do happen. If you find a mistake in one of our books—maybe a mistake in text or code—we would be grateful if you would report this to us. By doing this you can save other readers from frustration, and help to improve subsequent versions of this book. If you find any errata, report them by visiting http://www.packtpub.com/support, selecting your book, clicking on the **Submit Errata** link, and entering the details of your errata. Once your errata are verified, your submission will be accepted and the errata are added to the list of existing errata. The existing errata can be viewed by selecting your title from http://www.packtpub.com/support.

Questions

You can contact us at questions@packtpub.com if you are having a problem with some aspect of the book, and we will do our best to address it.

Introducing phpMyAdmin

1

Welcome to the evolved Web! In the last few years, the Web has changed dramatically. In its infancy, the Web was a medium used mainly to convey *static* information ("Look, my home page is on the Web!"). Now, large parts of the Web carry information that is *dynamically generated* by application programs, on which enterprises and even individuals rely for their intranets and public websites.

Because of the clear benefits of databases (better accessibility and structuring of information), web applications are mostly database driven. The front-end used is the well known (and quickly deployed) web browser, and there is a database system at the back-end. Application programs provide the interface between the browser and the database.

Those who are not operating a database-driven website today are not using the medium to its fullest capability. Also, they could be lagging behind competitors who have made the switch. So it is not a question of whether we *should* implement a database-driven site, but it is more about *when* and mostly *how* to implement it.

Why web applications? They improve user experience and involve them in the process by opening up possibilities such as:

- Gathering feedback about the site
- Letting users communicate with us and with each other through forums
- Ordering goods from our e-commerce site
- Enabling easily editable web-based information (content management)
- Designing and maintaining databases from the Web

Nowadays, WWW might stand for **World-Wide Wave**, a big wave that profoundly modifies the way developers think about user interface, data presentation, and most of all, the way data reaches users and comes back to the data center.

PHP and MySQL: The Leading Open-Source Duo

This chapter describes the place of phpMyAdmin in the context of PHP/MySQL, explains phpMyAdmin's history, and summarizes its features. Let us look at the solutions currently offered by host providers. The most prevalent is the PHP/MySQL combination.

Well-supported by their respective home sites, http://www.php.net and http://www.mysql.com, this duo has enabled developers to offer a lot of ready-made open-source web applications, and most importantly, enabled in-house developers to quickly put in place solid web solutions.

MySQL, which is mostly compliant with the SQL:2003 standard, is a database system well known for its speed, robustness, and small connection overhead, which is important in a web context where pages must be served as quickly as possible.

PHP, usually installed as a module inside the web server, is a popular scripting language in which applications are written to communicate with MySQL (or other database systems) on the back-end, and browsers on the front-end. Ironically, the acronym's signification has evolved itself along with the Web evolution, from **Personal Home Page** to **Professional Home Page** to its current recursive definition: **PHP: Hypertext Processor**. A reference about the successive name changes can be seen in PHP's source code itself at http://cvs.php.net/viewvc.cgi/php3/CHANGES?r1=1.23&r2=1.24. Available on millions of Web domains, PHP drives its own wave of quickly developed applications.

What is phpMyAdmin?

phpMyAdmin is a web application written in PHP and contains — like most web applications — XHTML, CSS, and JavaScript client code. It provides a complete web interface to administering MySQL databases and is widely recognized as the leading application in this field.

Being open source since the start of its existence, it has enjoyed support from numerous developers and translators world wide (being translated into 54 languages at the time of going to press). The project is currently hosted on SourceForge.

Host providers everywhere are showing their trust in phpMyAdmin (official home page at `http://www.phpmyadmin.net`) by installing it on their servers. In addition, we can install our own copy of phpMyAdmin inside our web space, as long as our provider respects the minimum requirements — see in Chapter 2 the *System Requirements* section. The popular Cpanel (a website control application) interfaces with phpMyAdmin.

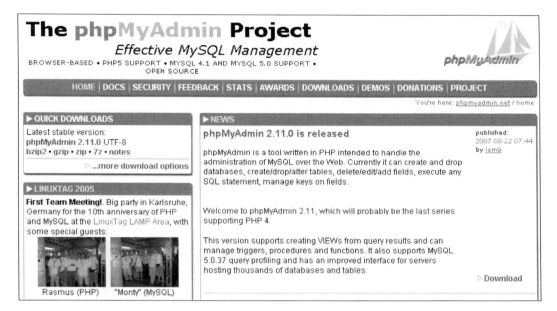

History

The first internal version (0.9.0) was coded by Tobias Ratschiller and bears the date 1998-09-09. He then released version 1.0.1 on 1998-10-26. The early versions were offered on Tobias's site: `http://www.phpwizard.net`. (This site is no longer associated with him.) Tobias wrote in the accompanying notes:

"This work is based on Peter Kuppelwieser's MySQL-Webadmin. It was his idea to create a web-based interface to MySQL using PHP3. Although I have not used any of his source-code, there are some concepts I've borrowed from him. phpMyAdmin was created because Peter told me he wasn't going to further develop his (great) tool."

Compared to today's version (nine years after the original), the first version was somewhat limited in features but could nonetheless be used to create databases and tables, edit their structure, and enter and retrieve data. Notice in the figure that follows that the left panel was already there to list database names (not table names yet), and the right panel was the workspace to manage a database or table. This is what the interface for databases looked like in version 1.3.0:

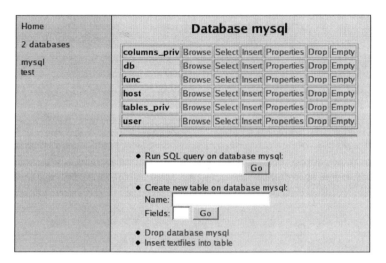

To work on a table, you had the following screen:

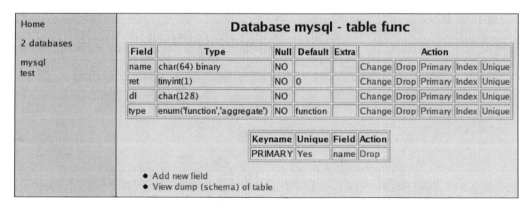

I started using phpMyAdmin at version 1.2.0 (released 1998-11-29) and was immediately hooked on the idea of being able to use a web application to maintain a remote database. However, students at Collège de Sherbrooke, where I work in Québec, Canada, are French-speaking folks, so I contacted Tobias and offered to transform his source code by outsourcing all messages in a message file. He accepted the offer and I created the English and the French message files. Then, on 1998-12-27, Tobias released version 1.3.1, the first multi-language version. (Meanwhile, he had managed to create the German message file.)

In 1999 and the first half of 2000, Tobias improved the navigation system, added features, and merged more language files. His project site maintained a discussion forum, so new ideas came along and patches were discussed. Version 2.1.0 was released on 2000-08-06, which was the last version released by Tobias, who had no more time to devote to this project.

However, users were already numerous and asked more of the product. Patches were floating on the Internet, with no way of coordinating them. A security alert (and fix) had been published by a third party, but no new version was being released. On 2001-03-31, Olivier Müller registered the phpMyAdmin project on `SourceForge.net`, and released a 2.2.0pre1 version. At this time, this was called the *unofficial* version. This restart of the project attracted some developers, who now had the SourceForge infrastructure (CVS server, forums, bug trackers, mailing lists) to help speed up the development. I personally "re-joined" the project in May 2001 and started fixing and improving the code, as my co-developers were doing.

We became "official" on 2001-05-28, as Tobias accepted our version as the new official one. I remember those months of very intense development effort, with daily improvements and bug fixes, along with new documentation sections. This effort culminated on 2001-08-31 with the release of version 2.2.0.

Here's an excerpt from the announcement file for 2.2.0:

"After 5 months, 5 beta releases, and 4 release candidate versions, the phpMyAdmin developers are pleased to announce the availability of phpMyAdmin 2.2.0. [...] on 31st March 2001, Olivier Müller (Switzerland), supported by Marc Delisle (Québec), Loïc Chapeaux (France) and a team of 8 other developers re-started the phpmyadmin project on SourceForge. net, with the authorization of the original package maintainer. Now, after 5 months of patches, bug fixes, new features and testing, the version 2.2.0 is finally ready."

This version had security fixes, seven new languages (with dynamic language-detection), and the code had been reworked to be CSS2 and XHTML 1.0 compliant, and follow the PEAR coding guidelines. The bookmarks feature appeared in this version—this came from a separate add-on called "phpMyBookmark".

During the following year, the development continued with the release of seven minor versions. The last version of the 2.2.x series is 2.2.7-pl1, which is also the last to have been fully tested under PHP 3. A date to note: 2002-04-03; we registered `phpmyadmin.net` as the official domain name for the project.

On 2002-08-11, version 2.3.0 was released. There had been so many new features that the pages were getting vertically too big, so this version was the "great split version", displaying sub-pages for each table and database group of features.

The team started a new schedule of releasing a new minor version (2.3.1, 2.3.2 ...) every two months. On 2003-02-23, version 2.4.0 included a new server/user management facility. Then on 2003-05-11, version number jumped to 2.5.0 to mark the new MIME-type cell transformation system.

Version 2.6.0 — released on 2004-09-27 — added support for the new `mysqli` extension available in PHP 5 for better performance and improved security. The interface for this version has been redesigned, including new icons and a theme manager. All these features are explained in this book. On 2005-04-16, version 2.6.2 was born, adding basic support for MySQL's **VIEW**s.

In June 2005, the first meeting of phpMyAdmin's development team took place in Karlsruhe, Germany during LinuxTag 2005. Six members of the team from Switzerland, Germany, Czech Republic, and Canada were present, displaying phpMyAdmin and discussing its features with the event's attendees. We also celebrated PHP's and MySQL's tenth anniversary on the same occasion.

On 2005-12-04, version 2.7.0 was released. With this version, we ended support for older configuration files — those before phpMyAdmin 2.3.0. Also, in 2.7.0 a new plug-in-based import module made its debut.

Version 2.8.0 was made available on 2006-03-06. It included a new web-based setup mechanism. With 2.8.0 the team started a new numbering scheme for version releases. The 2.8 family contains only fixes for the features already present in 2.8.0. Thus, after 2.8.0, here are some examples of the versions that can be released:

- 2.8.0.1, for anything urgent like a security fix
- 2.8.1, containing normal fixes for the 2.8 family
- 2.9.0, with new features

Version 2.9.0, released on 2006-09-20, added many small improvements like a font size selector, new export formats, and the possibility of using an external authentication method. On 2007-02-27, version 2.10.0's main attraction was the Designer, a new graphical Ajax-based relation manager. Version 2.11.0, released on 2007-08-21, offered support for creating views and for managing procedures, functions, and triggers.

In 2007, phpMyAdmin continues to be popular; the cumulative downloads since April 2001 have reached an impressive count of more than 14 million in September 2007 at the time of press.

Awards

phpMyAdmin has won some awards, as can be seen in the Awards section of the project's home page. First, it was awarded "Project of the Month" for December 2002 by the administrators of SourceForge. In the interview-style document we prepared to put on the SourceForge POTM page, I wrote that I was impressed by the download rate of our product, which was three per minute at that time. (Since then we have reached ten per minute on peak days.)

phpMyAdmin received 75% of the votes from the readers of both the German *PHP Magazin* and its international version, in the category "Best PHP Application/Tool" for 2003. This award was officially presented at the International PHP Conference held at Frankfurt in November 2003 to two members of the team. The German *PHP Magazin* hosted the readers choice again in 2005 and 2006; phpMyAdmin won for both years in the same category.

SourceForge.net hosted its *Community Choice Awards* for the first time in 2006 and phpMyAdmin won in two categories: Databases and System Administration. I represented the team at LinuxWorld, Boston in April for the awards presentation. The project also won "Best PHP Application of the Year" at the fifth Annual OS/2 World Awards. At the end of 2006, our project won a Silver Trophy at the third *Trophées du Libre* contest; I went to France to receive the trophy.

In 2007, at the SourceForge.net *Community Choice Awards*, phpMyAdmin was nominated in the "Best Tool or Utility for Developers" category, and won the "Best Tool or Utility for SysAdmins" award.

phpMyAdmin Features Summary

The goal of phpMyAdmin is to offer complete web-based management of MySQL servers and data, and to keep up with MySQL and web standards evolution. While the product is not perfect, it currently includes the most commonly requested features and lots of extra features as well.

The development team constantly develops the product based on the reported bugs and requested features, regularly releasing new versions.

phpMyAdmin offers features that cover basic MySQL database and table operations. It also has an internal relational system that maintains metadata to support advanced features. Finally, system administrators can manage users and privileges from phpMyAdmin. It is important to note that phpMyAdmin's choice of available operations depends on the rights the user has on a specific MySQL server.

The basic features consist of:

- Database creation, deletion, renaming, and attribute change
- Table creation, renaming, copying, and deletion
- Table structure maintenance, including indexes
- Special table operations (repair, optimization, changing type)
- Data insertion, modification, deletion
- Data display in horizontal/vertical mode, and Print view
- Data navigation and sorting
- Binary data uploading
- Data search (table or database)
- Querying by example (multi-table)
- Batch-loading of data (import)
- Exporting structure and data in various formats, with compression
- Multi-user and multi-server installation with web-based setup

The advanced features include:

- Field-level comments
- Foreign keys (with or without InnoDB)
- Browse foreign table
- Bookmarks of queries
- Data dictionary
- PDF relational schema and dictionary
- SQL queries history
- Connection to MySQL using either the traditional `mysql` extension or the new `mysqli` extension (in PHP 5)
- Character-set support for databases, tables, and fields (with MySQL 4.1)
- Column contents transformation based on MIME type
- Visual Designer for relations
- Support for MySQL 5.0 features: views, procedures, triggers, profiling
- **Theme management to customize the interface's look**

The server administration features consist of:

- User and privileges management
- Database privileges check
- Verify server's runtime information and obtain configuration hints
- Full server export

Summary

In this chapter, we saw how the Web has evolved as a means to deliver applications and why we should use PHP/MySQL to develop these applications. We also took a look at how phpMyAdmin is recognized as a leading application to interface MySQL from the Web, the history of phpMyAdmin, and a brief list of its features.

2
Installing phpMyAdmin

It's time to install the product and to configure it minimally for first-time use.

Our reason for installing phpMyAdmin could be one of the following:

- Our host provider did not install a central copy.
- Our provider installed it, but the version installed is not current.
- We are working directly on our enterprise's web server.

Some host providers offer an integrated web panel where we can manage accounts, including MySQL accounts, and also a file manager that can be used to upload web content. Depending on this, the mechanism we use to transfer phpMyAdmin to our web space will vary. We will need some specific information before starting the installation:

- The web server's name or address. Here, we will assume it is `www.mydomain.com`.
- Our web server's account information (username, password), which will be used either for FTP or SFTP transfer, SSH login, or web control panel login.
- The MySQL server's name or address. Often this is `localhost`, which means it is located on the same machine as the web server. We will assume this to be `mysql.mydomain.com`.
- Our MySQL server's account information (username, password).

System Requirements

The up-to-date requirements for a specific phpMyAdmin version are always stated in the accompanying `Documentation.html`. For phpMyAdmin 2.11, the minimum PHP version required is PHP 4.1.0 with **session** support. Moreover, the web server must have access to a MySQL server (version 3.23.32 or later) — either locally or on a remote machine. It is strongly recommended that the PHP **mcrypt** extension be present for improved performance in cookie authentication mode — more on this later in the chapter. In fact, on a 64-bit server, this extension is required.

On the browser side, cookie support must be activated, whatever authentication mode we use.

GoPHP5

phpMyAdmin is part of the GoPHP5 initiative — see `http://GoPHP5.org`. This means that the new feature releases of phpMyAdmin after 2008-02-05 will require a server running at least PHP 5.2.

This initiative promotes the adoption of PHP 5 among web hosts.

Downloading the Files

There are various files available in the **Downloads** section of `http://www.phpmyadmin.net`. There might be more than one version offered here; always download the latest stable version. We only need to download one file, which works regardless of the platform (browser, web server, MySQL, or PHP version). For the 2.11.0 version, there are three groups of files — `english`, `all-languages-utf-8-only`, and `all-languages`. If we only need the English interface, we can download a file containing "english", for example `phpMyAdmin-2.11.0-english.zip`. On the other hand, if we have the need for at least one other language, a choice containing "all-languages-utf-8-only" would be appropriate. Finally, on servers previous to MySQL 4.1, a file name containing "all-languages" (without the "utf-8-only" mention) that contains all character sets for all languages would be the best choice.

If we are using a server supporting only PHP3, the latest stable version of phpMyAdmin is not a good choice to download. I recommend using version 2.2.7-pl1, which is the latest version that supports PHP3. Thus we will have to download a file with .php3 in its name. These older files are available by following the **get older versions** link on the same **Downloads** section. In this case, while following the present instructions, we will have to transpose to .php3 each time we talk about `.php` files.

The files offered have various extensions: .zip, .tar.bz2, .tar.gz, .7z. Download a file with an extension for which you have the corresponding extractor. .zip is the most universal file format in the Windows world, although it is bigger than .gz or .bz2 (common in the Linux/Unix world). In the following examples, we will assume that the chosen file was phpMyAdmin-2.11.0-all-languages-utf-8-only.zip.

After clicking on the appropriate file, we will have to choose the nearest mirror. The file will start to download, and we can save it on our computer.

Installation

The next step depends on the platform you are using; the coming sections detail the procedure for some common platforms. You should proceed directly to the relevant section.

Installation on a Remote Server Using a Windows Client

Using the File explorer, we double-click the phpMyAdmin-2.11.0-all-languages-utf-8-only.zip file we just downloaded on the Windows machine; a file extractor should start, showing us all the scripts and directories inside a main phpMyAdmin-2.11.0-all-languages-utf-8-only directory, as shown in the following screenshot, using the **7-Zip File Manager**:

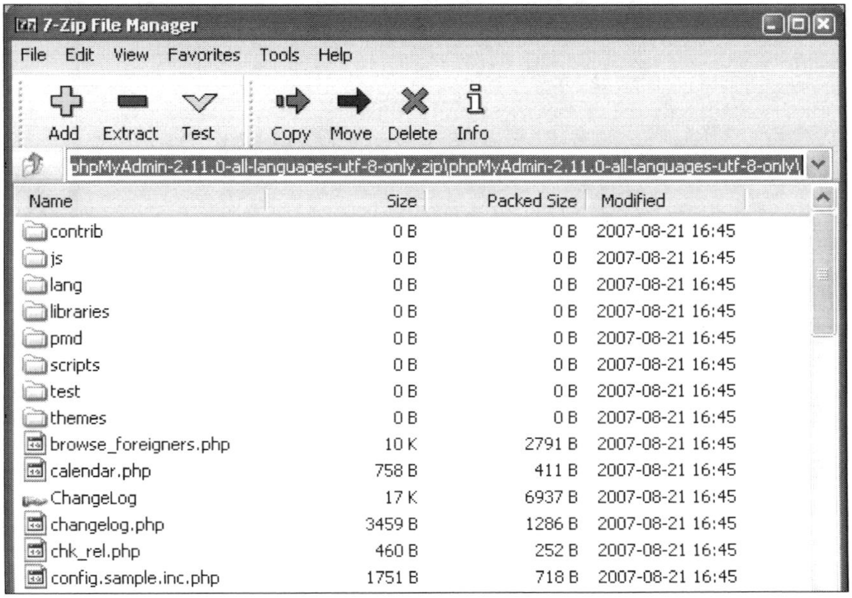

Use whatever mechanism your file extractor offers to save all the files, including subdirectories, to some location on your workstation. Here, we have chosen `c:\`, so a `c:\phpMyAdmin-2.11.0-all-languages-utf-8-only` directory has been created for extraction.

Now it's time to transfer the whole directory structure `c:\phpMyAdmin-2.11.0-all-languages-utf-8-only` to the web server in our web space. We use our favorite FTP software or the web control panel for the transfer.

The exact directory under which we transfer phpMyAdmin may vary: It could be our `public_html` directory or another directory where we usually transfer web documents. For further instructions about the exact directory to be used or the best way to transfer the directory structure, we can consult our host provider's help desk.

After the transfer is complete, these files are no longer needed on our Windows client, so we can remove them.

Installation on a Local Linux Server

Let's say we chose `phpMyAdmin-2.11.0-all-languages-utf-8-only.tar.gz` and downloaded it directly to some directory on the Linux server. We move it to our web server's document root directory (for example, `/var/www/html`) or to one of its subdirectories (for example, `/var/www/html/utilities`). Then we extract it with the following shell command or by using any graphical file extractor our window manager offers:

```
tar -xzvf phpMyAdmin-2.11.0-all-languages-utf-8-only.tar.gz
```

We ensure that the permissions and ownership of the directory and files are appropriate for our web server; the web server user or group must be able to read them.

Installation on Local Windows Servers (Apache, IIS)

The procedure here is similar to that described in the *Installation on a Remote Server Using a Windows Client* section, except that the target directory will be under our `DocumentRoot` (for Apache) or our `wwwroot` (for IIS). Of course, we do not need to transfer anything after the modifications of `config.inc.php`, as the directory is already on the web space.

Apache is usually run as a service, so we have to ensure that the user under which the service is running has normal read privileges to access our newly created directory. The same principle applies to IIS, which uses the **IUSR_machinename** user. This user *must* have read access to the directory. You can adjust permissions in the **Security/permissions** tab of the directory's properties.

First Connection Configuration

Here we learn how to prepare and use the configuration file which contains the parameters to connect to MySQL, and which can be customized as per our requirements. In this chapter, we will concentrate on the parameters that deal with connection and authentication. Other parameters will be discussed in the chapters where the corresponding features are explained.

Before configuring, we can rename the directory phpMyAdmin-2.11.0-all-languages-utf-8-only to something easier to remember, like phpMyAdmin, phpmyadmin, admin, or whatever. This way, we or our users will be able to visit an easily remembered URL to start phpMyAdmin. We can also use a symbolic link if our server supports this feature.

Configuration Principles

In versions before 2.8.0, a generic config.inc.php file was included in the downloaded kit. Since 2.8.0, this file is no longer present in the directory structure. Note that phpMyAdmin looks for this file in the first level directory—the same one where index.php is located.

Without a configuration file, phpMyAdmin uses its default settings as defined in libraries/config.default.php and tries to connect to a MySQL server on localhost, the same machine where the web server is running, with user root and password NO. This is the default setup produced by most MySQL installation procedures, even though it is not really secure. However, if our freshly installed MySQL server still has the default root account, we will be able to login easily and see a warning given by phpMyAdmin about such lack of security.

We can verify this fact by opening our browser and visiting http://www.mydomain.com/phpmyadmin—substituting the proper values for the domain part and the directory part. If we see phpMyAdmin's home page—as described in Chapter 3—it means the MySQL server is still configured by default.

If it's not the case, we should see these messages in the default language defined in our browser:

Error. MySQL said: Access denied for 'root'@'@localhost' (password: NO)

Probably reason of this is, that you did not create configuration file. You might want to use setup script to create one.

At this point we have two choices:

- Use the web-based setup script to generate a `config.inc.php` file
- Manually create a `config.inc.php` file

These options are presented in the following sections. We should note that even if we use the web-based setup script, we should familiarize ourselves with the `config.inc.php` file format, because the setup script does not cover all the possible configuration options.

Web-Based Setup Script

The web-based setup mechanism is strongly recommended in order to avoid syntax errors that could result from the manual creation of the configuration file. Indeed, since this file must respect PHP's syntax, it's common for new users to experience problems in this phase of the installation.

 A warning is in order here: even if phpMyAdmin contains translations for the user interface, the current version does not have a translation for the setup itself.

To access the setup script, we can click on the link available in the message we received previously, which points to `http://www.mydomain.com/phpmyadmin/scripts/setup.php`. The following screenshot shows what appears on the initial execution:

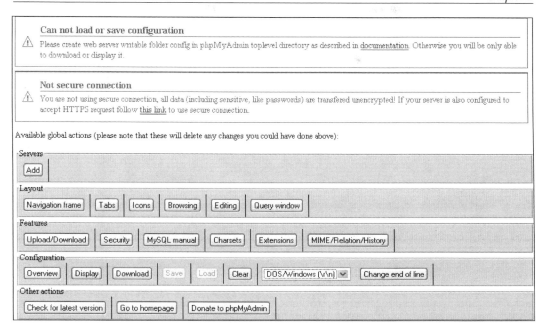

There are two warnings here. We will first deal with the second one—**Not secure connection**. This message appears if we are accessing the web server over HTTP, an insecure protocol. As we are possibly going to input confidential information like the user name and password in the setup phase, it's recommended to communicate over HTTPS at least for this phase. HTTPS uses SSL (Secure Socket Layer) to encrypt the communication and make eavesdropping impossible on the line. If our web server supports HTTPS, we can simply follow the proposed link, which will restart the setup process—this time over HTTPS. Our example supposes we do so.

The first warning tells us that phpMyAdmin did not find a writable directory with the name config and this is normal as it was not present in the downloaded kit. As the directory is not yet there, we observe that the **Save** and **Load** buttons in the interface are grey. In this config directory, we can:

- Save the working version of the configuration file during the setup process
- Load a previously prepared config.inc.php file

It's not absolutely necessary that we create this configuration directory, because we could download to our client machine the config.inc.php file produced by the setup procedure, then upload it to phpMyAdmin in the first-level directory via the same mechanism (say FTP) that we used to upload phpMyAdmin itself. However, we'll nonetheless create this directory.

The principle here is that the web server must be able to write to this directory. There is more than one way to achieve this. Here is one that would work on a Linux server (adding read, write, and execute permissions for everyone on this directory):

```
cd phpMyAdmin
mkdir config
chmod o+rwx config
```

Having done that, we refresh the page in our browser and we see:

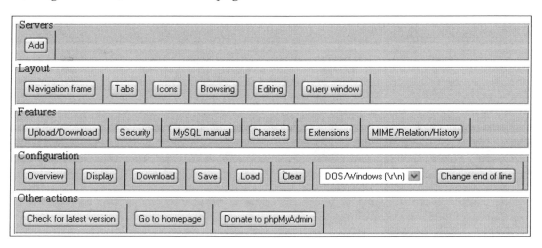

In the configuration dialog, a drop-down menu permits to choose the proper end-of-line format, according to the platform on which we plan to later open `config.inc.php` with a text editor.

A single copy of phpMyAdmin can be used to manage many MySQL servers. We will now define parameters describing our first MySQL server. In the **Servers** section, we click **Add** and the following screen is shown:

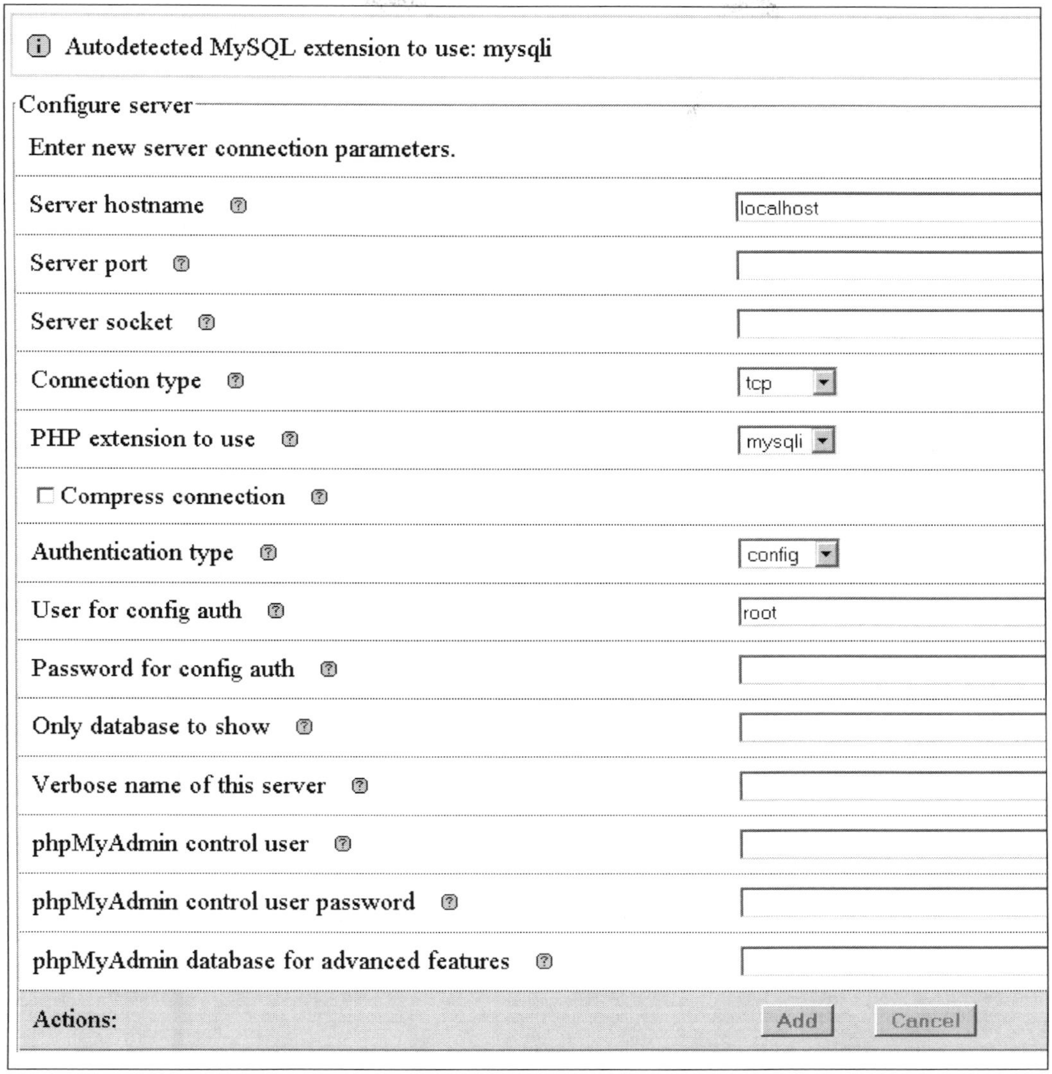

(i) Autodetected MySQL extension to use: mysqli

Configure server

Enter new server connection parameters.

Server hostname ⑦	localhost
Server port ⑦	
Server socket ⑦	
Connection type ⑦	tcp ▾
PHP extension to use ⑦	mysqli ▾
☐ Compress connection ⑦	
Authentication type ⑦	config ▾
User for config auth ⑦	root
Password for config auth ⑦	
Only database to show ⑦	
Verbose name of this server ⑦	
phpMyAdmin control user ⑦	
phpMyAdmin control user password ⑦	
phpMyAdmin database for advanced features ⑦	

| Actions: | Add | Cancel |

A complete explanation of these parameters can be found in the following sections
of this chapter and in Chapter 11. For now, we notice that the setup process has
detected that PHP supports the mysqli extension, so this is the one that is chosen
by default. This extension is the programming library used by PHP to communicate
with MySQL.

Let's enter the minimum parameters required for a first connection. We assume that our MySQL server is located on localhost, so we keep this value and all the proposed values intact, except for the following:

- **User for config auth**: we enter our user name, **marc**
- **Password for config auth**: we enter our password, **bingo**

We then click **Add**, and we get the **New server added** message. Now our setup process knows about one MySQL server, and there are sections of the interface that enable us to **Edit** or **Delete** these server settings:

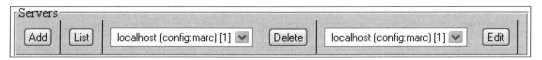

We can have a look at the generated configuration lines by using the **Configuration/ Display** button—then we can analyze these parameters using the explanations given in *The config.inc.php File* section later in this chapter.

At this point, this configuration is still just in memory, so we need to save it. This is done via the **Configuration/Save** button. It saves `config.inc.php` in the special `config` directory we created previously. This is a directory strictly used for configuration purposes.

The last step is to copy `config.inc.php` from the `config` directory to the top-level directory—the one that contains `index.php`. By copying this file, it becomes owned by the user instead of the web server, ensuring that further modifications are possible. This copy can be done via FTP or by commands such as:

```
cd config
cp config.inc.php ..
```

 As a security measure, it's recommended to change the permission on the `config` directory—for example, with the `chmod ugo-rwx config` command. This is to block any non-authorized writing in this directory.

Other configuration parameters can be set with these web-based setup pages. To do so, we would have to:

1. Enable read and write access to the `config` directory
2. Copy the `config.inc.php` there
3. Ensure that read and write access are provided to this file for the web server
4. Start the web-based setup tool

In order to keep this book's text lighter, we will only refer to the parameters' textual values in the following chapters.

Manual Creation of config.inc.php

We can create this text file from scratch using our favorite text editor. The exact procedure depends upon which client operating system we are using; we can refer to the *Tips for Editing config.inc.php on a Windows Client* section (below) for further information.

The default value of all the possible configuration parameters that can be located inside `config.inc.php` is defined in `libraries/config.default.php`. We can take a look at this file to see the syntax used and further comments about configuration. See the important note about this file in the *Upgrading phpMyAdmin* section of this chapter.

Tips for Editing config.inc.php on a Windows Client

This file contains special characters (Unix-style end of lines), so we must open it with a text editor that understands this format. If we use the wrong text editor, the file will be displayed with very long lines.

The best choice is a standard PHP editor. Another choice would be **WordPad**, **MetaPad** or **UltraEdit**, but we should be careful not to add any characters (even blank lines) at the beginning or end of the file. This would disturb the execution of phpMyAdmin and generate the **Cannot send header output...** error message. If this happens, refer to Chapter 20, *Troubleshooting and Support*.

Each time the `config.inc.php` file is modified, it will have to be transferred again to our web space. This transfer might have to be done explicitly with a specific transfer program, or it might be done by a feature of an editor like HomeSite, Komodo, or PHPEdit, which can save directly via FTP.

The config.inc.php File

This file contains valid PHP code, defining the majority of the parameters (expressed by PHP variables) that we can change to tune phpMyAdmin to our own needs. There are also normal PHP comments in it, and we can comment our changes.

 Be careful not to add any blank line at the beginning or end of the file; this would hamper the execution of phpMyAdmin.

Starting with phpMyAdmin 2.6.0, there is another configuration file: `layout.inc.php`. As this version offers theme management, this file contains the theme-specific colors and settings. There is one `layout.inc.php` per theme, located in `themes/themename`, for example, `themes/original`. We will cover the modification of some of those parameters in Chapter 4 under the *First Steps* section.

PmaAbsoluteUri

The first parameter to have a look at is `$cfg['PmaAbsoluteUri'] = '';`

In most cases we can leave this one empty, as phpMyAdmin tries to auto-detect the correct value. If we browse a table later and then edit a row and click **Save**, we will receive an error message from our browser—for example, **This document does not exist**. This means that the absolute URI that phpMyAdmin built in order to reach the intended page was wrong, indicating that we must manually put the correct value in this parameter.

For example, we would change it to:

```
$cfg['PmaAbsoluteUri'] = 'http://www.mydomain.com/phpMyAdmin/';
```

Server-Specific Sections

The next section of the file contains server-specific configurations, each starting with:

```
$i++;
$cfg['Servers'][$i]['host']           = '';
```

If we examine only the normal server parameters (other parameters will be covered starting with Chapter 11), we see a section like the following for each server:

```
$i++;
$cfg['Servers'][$i]['host']           = '';
$cfg['Servers'][$i]['port']           = '';
$cfg['Servers'][$i]['socket']         = '';
$cfg['Servers'][$i]['connect_type']   = 'tcp';
$cfg['Servers'][$i]['extension']      = 'mysql';
$cfg['Servers'][$i]['compress']       = FALSE;
$cfg['Servers'][$i]['controluser']    = '';
$cfg['Servers'][$i]['controlpass']    = '';
$cfg['Servers'][$i]['auth_type']      = 'config';
$cfg['Servers'][$i]['user']           = 'root';
$cfg['Servers'][$i]['password']       = '';
$cfg['Servers'][$i]['only_db']        = '';
$cfg['Servers'][$i]['hide_db']        = '';
$cfg['Servers'][$i]['verbose']        = '';
```

In this section, we have to enter in `$cfg['Servers'][$i]['host']` the hostname or IP address of the MySQL server—for example, `mysql.mydomain.com` or `localhost`. If this server is running on a non-standard port or socket, we fill in the correct values in `$cfg['Servers'][$i]['port']` or `$cfg['Servers'][$i]['socket']`. See the section on `connect_type` for more details about sockets.

The displayed server name inside phpMyAdmin's interface will be the one entered in `'host'` (unless we enter a non-blank value in the following parameter). For example:

```
$cfg['Servers'][$i]['verbose'] = 'Test server';
```

This feature can thus be used to hide the real server hostname as seen by the users.

extension

The traditional mechanism by which PHP can communicate with a MySQL server, as available in PHP before version 5, is the `mysql` extension. This extension is still available in PHP 5, but a new one called `mysqli` has been developed and should be preferred for PHP 5, because of its improved performance and its support of the full functionality of MySQL family 4.1.x. This extension is designed to work with MySQL version 4.1.3 and higher.

In phpMyAdmin version 2.6.0, a new library has been implemented, making possible the use of both extensions—choosing either for a particular server. We indicate the extension we want to use in `$cfg['Servers'][$i]['extension']`.

PersistentConnections

Another important parameter (which is not server-specific but applies to all server definitions) is `$cfg['PersistentConnections']`. For all servers to which we connect using the `mysql` extension, this parameter, when set to TRUE, instructs PHP to keep the connection to the MySQL server open. This speeds up the interaction between PHP and MySQL. However, it is set to FALSE by default in `config.inc.php`, because persistent connections are often a cause of resource depletion on servers—MySQL refusing new connections. For this reason, the option is not even available for the `mysqli` extension, so setting it to TRUE here would have no effect if you are connecting with this extension.

connect_type, socket and port

Both the `mysql` and `mysqli` extensions automatically use a socket to connect to MySQL if the server is on `localhost`. Consider this configuration:

```
$cfg['Servers'][$i]['host']          = 'localhost';
$cfg['Servers'][$i]['port']          = '';
```

```
$cfg['Servers'][$i]['socket']          = '';
$cfg['Servers'][$i]['connect_type']    = 'tcp';
$cfg['Servers'][$i]['extension']       = 'mysql';
```

The default value for connect_type is tcp. However, the extension will use a socket because it concludes that this is more efficient as the host is localhost, so in this case, we can use tcp or socket as the connect_type. To force a real tcp connection, we can specify 127.0.0.1 instead of localhost in the host parameter. Because the socket parameter is empty, the extension will try the default socket. If this default socket, as defined in php.ini, does not correspond to the real socket assigned to the MySQL server, we have to put the socket name (for example, /tmp/mysql.sock) in $cfg['Servers'][$i]['socket'].

If the hostname is not localhost, a tcp connection will occur—here, on the special port 3307. However, leaving the port value empty would use the default 3306 port:

```
$cfg['Servers'][$i]['host']            = 'mysql.mydomain.com';
$cfg['Servers'][$i]['port']            = '3307';
$cfg['Servers'][$i]['socket']          = '';
$cfg['Servers'][$i]['connect_type']    = 'tcp';
$cfg['Servers'][$i]['extension']       = 'mysql';
```

compress Configuration

Starting with PHP 4.3.0 and MySQL 3.23.49, the protocol used to communicate between PHP and MySQL allows a compressed mode. Using this mode provides better efficiency. To take advantage of this mode, simply specify:

```
$cfg['Servers'][$i]['compress']        = TRUE;
```

Authentication Type: config

For our first test, we will use the config authentication type, which is easy to understand. However, in the *Multi-User Installation* section, we will see more powerful and versatile ways of authenticating.

Although it seems that we are logging in to phpMyAdmin, we are not! The authentication system is a function of the MySQL server. We are merely using phpMyAdmin (which is running on the web server) as an interface that sends our user and password information to the MySQL server. Strictly speaking, we do not log in *to* phpMyAdmin but *through* phpMyAdmin.

 Using the config authentication type leaves our phpMyAdmin open to intrusion, unless we protect it, as explained in the *Security* section of this chapter.

Here we enter our username and password for this MySQL server:

```
$cfg['Servers'][$i]['user']          = 'marc';
$cfg['Servers'][$i]['password']      = 'bingo';
```

We can then save the changes we made in config.inc.php.

Testing the First Connection

Now it's time to start phpMyAdmin and try connecting for the first time. This will test the following:

- The values we entered in the config file or on the web-based setup
- The setup of the PHP component inside the web server — if we did a manual configuration
- Communication between web and MySQL servers

Due to a problem in phpMyAdmin 2.8.0 to 2.8.2, for these versions we should close all windows of our browser at this point.

We start our browser and point it to the directory where we installed phpMyAdmin, as in http://www.mydomain.com/phpMyAdmin. If this does not work, we try http://www.mydomain.com/phpMyAdmin/index.php. (This would mean that our web server is not configured to interpret index.php as the default starting document.)

If you still get an error, refer to Chapter 19, the *Troubleshooting and Support*. We should now see phpMyAdmin's home page. Chapter 3 gives an overview of the panels seen now.

Multi-Server Configuration

The config.inc.php file contains at least one server-specific section but we can add more, enabling a single copy of phpMyAdmin to manage many servers. Let us see how to configure more servers.

Servers Defined in the Configuration File

In the server-specific sections of the config.inc.php file, we see lines referring to $cfg['Servers'][$i] for each server. Here, the variable $i is used so that one can easily cut and paste whole sections of the configuration file to configure more servers. While copying such sections, we should take care that the $i++; instruction that precedes each section and is crucial to delimit the server sections is also copied.

Then, at the end of the sections, the following line controls what happens at startup:

```
$cfg['ServerDefault'] = 1;
```

The default value, 1, means that phpMyAdmin will connect by itself to the first server defined or present this server choice by default when using advanced authentication—more on this later in this chapter. We can specify any number, for the corresponding server-specific section. We can also enter the value 0, signifying no default server, in which case phpMyAdmin will present a server choice:

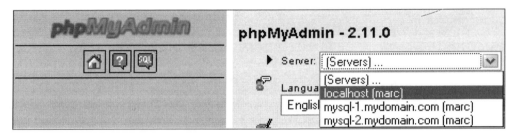

Arbitrary Server

Another mechanism can be used if we want to be able to connect to an undefined MySQL server. First, we have to set the following parameter:

```
$cfg['AllowArbitraryServer']    = TRUE;
```

We also have to put back the default value of 1 into $cfg['ServerDefault']. Then, we need to use the cookie authentication type, explained in the next section. We will be able to choose the server and enter a username and a password.

 This mechanism should probably be used in conjunction with a reinforced security mechanism (see the *Security* section), because any MySQL server accessible from our web server could be connected to.

As seen here, we still can choose one of the defined servers in **Server Choice**, but we can enter an arbitrary server name, a username, and a password:

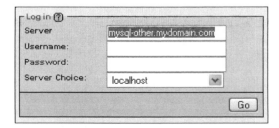

Advanced Authentication

We might want to allow a single copy of phpMyAdmin to be used by a group of persons, each having their own MySQL username and password and seeing only the databases they have rights to. Or we might prefer to avoid having our username and password in clear text in `config.inc.php`.

Authentication Types Offered

Instead of relying on a username/password pair stored in `config.inc.php`, phpMyAdmin will communicate with the browser and get authentication data from it. This enables **true login** for all users defined in a specific MySQL server, without having to define them in the configuration file. There are three modes offered that allow a controlled login to MySQL via phpMyAdmin: `http`, `cookie` and `signon`. We will have to choose the one that suits our specific situation and environment (more on this in a moment). The `http` and `cookie` modes may require that we first define a control user.

The Control User

> Defining the control user for authentication purposes only applies to a MySQL server previous to version 4.1.2; however, there is another reason to define a control user: to be able to use the advanced relational features of phpMyAdmin, which are described starting at Chapter 11.

To be able to use authentication types for every kind of MySQL user (in MySQL, user privileges may be expressed in various ways), we should define a control user and password in the server-specific section of a server. If we do not define one, users who have been defined in MySQL with a syntax of `'user'@'hostname'` or `'user'@'%'` will be able to function normally with phpMyAdmin's features like creating a database, and others won't.

The control user is a special user (the usual name we choose for it is **pma**, a familiar abbreviation for phpMyAdmin) who has the rights to read some fields in the special **mysql** database (which contains all the user definitions). phpMyAdmin sends queries with this special control user only for the specific needs of authentication, and not for normal operation. The commands to create the control user are available in phpMyAdmin's `Documentation.html` and may vary from version to version. This documentation contains the most current commands.

When our control user is defined, we fill in the parameters as in the following example:

```
$cfg['Servers'][$i]['controluser']     = 'pma';
$cfg['Servers'][$i]['controlpass']     = 'bingo';
```

 I use the bingo password when I teach phpMyAdmin; it is recommended to avoid using the same password for your own installation.

Logging Out

Since version 2.10, a mechanism is available to indicate to phpMyAdmin which URL it should pass control after a logout. This feature works for all authentication types. Here is an example:

```
$cfg['Servers'][$i]['LogoutURL']       = 'http://www.mydomain.com';
```

This directive must contain an absolute URL, including the protocol.

HTTP Authentication

This mode, http, is the traditional mode offered in HTTP, in which the browser asks for the username and password, sends them to phpMyAdmin, and keeps sending them until all the browser's windows are closed.

To enable this mode, we simply use the following line:

```
$cfg['Servers'][$i]['auth_type']       = 'http';
```

This mode has some limitations:

- PHP, depending on the version, might not support HTTP authentication. It works when PHP is running as a module under Apache; for other cases, we should consult the PHP documentation for our version.
- If we want to protect phpMyAdmin's directory with a .htaccess file (see the *Security* section in this chapter), this will interfere with HTTP authentication type; we cannot use both.

There is not a true logout; we will have to close all browser windows to be able to login again with the same username. Even considering those limitations, this mode may be a valuable choice for the following reasons:

- Some browsers (like Mozilla) can store the authentication information in an encrypted form.
- It is a bit faster than cookie processing.

Cookie Authentication

The cookie authentication mode is superior to http in terms of the functionalities offered. It offers true login and logout, and can be used with PHP running on any kind of web server. It presents a login panel (see the following figure) from within phpMyAdmin. This can be customized because we have the application source code. However, as you may have guessed, for cookie authentication, the browser must accept cookies coming from the web server—but this is true for all authentication modes starting with phpMyAdmin 2.8.0:

This mode stores the username typed in the login screen into a permanent cookie in our browser. The password is stored as a temporary cookie. In a multi-server configuration, the username/password pair corresponding to each server is stored separately. To protect the username/password secrecy against some attack methods that target cookie content, they are encrypted using the Blowfish mechanism. So, to use this mode, we have to define (once) in config.inc.php a secret password that will be used to securely encrypt all passwords stored as cookies from this phpMyAdmin installation.

This is done by putting a secret password here:

```
$cfg['blowfish_secret'] = 'SantaLivesInCanada';
```

Then, for each server-specific section, use the following:

```
$cfg['Servers'][$i]['auth_type']       = 'cookie';
```

The next time we start phpMyAdmin, we will see the login panel.

By default, phpMyAdmin displays (in the login panel) the last username for which a successful login was achieved for this particular server, as retrieved from the permanent cookie. If this behavior is not acceptable (if we would prefer that someone else who logs in from the same workstation should not see the previous username), we can set the following parameter to FALSE:

```
$cfg['LoginCookieRecall']        = FALSE;
```

A security feature was added in phpMyAdmin 2.6.0: a time limit for the validity of the entered password. This feature helps to protect the working session. After a successful login, our password is stored in a cookie, along with a timer. Every action in phpMyAdmin resets the timer. If we stay *inactive* a certain number of seconds, as defined in $cfg['LoginCookieValidity'], we are disconnected and have to login again. The default is 1800 seconds.

> The Blowfish algorithm used to protect the username and password requires many computations. To achieve the best possible speed, the PHP's **mcrypt** extension and its accompanying library must be installed on our web server. Otherwise, phpMyAdmin relies on an internally coded algorithm, which works but causes *delays of several seconds* on almost every operation done from phpMyAdmin! This is because the username and password information must be decoded on every mouse click to be able to connect to MySQL.

Signon

Since version 2.10, the signon mode enables us to use the credentials from another application to authenticate to MySQL. Some applications have their own authentication mechanism, so it's convenient to be able to use this fact to avoid another cumbersome login panel. In order for this to work, this other application has to store the proper credentials into PHP's session data to be retrieved later by phpMyAdmin.

To enable this mode, we start with this directive:

```
$cfg['Servers'][$i]['auth_type'] = 'signon';
```

Let's suppose that the authenticating application has used a session named FirstApp to store the credentials. We tell phpMyAdmin this fact:

```
$cfg['Servers'][$i] ['SignonSession'] = 'FirstApp';
```

We must take care of users that would try to access phpMyAdmin before the other application; in this case, phpMyAdmin will redirect users to the authenticating application. This is done with:

```
$cfg['Servers'][$i] ['SignonURL'] = 'http://www.mydomain.com/
FirstApp';
```

How does the authenticating application store credentials in a format that phpMyAdmin can understand? An example is included as `scripts/signon.php`. In this script, there is a simple HTML form to input the credentials and logic that initializes the session—we would use `FirstApp` as a session name—and creates the user, password, and host information into this session:

```
$_SESSION['PMA_single_signon_user'] = $_POST['user'];
$_SESSION['PMA_single_signon_password'] = $_POST['password'];
$_SESSION['PMA_single_signon_host'] = $_POST['host'];
```

Note that `FirstApp` does not need to ask the MySQL's credentials to the user. These could be hard-coded inside the application because they are secret or there is a known correspondence between this application's credentials and MySQL's ones.

The authenticating application then uses a way of its choosing—a link or button—to let its users start phpMyAdmin.

Security

Security can be examined at various levels:

- Directory-level protection for phpMyAdmin
- IP-based access control
- The databases that a legitimate user can see
- In-transit data protection

Directory-Level Protection

Suppose an unauthorized person is trying to execute our copy of phpMyAdmin. If we used the simple `config` authentication type, anyone knowing the URL of our phpMyAdmin will have the same effective rights on our data as us. In this case, we should use the directory-protection mechanism offered by our web server (for example, `.htaccess`, a file with a leading dot) to add a level of protection.

If we chose to use `http` or `cookie` authentication types, our data would be safe enough, but we should take the normal precautions with our password (including its periodic change).

The directory where phpMyAdmin is installed contains sensitive data. Not only the configuration file but also ultimately all scripts stored there must be protected from alteration. We should ensure that apart from us, only the web server effective user has read access to the files contained in this directory and that only we can *write* to them.

 phpMyAdmin's scripts never have to modify anything inside this directory, except when we use the **Save export file to server** feature, which is explained in Chapter 7.

Another possible attack is from other developers having an account on the same web server as us. In this kind of attack, someone can try to open our `config.inc.php` file. Since this file is readable by the web server, someone could try to include our file from their PHP scripts. This is why it is recommended to use PHP's `open_basedir` feature, possibly applying it to all directories from which such attacks could originate.

IP-Based Access Control

An additional level of protection can be added, this time verifying the **Internet Protocol (IP)** address of the machine from which the request to use phpMyAdmin is received.

To achieve this level of protection, we construct rules allowing or denying access, and specify the order in which these rules will be applied.

Rules

The format of a rule is:

```
<'allow' | 'deny'> <username> [from] <source>
```

`from` being optional. Here are some examples:

```
allow Bob from 1.2.3.4
```

User `Bob` is allowed access from IP address `1.2.3.4`.

```
allow Bob from 1.2.3/24
```

User `Bob` is allowed from any address matching the network `1.2.3` (this is CIDR IP matching).

```
deny Alice from 4.5/16
```

User `Alice` cannot access when located on network `4.5`.

```
allow Melanie from all
```

User `Melanie` can login from anywhere.

```
allow Julie from localhost
```

Equivalent to 127.0.0.1

```
deny % from all
```

`all` can be used as an equivalent to 0.0.0.0/0, meaning any host. Here, the `%` sign means any user.

The source part can also be formed with the special names `localnetA`, `localnetB`, or `localnetC`. These represent the complete class A, B, or C network in which the web server is located. Note that phpMyAdmin relies on the `$_SERVER["SERVER_ADDR"]` PHP parameter for this feature. Usually we will have several rules. Let's say we wish to have the two rules that follow:

```
allow Marc from 45.34.23.12
allow Melanie from all
```

We have to put them in `config.inc.php` (in the related server-specific section) as follows:

```
$cfg['Servers'][$i]['AllowDeny']['rules'] =
  array('allow Marc from 45.34.23.12',
    'allow Melanie from all');
```

When defining a single rule or multiple rules, a PHP array is used, and we must follow its syntax enclosing each complete rule within single quotes and separating each rule from the next with a comma. Thus, if we have only one rule, we must still use an array to specify it like this:

```
$cfg['Servers'][$i]['AllowDeny']['rules'] =
  array('allow Marc from 45.34.23.12');
```

The next parameter explains the order in which rules are interpreted.

Order of Interpretation for Rules

By default, this parameter is empty:

```
$cfg['Servers'][$i]['AllowDeny']['order'] = '';
```

This means that *no* IP-based verification is made.

Suppose we want to allow access by default, denying access only to some username/ IP pairs. We should use:

```
$cfg['Servers'][$i]['AllowDeny']['order'] = 'deny,allow';
```

In this case, all `deny` rules will be applied first, followed by `allow` rules. If a case is not mentioned in the rules, access is granted. Being more restrictive, we'd want to deny by default. We can use:

```
$cfg['Servers'][$i]['AllowDeny']['order'] = 'allow,deny';
```

This time, all `allow` rules are applied first, followed by `deny` rules. If a case is not mentioned in the rules, access is denied.

The third (and most restrictive) way of specifying rules order is:

```
$cfg['Servers'][$i]['AllowDeny']['order'] = 'explicit';
```

`deny` rules are applied before `allow` rules, but to be accepted, a username/IP address *must be listed* in the allow rules and not in the `deny` rules.

Simplified Rule for Root Access

Since the `root` user is present in almost all MySQL installations, it's often the target of attacks. Starting with phpMyAdmin 2.6.1, a parameter permits us to easily block all logins of the MySQL's `root` account, using the following:

```
$cfg['Servers'][$i]['AllowRoot']      = FALSE;
```

Restricting the List of Databases

Sometimes it is useful to avoid showing in the left panel all the databases to which a user has access. phpMyAdmin offers two ways of restricting: `only_db` and `hide_db`.

To specify the list of what can be seen, the `only_db` parameter is used. It may contain a database name or a list of database names. Only these databases will be seen in the left panel:

```
$cfg['Servers'][$i]['only_db']          = 'payroll';
$cfg['Servers'][$i]['only_db']          = array('payroll', 'hr');
```

The database names can contain MySQL wildcard characters like _ and %.

We can also indicate which database names must be hidden with the `hide_db` parameter. It contains a regular expression (http://en.wikipedia.org/wiki/Regular_expression) representing what to exclude. If we do not want users to see all databases whose names begin with `secret` we would use:

```
$cfg['Servers'][$i]['hide_db']          = '^secret';
```

These parameters apply to all users for this server-specific configuration.

These mechanisms do not replace the MySQL privilege system. Users' rights on other databases still apply, but they cannot use phpMyAdmin's left panel to navigate to their other databases or tables.

Protecting In-Transit Data

HTTP is not inherently immune to network sniffing (grabbing sensitive data off the wire), so if we want to protect not only our username and password but all the data that travels between our web server and browser, we have to use HTTPS.

To do so, assuming that our web server supports HTTPS, we just have to start phpMyAdmin by putting `https` instead of `http` in the URL as follows:

```
https://www.mydomain.com/phpMyAdmin
```

If we are using `PmaAbsoluteUri` auto-detection:

```
$cfg['PmaAbsoluteUri'] = '';
```

phpMyAdmin will see that we are using HTTPS in the URL and react accordingly. If not, we must put the `https` part in this parameter as follows:

```
$cfg['PmaAbsoluteUri'] = 'https://www.mydomain.com/phpMyAdmin';
```

Also, since phpMyAdmin 2.7.0, we can *automatically* switch users to an HTTPS connection with this setting:

```
$cfg['ForceSSL'] = TRUE;
```

Upgrading phpMyAdmin

Normally, upgrading is just a matter of installing the newer version into a separate directory and copying the previous version's `config.inc.php` to the new directory. If the previous version is phpMyAdmin 2.6.0 or older, we cannot copy its `config.inc.php` to the new version because the file format has changed too much.

 An upgrade—or first-installation—path that *should not* be taken is to copy `libraries/config.default.php` to `config.inc.php`, since this default configuration file is version-specific and is not guaranteed to work for future versions.

New parameters appear from version to version. They are documented in
`Documentation.html` and defined in `libraries/config.default.php`. If
a configuration parameter is not present in `config.inc.php`, its value from
`libraries/config.default.php` will be used; so we do not have to include it
into `config.inc.php` if the default value suits us.

Special care must be taken to propagate the changes we might have made to the
`layout.inc.php` files, depending on the themes used. We may even have to copy
our custom themes subdirectories if we added our own themes to the structure.

Summary

In this chapter, we took a look at the common reasons for installing phpMyAdmin,
the steps for downloading it from the main site, basic configuration, and uploading it
to our web server. We learned how to use a single copy of phpMyAdmin to manage
multiple servers, and also the usage of authentication types to fulfill the needs of a
users' group while protecting authentication credentials. Securing our phpMyAdmin
installation and upgrading phpMyAdmin were also covered.

3
Interface Overview

Panels and Windows

The phpMyAdmin interface is composed of various panels and windows, each one having a specific function. We will first provide a quick overview of each panel and then take a detailed look, later in this chapter.

Login Panels

The login panel that appears depends on the authentication type chosen. For the `http` type, it will take the form of our browser's HTTP authentication pop-up screen. For the `cookie` type, the phpMyAdmin-specific login panel will be displayed. (This is covered in Chapter 2.) For the external authentication (`signon`), the login panel is handled by the external application itself. By default, a **Server** choice dialog and a **Language** selector are present on this panel.

However, if we are using the `config` authentication type, no login panel is displayed, and the first displayed interface contains the left and right panels.

Left and Right Panels

These panels go together and are displayed during most of our working session with phpMyAdmin. The **left panel** is our navigation guide through the databases and tables. The **right panel** is the main working area where the data is managed and results appear. Its exact layout depends on the choices made from the left panel, and the sequence of operations performed. For right-to-left languages like Hebrew, the navigation panel is located on the right side and the main panel is on the left.

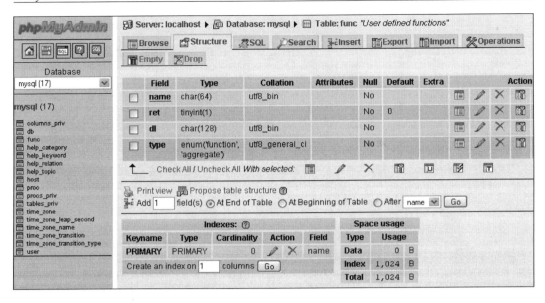

Home Page

The right panel can take the form of the **Home** page, which contains various links related to MySQL operations or phpMyAdmin information, a **Language** selector, and possibly the themes selector.

Views

In the right panel, we can see the Database view, where we can take various actions about a specific database, or the Table view, where we can access many functions to manage a table. There is also a Server view, useful for both system administrators and non-administrator users. All these views have a top menu, which takes the form of tabs that lead to different sub-pages used to present information regrouped by common functions (table structure, privileges, and so on).

 Please do not confuse the term *view* — used here in the interface sense — with the MySQL 5.0's notion of SQL views, which are covered in Chapter 18.

Query Window

This is a distinct window that is usually opened from the left panel—and sometimes from the right panel when editing a SQL query. Its main purpose is to facilitate work on queries and display the results on the right panel.

Starting Page

When we start phpMyAdmin, we will see the following (depending on the authentication type specified in `config.inc.php` and on whether it has more than one server defined in it):

- One of the login panels
- The left and right panels with the home page displayed in the right panel

Window Titles Configuration

When the left and right panels are displayed, the window's title changes to reflect *which* MySQL server, database, and table are active. phpMyAdmin also shows some information about the web server's host name if `$cfg['ShowHttpHostTitle']` is set to TRUE. What is displayed depends on another setting, `$cfg['SetHttpHostTitle']`. If this setting is empty (as it is by default), the true web server's host name appears in the title. We can put another string here, like 'my Web server', and this will be shown instead of the true host name.

Seeing the web server's host name can come in handy when we have many phpMyAdmin windows open, thus being connected to more than one *web* server. Of course, each phpMyAdmin window can itself give access to many *MySQL* servers.

General Icon Configuration

When various warning, error, or information messages are displayed, they can be accompanied by an icon, if `$cfg['ErrorIconic']` is set to TRUE. Another parameter, `$cfg['ReplaceHelpImg']`, when set to TRUE, displays a small icon containing a question mark at every place where documentation is available for a specific subject. These two parameters are set to TRUE by default, thus producing:

They can be independently set to FALSE. Setting both to FALSE would give:

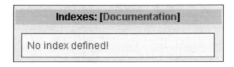

Natural Sort Order for Database and Table Names

Usually, computers sort items in lexical order, which gives the following results for a list of tables:

```
table1
table10
table2
table3
```

phpMyAdmin implements 'natural sort order' by default, as specified by $cfg['NaturalOrder'] being TRUE. Thus the database and table lists in left and right panels are sorted as:

```
table1
table2
table3
table10
```

Language Selection

A **Language** selector appears on the login panel (if any) and on the **Home** page. The default behavior of phpMyAdmin is to use the language defined in our browser's preferences, if there is a corresponding language file for this version.

The default language used in case the program cannot detect one is defined in config.inc.php in the $cfg['DefaultLang'] parameter with 'en-iso-8859-1'. This value can be changed. The possible values for language names are defined in the libraries/select_lang.lib.php script as an array.

Even if the default language is defined, each user (especially on a multi-user installation) can choose his or her preferred language from the selector:

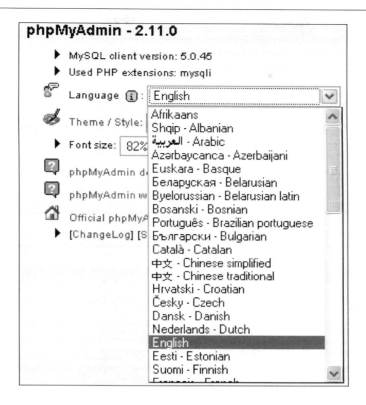

The user's choice will be remembered in a cookie whenever possible.

We can also force a single language by setting the $cfg['Lang'] parameter with a value, such as 'en-iso-8859-1'. Starting with version 2.7.0, another parameter, $cfg['FilterLanguages'], is available. Suppose we want to shorten the list of available languages to **English** and **Français — French** because those are the ones used exclusively by our users. We build a regular expression indicating which languages we want to display based on the ISO codes of these languages. To continue with our example, we would use:

```
$cfg['FilterLanguages']  = '^(fr|en)';
```

In this expression, the caret (^) means *starting with* and the (|) means *or*. The expression indicates that we are restricting the list to languages whose corresponding ISO codes start with fr or en.

By default, this parameter is empty, meaning that no filter is applied to the list of available languages.

The small information icon beside **Language** gives access to phpMyAdmin's translator page, which lists, by language, the official translator and the contact information. This way we can reach the translator for corrections or to offer help on untranslated messages.

On the **Home** page, we might also see a **MySQL Charset** selector or **MySQL Charset** information (not in a selector). You can refer to Chapter 17, *Character Sets and Collations*, for full details on this subject.

Themes

A theme system is available in phpMyAdmin starting with version 2.6.0. The color parameters and the various icons are located in a directory structure under the `themes` subdirectory. For each available theme, there is a subdirectory named after the theme. It contains:

- `layout.inc.php` for the theme parameters
- `css` directory with the various CSS scripts
- `img` directory containing the icons
- `screen.png`, a screenshot of this theme

The downloaded kit contains two themes, and more themes are available at `http://www.phpmyadmin.net/home_page/downloads.php?themes`.

Theme Configuration

In `config.inc.php`, the `$cfg['ThemePath']` parameter contains `'themes'` by default, which indicates *which* subdirectory the required structure is located in. This could be changed to point to another directory where our company's specific phpMyAdmin themes are located.

The default chosen theme is specified in `$cfg['ThemeDefault']`, and is set to `'original'`. If no theme selection is available for users, this theme will be used.

 The `original` subdirectory should *never* be deleted; phpMyAdmin relies on it for normal operations.

Theme Selection

On the **Home** page, we can offer a theme selector to users. Setting `$cfg['ThemeManager']` to TRUE (the default) shows the selector:

To help choose a suitable theme, the color palette icon next to **Theme/Style** brings us screenshots of the available themes. We can then click on **take it** under the theme we want. The chosen theme is remembered in a cookie. By default, the remembered theme applies to all servers we connect to. To make phpMyAdmin remember one theme per MySQL server, we set `$cfg[ThemePerServer]` to TRUE.

Left Panel

The left panel contains the following elements:

- The logo (see *Logo Configuration* over the page)
- The server list (if `$cfg['LeftDisplayServers']` is set to TRUE)
- The **Home** link or icon (takes you back to the phpMyAdmin home page)
- A **Log out** link or icon
- A link or icon leading to the **Query** window
- Icons to display phpMyAdmin and MySQL documentation
- The databases and tables choices with statistics about the number of tables per database

If `$cfg['MainPageIconic']` is set to TRUE (the default), we see the *icons*. If it is set to FALSE, we see the **Home**, **Log out**, and **Query** window *links*.

The left panel can be resized by clicking and moving the vertical separation line in the preferred direction to reveal more data, in case the database or table names are too long for the default left panel size.

We can customize the appearance of this panel—all parameters are located in `themes/themename/layout.inc.php` except where noted otherwise. `$cfg['LeftWidth']` contains the default width of the left frame, in pixels. The background color is defined in `$cfg['LeftBgColor']` with a default value of `'#D0DCE0'`. The `$cfg['LeftPointerColor']` parameter, with a default value of `'#CCFFCC'`, defines the pointer color. (The pointer appears when we are using the Full mode, discussed shortly.) To activate the left pointer for any theme being used, a master setting, `$cfg['LeftPointerEnable']`, exists in `config.inc.php`. Its default value is TRUE.

Logo Configuration

The logo display behavior is controlled by a number of parameters. First, `$cfg['LeftDisplayLogo']` has to be set to TRUE to enable any displaying of the logo—it is `true` by default. A click on this logo brings the interface to the page listed in the `$cfg['LeftLogoLink']` parameter, which is usually the main phpMyAdmin page (default value `main.php`), but can be any URL. Finally, the `$cfg['LeftLogoLinkWindow']` parameter indicates in which window the new page appears after a click on the logo. By default, it's on the main page (value `main`) but it could be on a brand-new window by using the value `new`.

The logo image itself comes from the `logo_left.png` file, which is located in each specific theme directory structure.

Database and Table List

The following examples show that no database has been chosen from the drop-down menu:

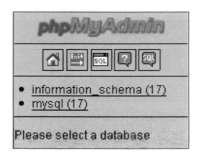

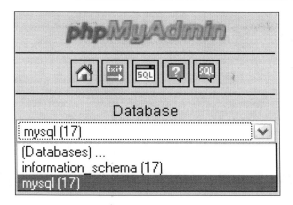

It is also possible to see the following screen:

This means that our current MySQL rights do not allow us to see any existing databases.

 A MySQL server always has *at least* one database (named **mysql**), but in this case, we do not have the right to see it. Moreover, since MySQL 5.0.2, a special database called **information_schema** appears at all times in the database list. It contains a set of views describing the metadata visible for the logged-in user.

We may have the right to create one, as explained in Chapter 4.

Light Mode

The left panel can be shown in two ways: the Light mode and the Full mode. The Light mode is used by default, defined by a TRUE value in $cfg['LeftFrameLight']. This mode shows a drop-down list of the available databases, and only tables of the currently chosen database are displayed. It is more efficient than Full Mode; the reason is explained in the *Full Mode* section.

Here we have chosen the **mysql** database:

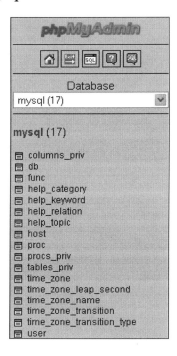

Clicking on the database name opens the right panel in the Database view, and clicking on a table name opens the right panel in the Table view. (See the *Right Panel* section for details.)

Tree Display of Database Names

A user might be allowed to work on a single database, for example `marc`. Some system administrators offer a more flexible scheme by allowing user `marc` to create many databases, provided their names all start with **marc**—like **marc_airline** and **marc_car**. In this situation, the left panel can be set to display a tree of these database names.

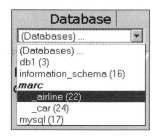

This feature is currently offered only in light mode and is controlled by these parameters:

```
$cfg['LeftFrameDBTree']        = TRUE;
$cfg['LeftFrameDBSeparator']   = '_';
```

The default value of TRUE in `$cfg['LeftFrameDBTree']` ensures that this feature is activated. A popular value for the separator is '_'.

Full Mode

The previous examples were shown in Light mode, but setting the `$cfg['LeftFrameLight']` parameter to FALSE produces a complete layout of our databases and tables using collapsible menus (if supported by the browser):

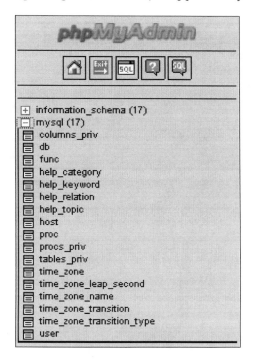

The number of tables per database is shown in brackets. The Full mode is not selected by default; it can increase network traffic and server load if our current rights give us access to a large number of databases and tables. Links must be generated in the left panel to enable table access and quick-browse access to every table, and the server has to count the number of rows for all tables.

Table Short Statistics

Moving the cursor over a table name displays comments about the table (if any) and the number of rows currently in it:

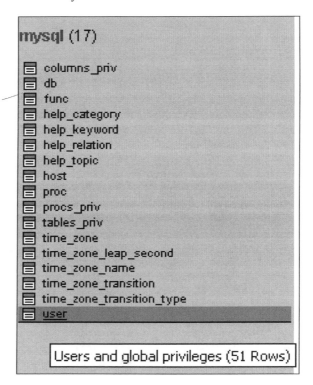

Quick-Browsing a Table

The small icon beside each table name is a quick way to browse the table's rows. It opens the right panel in the Table view, browsing the first page of data from the table.

Nested Display of Tables within a Database

MySQL's data structure is based on two levels: databases and tables. This does not allow subdivisions of tables per project, a feature often requested by MySQL users. They must rely on having multiple databases, but this is not always allowed by their provider. To help them with this regard, phpMyAdmin introduces a **nested-levels** feature, based on the table naming.

Let's say we have access to the **db1** database and we want to represent two projects, **marketing** and **payroll**. Using a special separator (by default a double underscore) between the project name and the table name, we create the **payroll__employees** and **payroll__jobs** tables achieving a visually interesting effect:

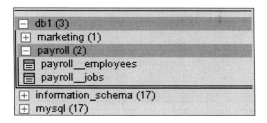

This feature is parameterized with $cfg['LeftFrameTableSeparator']$ (set here to '__') to choose the characters that will mark each level change, and $cfg['LeftFrameTableLevel']$ (set here to '1') for the number of sub-levels.

 The nested-level feature is only intended for improving the left panel look. The proper way to reference the tables in MySQL statements stays the same: for example, db1.payroll__jobs.

Beginning with phpMyAdmin 2.6.0, a click in the left panel *on the project name* (here **payroll**) opens this project in the right panel, showing only those project's tables.

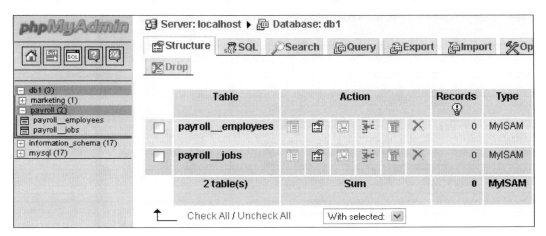

Server-List Choice

If we have to manage multiple servers from the same phpMyAdmin window and often need to switch between servers, it might prove useful to always have the list of servers in the left frame:

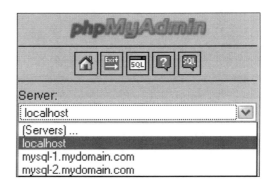

For this, the $cfg['LeftDisplayServers']$ parameter must be set to TRUE. The list of servers can have two forms: a drop-down list or links. Which form appears depends on $cfg['DisplayServersList']$. By default, this parameter is set to FALSE, so we see a drop-down list of servers. Setting $cfg['DisplayServersList']$ to TRUE produces a list of links to all defined servers:

Handling Many Databases or Tables

Before phpMyAdmin 2.11, it was difficult to work with the interface if we had access to hundreds or even thousands of databases, or hundreds of tables in the same database. Loading of the navigation panel was slow or did not work at all. In 2.11, the interface has been reworked to take care of this.

Two new parameters, shown here with their default values, establish a limit on the number of databases and tables displayed, by adding a page selector and navigation links:

```
$cfg['MaxDbList'] = 100;
$cfg['MaxTableList'] = 250;
```

The effect of `$cfg['MaxDbList']` can be seen on the main panel in Server view:

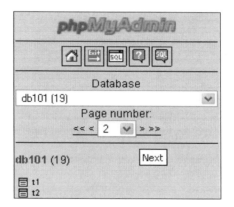

...as well as in the navigation panel:

In version 2.11.0, the `$cfg['MaxTableList']` feature has not been completely implemented. Nonetheless, the number of tables displayed in Database view and in the navigation panel is limited by this parameter, and there is a page selector in the main panel.

Right Panel

The right panel is the main working area, and all the possible views for it are explained in the following sections. Its appearance can be customized. The background color is defined in `$cfg['RightBgColor']`, and the default color is #F5F5F5. We can also select a background image by setting the URI of the image we want (for example, `http://www.domain.com/images/clouds.jpg`) in `$cfg['RightBgImage']`.

Home Page

The home page may contain a varying number of links depending on the login mode and the user's rights. A normal user may see it as:

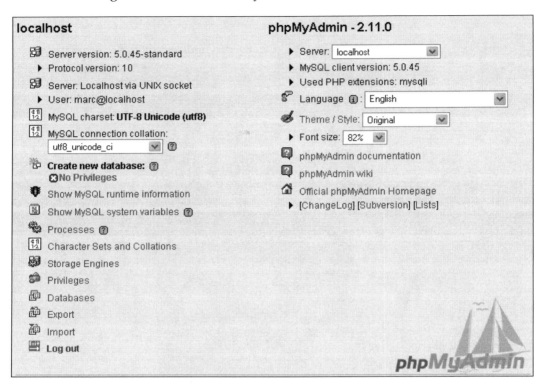

The **Home** link from the left panel is used to display this page. It shows the phpMyAdmin and MySQL versions, the MySQL server name, and the logged-in user. We also see that this user does not have the privileges to create a database. We see some links that relate to MySQL or phpMyAdmin itself. The **Log out** link might not be there if automatic login was done, as indicated by the configuration file.

In this example, a normal user is not allowed to change his or her password from the interface. To allow this password change, we set $cfg['ShowChgPassword']$ to TRUE. Privileged users have more options on the home page. They can always create databases and have more links to manage the server as a whole (Server view):

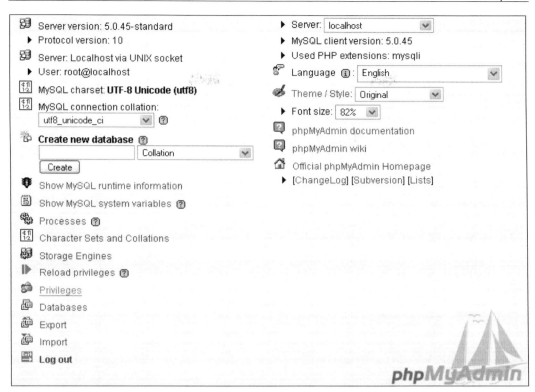

Another setting, $cfg['ShowPhpInfo']$, can be set to TRUE if we want to see the
Show PHP Information link on the Home page.

Database View

phpMyAdmin goes into this view (shown in the screenshot that follows) every time
we click on a database name from the left frame, or if the USE command followed by
a database name is typed in a SQL box.

This is where we can see an overview of the database: the existing tables, a link to
create a table, the tabs to the Database view sub-pages, and some special operations
we might do on this database to generate documentation and statistics. There is
a checkbox beside each table to make global operations on that table (covered in
Chapter 10). The table is chosen by using the checkbox or by clicking anywhere on
the row's background. We can also see each table's size, if $cfg['ShowStats']$ is
set to TRUE. This parameter also controls the display of table-specific statistics in the
Table view.

The initial screen that appears here is the database **Structure** sub-page. We might want a different initial sub-page to appear when entering the Database view. This is controlled by the `$cfg['DefaultTabDatabase']` parameter, and the available choices are given in the configuration file as comments.

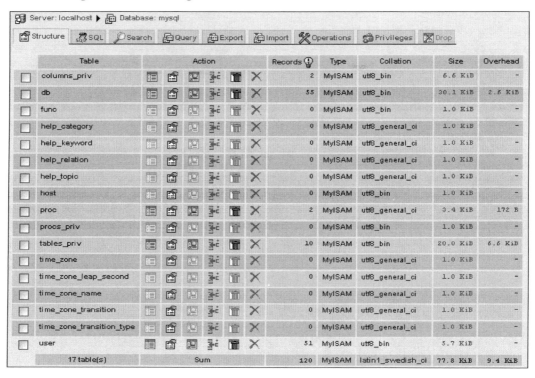

The number of records is obtained using a quick method, the SHOW TABLE STATUS statement—*not* by using a SELECT COUNT(*) FROM TABLENAME. This quick method is usually accurate, except for InnoDB tables, which returns an approximate number of records. To help get the correct number of records, even for InnoDB, the `$cfg['MaxExactCount']` parameter is available. If the approximate number of records is lower than this parameter's value—by default, 20000—the slower SELECT COUNT(*) method will be used.

 Do *not* put a value too high for this parameter. You would get correct results, but only after waiting for a few minutes, if there are hundreds of thousands of records in your InnoDB table.

A user might be surprised when seeing the term **KiB** in the **Size** and **Overhead** columns. phpMyAdmin has adopted the International Electrotechnical Commission (IEC) binary prefixes (see `http://en.wikipedia.org/wiki/Binary_prefix`). The displayed values are defined in each language file; here is the definition for English:

```
$byteUnits = array('B', 'KiB', 'MiB', 'GiB', 'TiB', 'PiB', 'EiB');
```

Table View

This is a commonly used view, giving access to all table-specific sub-pages. Usually, the initial screen is the table's **Structure** screen, which shows (note the upper part) all fields and indexes. Note that the header for this screen always shows the current database and table names. We also see the comments set for the table:

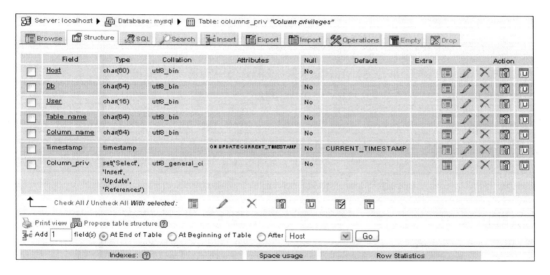

The `$cfg['DefaultTabTable']` parameter defines the initial sub-page on the Table view. Some users prefer to avoid seeing the structure, because in production they routinely run saved queries or enter the **Search** sub-page (explained in Chapter 9).

Server View

This view is entered each time we choose a MySQL-related option from the **Home** page—for example, **Databases** or **Show MySQL runtime information**. A privileged user will of course see more choices in the Server view. The Server view panel was created to group together related server management sub-pages and enable easy navigation between them.

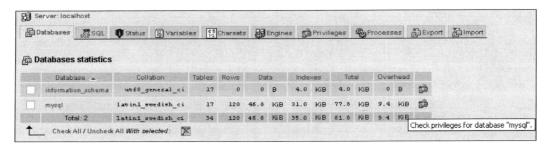

The default Server page is controlled by the $cfg['DefaultTabServer'] parameter. This parameter defines the initial starting page as well. For multi-user installations, it is recommended to keep the default value (main.php), which displays the traditional home page. We could choose to display server statistics instead by changing this parameter to server_status.php, or to see the users list with server_privileges. php. Other possible choices are explained in the configuration file, and the server administration pages are explained in Chapter 19.

Icons for Home Page and Menu Tabs

A configuration parameter, $cfg['MainPageIconic'], controls the appearance of icons at various places on the right panel:

- On the home page
- At top of page when listing the **Server**, **Database**, and **Table** information
- On the menu tabs in Database, Table, and Server views

This parameter is set to TRUE by default producing, for example:

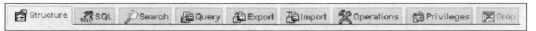

We can also display menu items without tabs by setting the $cfg['LightTabs'] parameter to true, producing:

Query Window

It is often convenient to have a *distinct window* in which we can type and refine queries and which is synchronized with the right panel. This window is called the **Query** window. We can open this window by using the small SQL icon or the **Query** window link from the left panel's icons or links zone.

This link or icon is displayed if `$cfg['QueryFrame']` is set to TRUE. The TRUE for `$cfg['QueryFrameJS']` tells phpMyAdmin to open a distinct window and update it using JavaScript commands; of course, this only works for a JavaScript-enabled browser. If this is set to FALSE, clicking on **Query** window will only open the right panel and will display the normal SQL sub-page.

 The full usability of the **Query** window is only achieved with the distinct window mode.

The **Query** window itself has sub-pages, and it appears here over the right panel:

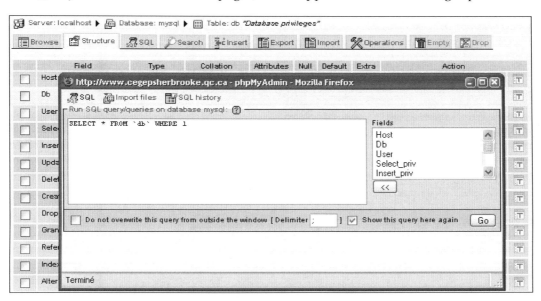

We can choose the dimensions (in pixels) of this window with `$cfg['QueryWindowWidth']` and `$cfg['QueryWindowHeight']`. Chapter 12 explains the **Query** window in more details, including the available SQL query history features.

Site-Specific Header and Footer

Some users may want to display a company logo, a link to the helpdesk, or other information on the phpMyAdmin interface. In the main `phpMyAdmin` directory, two scripts—`config.header.inc.php` and `config.footer.inc.php`—are available for this purpose. We can add our own PHP or XHTML code in these scripts, and it will appear at the beginning (for header) or end of page (for footer) of the page:

- On the cookie login page
- On the right panel

MySQL Documentation Links

phpMyAdmin displays links to the MySQL documentation at various places on its interface. These links refer to the exact point in the official MySQL documentation to learn about a MySQL command. We can customize the location, language, and manual type referred to, with the following configuration parameters:

```
$cfg['MySQLManualBase'] = 'http://www.mysql.com/doc/en';
$cfg['MySQLManualType'] = 'searchable';
```

You may take a look at `http://www.mysql.com/documentation` to see the languages in which the manual is available and change the parameters accordingly. For the manual type, the most up-to-date possible values are explained as comments in `config.inc.php`. Users who prefer to keep a copy of this documentation on a local server would specify a local link here.

The `$cfg['ReplaceHelpImg']` parameter controls how the links are displayed. Its default value of TRUE makes phpMyAdmin display small question-mark icons, and FALSE shows **Documentation** links.

Summary

In this chapter, we covered the language selection system, the purpose of the left and right panels, the contents of the left panel, including Light mode and Full mode, and the contents of the right panel, with its various views depending on the context. We also took a look at the **Query** window and the customization of MySQL documentation links.

4
First Steps

Database Creation

Having seen the overall layout of phpMyAdmin's panel, we are ready to create a database and our first table, insert some data in it, and browse it. Before creating a table, we must ensure that we have a database for which the MySQL server's administrator has given us the CREATE privilege. Various possibilities exist:

- The administrator has already created a database for us, and we see its name in the left panel; we don't have the right to create an additional database.
- We have the right to create databases from phpMyAdmin.
- We are on a shared host, and the host provider has installed a general Web interface (for example, Cpanel) to create MySQL databases and accounts.

Note that a configuration parameter, $cfg['ShowCreateDb']$, controls the display of the **Create new database** dialog. By default, it is set to true which shows this dialog.

No Privileges?

In this case, the **Home** page looks like the following screenshot:

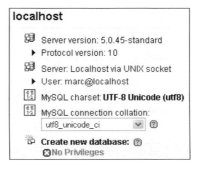

This means that we must work with the databases already created for us, or ask the MySQL server's administrator to give us the necessary CREATE privilege.

 If you *are* the MySQL server's administrator, refer to Chapter 19, the *MySQL Server Administration* section.

First Database Creation Is Authorized

If phpMyAdmin detects that we have the right to create a database, the home page looks as shown in the following screenshot:

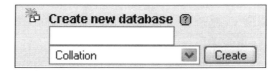

In the input field, a suggested database name appears if the $cfg['SuggestDBName'] parameter is set to TRUE—this is the default setting. The suggested database name is built according to the privileges we possess.

If we are restricted to the use of a prefix, the prefix might be suggested in the input field. (A popular choice for this prefix is the username.) Note that, in this case, the prefix is followed by an ellipsis mark; we should remove this ellipsis mark and complete the input field with an appropriate name.

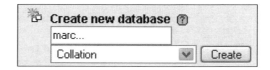

The **Collation** choice can be left unchanged for now — more details on this in Chapter 17.

We will assume here that we have the right to create a database named **marc_book**. We enter **marc_book** in the input field and click on **Create**. Once the database is created, we will see the following screen:

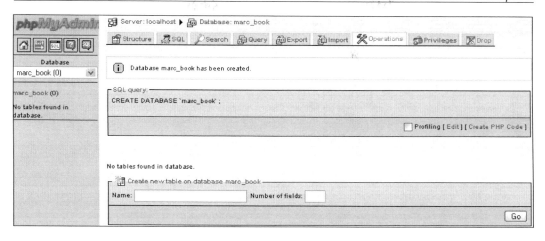

Notice the following:

- The main title of the right panel has changed to reflect the fact that we are now located in this database.

- A confirmation message regarding the creation is displayed.

- The left panel has been updated; we see **marc_book (0)**. Here, the name indicates that the **marc_book** database has been created, and the number 0 indicates that it contains no tables.

- By default, the SQL query sent to the server by phpMyAdmin to create the database is displayed in color.

 phpMyAdmin displays the query it generated, because `$cfg['ShowSQL']` is set to TRUE. Looking at the generated queries can be a good way of learning SQL.

As the generated queries could be large and take much room on-screen, the `$cfg['MaxCharactersInDisplayedSQL']` acts as a limit. Its default value of `1000` should be a good balance between seeing too few and seeing too much of the queries, especially when doing large imports.

It is important to examine the phpMyAdmin feedback to ascertain the validity of the operations we make through the interface. This way, we can detect errors like typos in the names, or creation of a table in the wrong database.

Creating Our First Table

Now that we have a new database, it's time to create a table in it. The example table we will use is the familiar **book** table.

Choosing the Fields

Before creating a table, we should plan the information we want to store. This is usually done during database design. In our case, a simple analysis leads us to the following book-related data we want to keep:

- International Standard Book Number (ISBN)
- Title
- Number of pages
- Author identification

For now, it is not important to have the complete list of fields (or columns) for our **book** table; we will modify it by prototyping the application and refine it later. At the end of the chapter, we will add a second table, **author**, containing information about each author.

Table Creation

We have chosen our table name and we know the number of fields. We enter this information in the **Create new table** dialog and click **Go** to start creating the table:

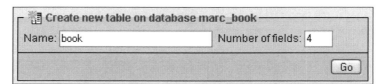

We then see a panel specifying field information. Since we asked for four fields, we get four rows, each row referring to information specific to one field:

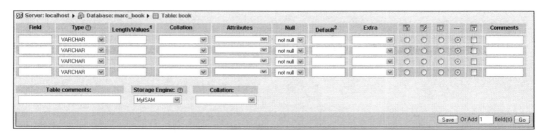

The two following images are enlargements of the left and right sides for this panel:

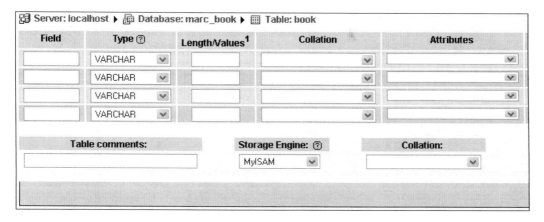

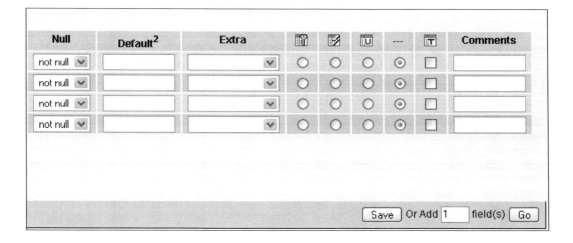

 On pre-4.1 MySQL versions, the **Collation** and **Comments** columns might not be shown at this point. Please refer to Chapter 17, *Character Sets and Collations*, for collation issues, and to Chapter 11, *Relational System*, for column commenting.

The MySQL documentation explains valid characters for table and field names (if we search for **Legal names**). This may vary depending on the MySQL version. Usually, any character that is allowed in a file name (except the dot and the slash) is acceptable in a table name, and the length of the name must not exceed 64 characters. The 64-character limit exists for field names as well, but we can use any character.

We enter our field names under the **Field** column. Each field has a type, the **VARCHAR** type (variable character) being the default since it is the most commonly used.

The **VARCHAR** type is widely used when the field content is alphanumeric, because the contents will occupy only the space needed for it. This type requires a maximum length, which we specify. If we forget to do so, a small pop-up message reminds us later when we save. For the page count and the author identification, we have chosen **INT** type (integer), as depicted in the following screenshot:

Field	Type ⑦	Length/Values[1]
isbn	VARCHAR ∨	25
title	VARCHAR ∨	100
page_count	INT ∨	
author_id	INT ∨	

There are other attributes for fields, but we will leave them empty in this short example. You might notice the **Add 1 Field(s)** dialog at the bottom of the screen. We can use it to add some fields to this table creation panel by entering the appropriate value and hitting **Go**. The number of rows would change according to the new number of fields, *leaving intact the information already entered* about the first four Fields. Before saving the page, let's define some keys.

Choosing Keys

A table should normally have a primary key (a field with unique content that represents each row). Having a primary key is recommended for row identification, better performance, and possible cross-table relations. A good value here is the ISBN; so we select **Primary** for the **isbn** field. As $cfg['PropertiesIconic']$ is set to TRUE by default, we see icons indicating the various index possibilities. Moving the mouse over them, or over the radio buttons, reveals **Primary**, **Index**, **Unique**, and **Full text**.

 Index management (also referred to as **Key** management) can be done at initial table creation, or later in the **Structure** sub-page of Table view.

To improve the speed of queries we will make by author ID, we should add an index on this field. Our screen now looks like this:

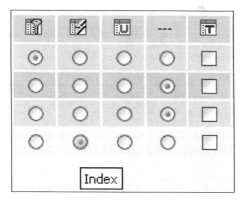

At this point, we could change the table type using the **Type** drop-down menu, but for now we will just accept the default type.

Now we are ready to create the table by clicking on **Save**. If all goes well, the next screen confirms that the table has been created; we are now in the **Structure** sub-page of Table view.

If we forget to specify a value in the **Length** column for a **CHAR** or **VARCHAR**, phpMyAdmin would remind us before trying to create the table.

Of the various tabs leading to other sub-pages, some are not active, because it would not make sense to browse or search a table if there are no rows in it. It would, however, be acceptable to export, because we can export a table's structure even if it contains no data.

(i) Table `marc_book`.`book` has been created.

SQL query:
```
CREATE TABLE `marc_book`.`book` (
  `isbn` VARCHAR( 25 ) NOT NULL ,
  `title` VARCHAR( 100 ) NOT NULL ,
  `page_count` INT NOT NULL ,
  `author_id` INT NOT NULL ,
  PRIMARY KEY ( `isbn` ) ,
  INDEX ( `author_id` )
) ENGINE = MYISAM
```

☐ Profiling [Edit] [Create PHP Code]

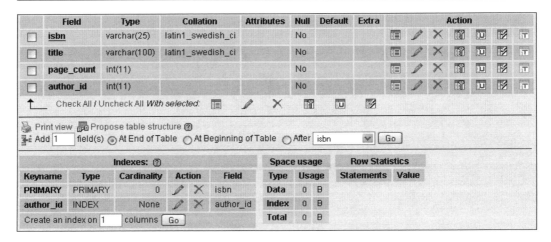

	Field	Type	Collation	Attributes	Null	Default	Extra	Action
☐	**isbn**	varchar(25)	latin1_swedish_ci		No			
☐	**title**	varchar(100)	latin1_swedish_ci		No			
☐	**page_count**	int(11)			No			
☐	**author_id**	int(11)			No			

↑ Check All / Uncheck All *With selected:*

🖶 Print view 🗔 Propose table structure ⑦
Add 1 field(s) ⊙ At End of Table ○ At Beginning of Table ○ After isbn ▾ Go

Indexes: ⑦						Space usage		Row Statistics	
Keyname	Type	Cardinality	Action		Field	Type	Usage	Statements	Value
PRIMARY	PRIMARY	0	✎ ✕		isbn	Data	0 B		
author_id	INDEX	None	✎ ✕		author_id	Index	0 B		
Create an index on 1 columns Go						Total	0 B		

Manual Data Insertion

Now that we have a table, let's put some data in it manually. Before doing so, here are some useful references on data manipulation within this book:

- Chapter 5 explains how to change data.
- Chapter 8 explains how to import data from existing files.
- Chapter 10 explains how to copy data from other tables.
- Chapter 11 explains the relational system (in our case, we will want to link to the **author** table).

For now, click on the **Insert** link, which will lead us to the data-entry (or edit) panel (shown in the screenshot that follows).

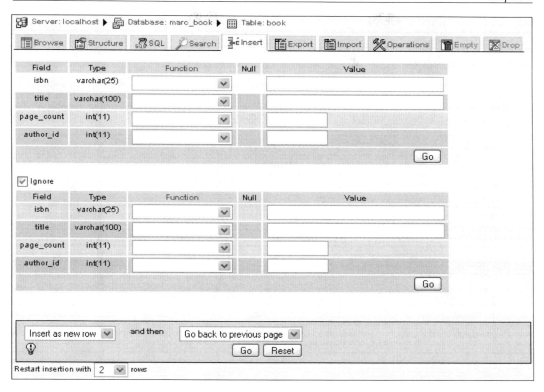

This screen has room to enter information for two rows—two books. This is because the default value of $cfg['InsertRows']$ is 2. In the lower part of the screen, the dialog **Restart insertion with 2 rows** can be used if the default number of rows does not suit our needs—but be warned, any data already on-screen would be lost. By default, the **Ignore** checkbox is ticked, which means that the second group of fields will be ignored. But as soon as we enter some information in one field of this group and exit the field, the **Ignore** box is unchecked.

We can enter the following sample information for two books:

- ISBN: 1-234567-89-0, title: A hundred years of cinema (volume 1), 600 pages, author ID: 1

- ISBN: 1-234567-22-0, title: Future souvenirs, 200 pages, author ID: 2

We start by entering data for the first and second rows. The **Value** column width obeys the maximum length for the character fields. For this example, we keep the lower drop-down selector to its default value of **Insert as new row**. We then click on **Go** to insert the data. There is a **Go** button after each set of columns that represent a row, and another one on the lower part of the screen; all these perform the same effect of saving the entered data:

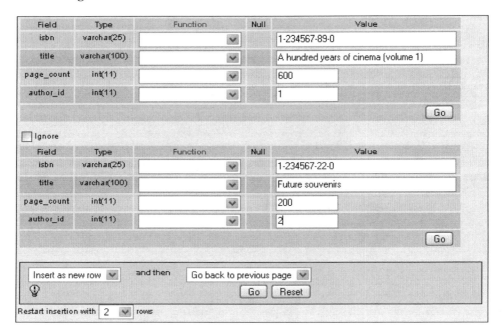

If our intention had been to enter data for more books after these two, we would have selected **Insert another new row** from the first drop-down before clicking on **Go.**

Data Entry Panel Tuning for CHAR and VARCHAR

By default, phpMyAdmin displays an input field on a single line for the field types, CHAR and VARCHAR. This is controlled by setting $cfg['CharEditing'] to 'input'. Sometimes we may want to insert line breaks (new lines) within the field. (This insertion might be done manually with the *Enter* key, or while copying and pasting lines of text from another on-screen source.) This can be done by changing $cfg['CharEditing'] to 'textarea'. This is a global setting and will apply to all fields of all tables, for all users of this copy of phpMyAdmin.

We can tune the number of columns and rows of this text area with:

```
$cfg['CharTextareaCols']    = 40;
$cfg['CharTextareaRows']    = 2;
```

Here, 2 for `$cfg['CharTextareaRows']` means that we should be able to see at least two lines before the browser starts to display a vertical scroll bar. These settings apply to all **CHAR** and **VARCHAR** fields, and using them would generate a different **Insert** screen as follows:

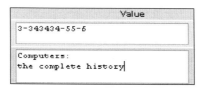

 With this entry mode, the maximum length of each field no longer applies visually, but would be enforced by MySQL at insert time.

Browse Mode

There are many ways to enter this mode. In fact, it is used each time query results are displayed. We can enter this mode manually using the quick-browse icon on the left panel, or by going to Table view for a specific table and clicking **Browse**:

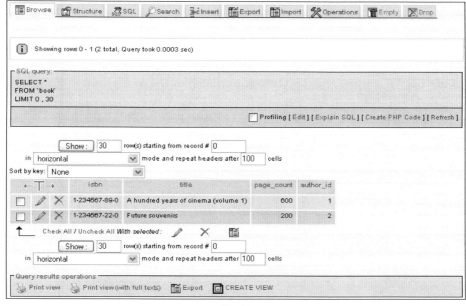

The checkboxes beside each row of results and the **With selected** menu will be explained in Chapter 5.

SQL Query Links

In the **Browse** results, the first part displayed is the query itself, along with a few links. The displayed links may vary depending on our actions and some configuration parameters:

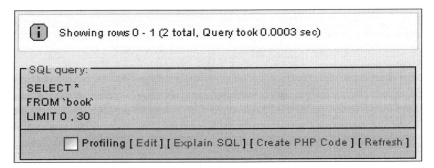

The **Profiling** checkbox will be covered in Chapter 18, *MySQL 5.0 Features*.

The **Edit** link appears if $cfg['SQLQuery']['Edit']$ is set to TRUE. Its purpose is to open the **Query window**, so that you can edit this query. (See Chapter 12, *Entering SQL Commands*.)

Explain SQL is displayed if $cfg['SQLQuery']['Explain']$ is set to TRUE. We will see in Chapter 6, *Changing Table Structure*, what this link can be used for.

The **Create PHP Code** link can be clicked to reformat the query to the syntax expected in a PHP script. It can then be copied and pasted directly at the place where we need the query in the PHP script we are working on. Note that after a click, this link changes to **Without PHP Code**, which would bring back the normal query display. This link is available if $cfg['SQLQuery']['ShowAsPHP']$ is set to TRUE:

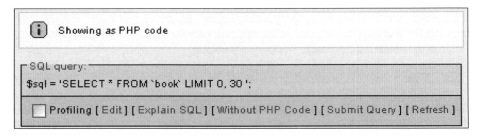

Refresh is used to execute the same query again. The results might change, since a MySQL server is a multi-user server, and other users might be modifying the same tables. This link is shown if `$cfg['SQLQuery']['Refresh']` is set to TRUE.

All these four parameters have a default value of TRUE in `config.inc.php`.

Navigation Bar

This bar is displayed at the top of results and also at the bottom. Column headers can be repeated at certain intervals among results depending on the value entered in **repeat headers after...**.

In the previous example, the bar was simple:

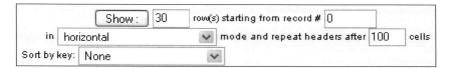

The bar enables us to navigate from page to page, displaying an arbitrary number of records (or rows), starting at some point in the results. Since we entered browse mode by clicking **Browse**, the underlying query that generated the results includes the whole table. However, this is not always the case.

Notice that we are positioned at record number **0** and are seeing records in **horizontal** mode.

The default display mode is 'horizontal', as defined in `$cfg['DefaultDisplay']`. We can also set this to 'vertical' if we usually prefer this mode. Even if our preferred mode is set in this configuration parameter, we can always use the **Show** dialog to change it on-the-fly:

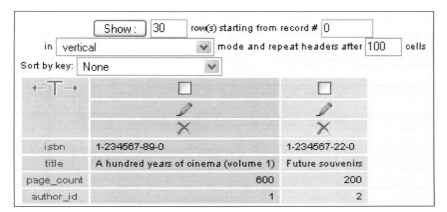

Another possibility is the 'horizontalflipped' choice, which rotates the column headers by 90 degrees. If we try this choice, another parameter, $cfg['HeaderFlipType']$, plays a role. Its default value, 'css', displays true rotated headers, but not every browser supports this—Internet Explorer 7 does and produces:

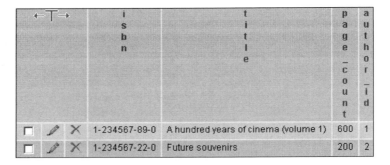

On other browsers, it seems the best we can achieve is by setting $cfg['HeaderFlipType']$ to 'fake':

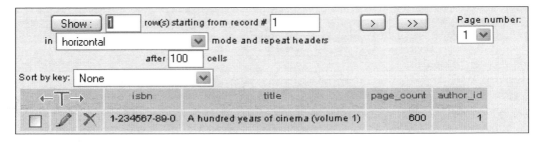

We are currently using a table containing a small number of rows. With larger tables, we could see a more complete set of navigation buttons. To simulate this, let's use the **Show** dialog to change the default number of rows from 30 to 1; we then click **Show**. We can see that the navigation bar adapts itself:

This time, there are buttons labeled **<<**, **<**, **>**, and **>>** for easy access to the first page, previous page, next page, and last page of the results. The buttons only appear when necessary; for example, the **first page** button is not displayed if we already are on the first page. These symbols are displayed in this manner because the default setting of $cfg['NavigationBarIconic']$ is TRUE. A FALSE here would produce a different set of labels:

There is also a **Page number** drop-down menu, to go directly to one of the pages located near the current page. Since there can be hundreds or thousands of pages, this menu is kept small with only a few page numbers before and after the current page.

By design, phpMyAdmin always tries to give quick results, and one way to achieve this result is by adding a **LIMIT** clause in **SELECT**. If there is already a **LIMIT** clause in the original query, phpMyAdmin will respect it. The default limit is 30 rows, set in $cfg['MaxRows']$. With multiple users on the server, this helps keeping the server load to a minimum.

Another button is available on the navigation bar, but must be activated by setting $cfg['ShowAll']$ to TRUE. It would be very tempting for users to use this button often, so on a multi-user installation of phpMyAdmin, it is recommended that it be disabled (FALSE). When enabled, the navigation bar is augmented as shown:

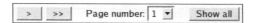

Clicking on the **Show all** button retrieves all the rows of the current results set, which might hit the execution time limit in PHP or a memory limit in the server or browser.

 If we enter a big number in the **Show...rows** dialog, the same results will be achieved (and we may face the same potential problems).

Query Results Operations

A section labelled **Query results operations** is located under the results. It contains links to print the results (without or with the FULL TEXT columns), to export these results (see Chapter 7, section *Exporting Partial Query Results*) or to create a view from this query (more on this in Chapter 18, *MySQL 5.0 Features*).

Sorting Results

In SQL, we can never be sure of the order in which the data is retrieved, unless we explicitly sort the data. Some implementations of the retrieving engine may show results in the same order as when data was entered, or by primary key, but a sure way to get results in the order we want is by sorting them explicitly.

When browsing results are displayed, any column header can be clicked to sort on this column, even if it is not part of an index. Let's click on the **author_id** column header.

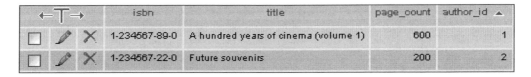

We can confirm that the sort occurred by watching the SQL query at the top of screen; it should contain an **ORDER BY** clause.

We now see a small red triangle pointing upwards beside the **author_id** header. This means that the current sort order is 'ascending'. Moving the mouse cursor over the **author_id** header makes the red triangle change direction, to indicate what will happen if we click on the header: a sort by descending **author_id**.

Another way to sort is by key. The **Sort** dialog shows all the keys already defined. Here we see a key named **PRIMARY**, the name given to our primary key on the **isbn** field when we checked **Primary** for this field at creation time:

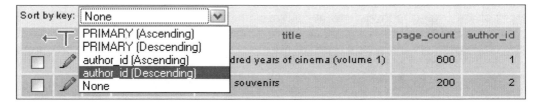

This might be the only way to sort on multiple fields at once (for multi-fields indexes).

The default initial sort order is defined in $cfg['Order']$ with ASC for ascending, DESC for descending, or SMART, which means that fields of type DATE, TIME, DATETIME, and TIMESTAMP would be sorted in descending order, and other field types in ascending order.

Color-Marking Rows

When moving the mouse between rows, the row background color may change to the color defined in $cfg['BrowsePointerColor']. This parameter can be found in themes/themename/layout.inc.php. To enable this browse pointer for all themes, $cfg['BrowsePointerEnable'] must be set to TRUE (the default) in config.inc.php.

It may be interesting to visually mark some rows to highlight their importance for personal comparison of data, or when showing data to people. Highlighting is done by clicking the row. Clicking again removes the mark on the row. The chosen color is defined by $cfg['BrowseMarkerColor'] (see themes/themename/layout.inc. php). This feature must be enabled by setting $cfg['BrowseMarkerEnable'] to TRUE, this time in config.inc.php—this sets the feature for all themes. We can mark more than one row. Marking the row also activates the checkbox for this row:

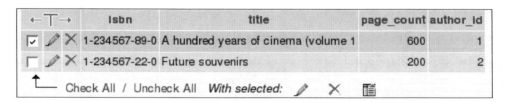

Limiting the Length of Each Column

In the previous examples, we always saw the full contents of each column, because their number of characters was within the limit defined by $cfg['LimitChars']. This is a limit enforced on all non-numeric fields. If this limit was lower (say 10), the display would be as follows:

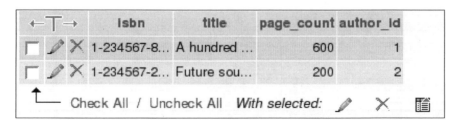

This would help us see more columns at the same time (at the expense of seeing less of each column).

To reveal the full texts, we can click the **T** besides the column header, which toggles between the full-text mode and the partial-text mode:

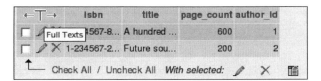

Browsing Distinct Values

There is a quick way to display all distinct values and the number of occurrences for each value for each field. This feature is available on the **Structure** page. For example, we want to know how many different authors we have in our book table and how many books each one wrote. On the line describing the field we want to browse — here **author_id** — we click the **Browse distinct values** icon or link.

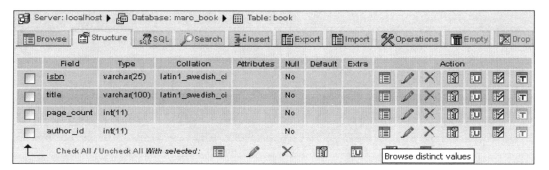

We have a limited test set but we can nonetheless see the results:

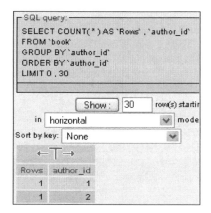

Browse-Mode Customization

Here are more parameters that control the appearance of results. These parameters — except $cfg['RepeatCells'] — are located in themes/themename/layout.inc.php.

- $cfg['Border']: The HTML tables used to present results have no border by default because this parameter is set to 0; we can put a higher number (for example 1 or 2) to add borders to the tables.

- $cfg['ThBgcolor']: The tables mentioned have headers with #D3DCE3 as the default background color.

- $cfg['BgcolorOne'], $cfg['BgcolorTwo']: When displaying rows of results, two background colors are used alternately; by default, those are #CCCCCC and #DDDDDD.

- $cfg['RepeatCells']: When many rows of data are displayed, we may lose track of the meaning of each column; by default, at each 100th cell, column headers are displayed.

Creating an Additional Table

In our (simple) design, we know that we need another table: the **author** table. The **author** table will contain:

- Author identification
- Full name
- Phone number

To create this table, we must go back to the Database view in the left panel. We click on **marc_book** in the left panel, and request the creation of another table with three fields:

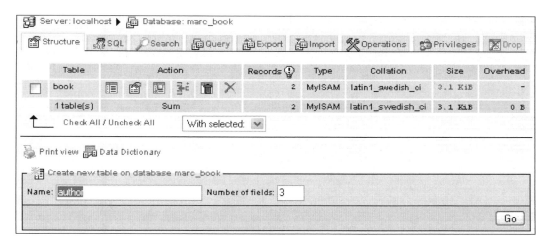

Using the same techniques used when creating the first table, we get:

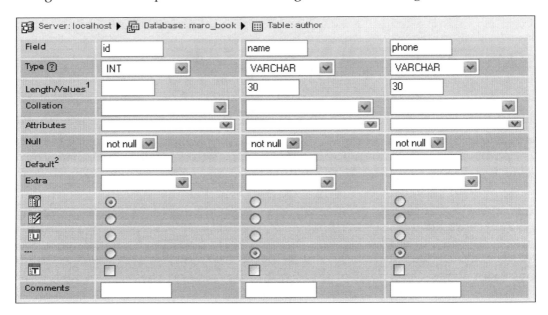

Since we have three fields or less, the display is now in vertical mode (more details on this in Chapter 6, *Vertical Mode* section).

Here the field name **id**, which is our primary key in this new table, relates to the author_id field from the book table. After saving the table structure, we enter some data for authors 1 and 2. Use your imagination for this!

Summary

In this chapter, we explained how to create a database and tables, and how to enter data manually in the tables. We also saw how to confirm the presence of data by using the browse mode; including the SQL query links, navigation bar, sorting options, and row marking.

5
Changing Data

Data is not static; it often changes. This chapter focuses on editing and deleting data and its supporting structures: tables and databases.

Edit Mode

When we browse a table or view results from a search on any single-table query, small icons appear on the left or right of each table row:

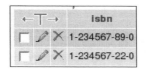

The row can be edited with the pencil-shaped icon and deleted with the X-shaped icon. The exact form and location of these controls are governed by:

```
$cfg['PropertiesIconic']      = TRUE;
$cfg['ModifyDeleteAtLeft']    = TRUE;
$cfg['ModifyDeleteAtRight']   = FALSE;
```

We can decide whether to display them on the left, the right, or both sides. The $cfg['PropertiesIconic'] parameter can have the values TRUE, FALSE, or 'both'. TRUE displays icons as seen in the previous image, FALSE displays **Edit** and **Delete** (or their translated equivalent) as links, and 'both' displays the icon *and* the text.

The small checkbox beside each row is explained in the *Multi-Row Edit* and the *Deleting Many Rows* sections later in this chapter.

Clicking on the **Edit** icon or link brings the following panel, which is similar to the data entry panel (except for the lower part):

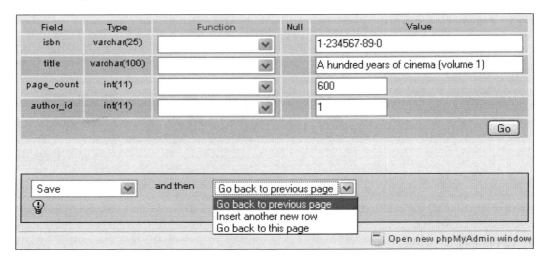

In this panel, we can change data by directly typing (or by cutting and pasting via the normal operating system mechanisms). We can also revert to the original contents using the **Reset** button.

By default, the lower drop-down menus are set to **Save** (so that we make changes to *this* row) and **Go back to previous page** (so that we can continue editing another row on the previous results page). We might want to stay on the current page after clicking **Go**—if we wanted to save and then continue editing—so we can choose **Go back to this page**. If we want to insert yet another new row after saving the current row, we just have to choose **Insert another new row** before saving. The **Insert as new row** choice—below the **Save** choice—is explained in the section *Duplicating Rows of Data* of this chapter.

Moving to Next Field with the Tab Key

People who prefer to use the keyboard can use the *Tab* key to go to the next field. Normally, the cursor goes from left to right and from top to bottom, so it would travel into the fields in the **Function** column (more on this in a moment). However, to ease data navigation in phpMyAdmin, the normal order of navigation has been altered; the *Tab* key first goes through each field in the **Value** column and then through each one in the **Function** column.

Moving with Arrows

Another way of moving between fields is with the *Ctrl+arrows* keys. This method might be easier than using the *Tab* key when many fields are on-screen. For this to work, the `$cfg['CtrlArrowsMoving']` parameter must be set to `true`; this is the default value.

 On a Mac OS X 10.5 with Spaces enabled, *Ctrl+arrows* are the default shortcut to switch between virtual desktops, so this technique cannot be used for moving between fields.

Handling NULL Values

If the table's structure permits a `NULL` value inside a field, a small checkbox appears in the field's **Null** column. Checking it puts a `NULL` value in the field. A special mechanism has also been added to phpMyAdmin to ensure that, if data is typed into the **Value** column for this field, the **Null** checkbox is cleared automatically. (This is possible in JavaScript-enabled browsers.)

Here, we have modified the structure (as explained in Chapter 6) of the **phone** field in the `author` table to permit a `NULL` value. The **Null** checkbox is not checked here:

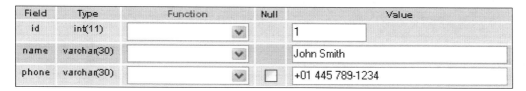

The data is erased after checking the **Null** box, as shown in the following screenshot:

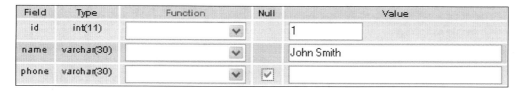

The **Edit** panel will appear this way if this row is ever brought on-screen again.

Applying a Function to a Value

The MySQL language offers some functions that we may apply to data before saving, and some of these functions appear in a drop-down menu beside each field if `$cfg['ShowFunctionFields']` is set to `TRUE`.

The function list is defined in the `$cfg['Functions']` array. The most commonly used functions for a certain data type are displayed first in the list. Some restrictions are defined in the `$cfg['RestrictColumnTypes']` and `$cfg['RestrictFunctions']` arrays to control which functions are displayed first.

Here are the definitions that restrict the function names to be displayed for the VARCHAR type:

```
$cfg['RestrictColumnTypes'] = array(
        'VARCHAR'       => 'FUNC_CHAR',   [...]
$cfg['RestrictFunctions'] = array(
        'FUNC_CHAR'    => array(
            'ASCII',
            'CHAR',
            'SOUNDEX',
            'LCASE',
            'UCASE',
            'PASSWORD',
            'OLD_PASSWORD',
            'MD5',
            'SHA1',
            'ENCRYPT',
            'COMPRESS',
            'UNCOMPRESS',
            'LAST_INSERT_ID',
            'USER',
            'CONCAT'
        ),   [...]
```

As depicted in the following screenshot, we apply the UCASE function to the title when saving this row:

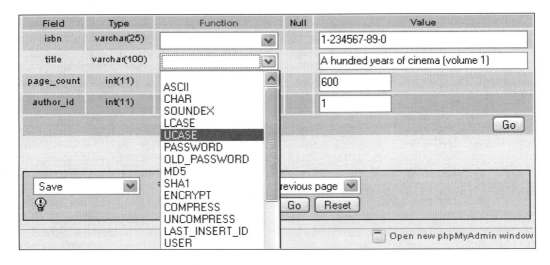

This feature may be disabled by setting `$cfg['ShowFunctionFields']` to FALSE to gain some screen space (to be able to see more of the data). Moreover, the **Function** column header is clickable so we can disable this feature on the fly.

When the feature is disabled, either by clicking or via the configuration parameter, a **Show: Function** link appears in order to display this **Function** column with a single click.

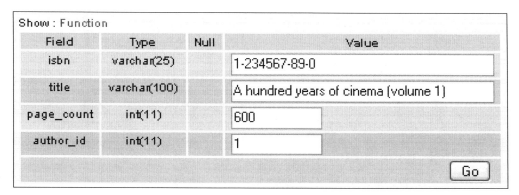

Duplicating Rows of Data

During the course of data maintenance (for permanent duplication or for test purposes), we often have to generate a copy of a row. If this is done in the same table, we must respect the rules of key uniqueness.

An example is in order here. Our author has written Volume 2 of his book about cinema, so the fields that need a slight change are the ISBN, title, and page count. We bring the existing row on-screen, change these three fields, and choose **Insert as new row**, as shown in the following screenshot:

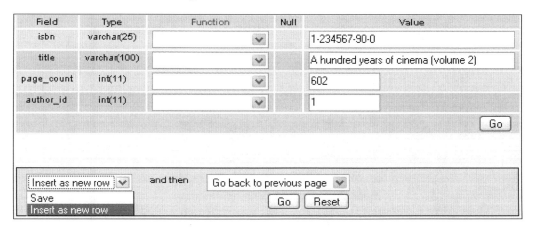

When we click **Go**, another row is created with the modified information, leaving the original row unchanged:

←T→			isbn	title	page_count	author_id
☐	🖉	✕	1-234567-89-0	A hundred years of cinema (volume 1)	600	1
☐	🖉	✕	1-234567-22-0	Future souvenirs	200	2
☐	🖉	✕	1-234567-90-0	A hundred years of cinema (volume 2)	602	1

Multi-Row Editing

Starting with phpMyAdmin 2.5.5, the multi-row edit feature enables us to use checkboxes on the rows we want to edit, and use the **Change** link (or the pencil-shaped icon) in the **With selected** menu. The **Check All / Uncheck All** links can also be used to quickly check or uncheck all the boxes. We can also click anywhere on the row's data to activate the corresponding checkbox.

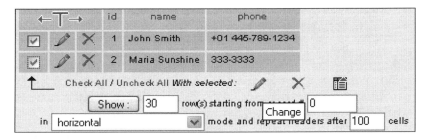

This brings up an Edit panel containing all the chosen rows, and the editing process may continue while the data from these rows is seen, compared, and changed.

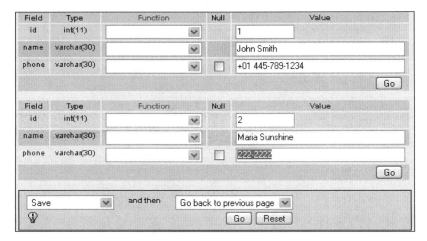

When we mark some rows with the checkboxes, we can also perform two other actions on them: delete (see the *Deleting Many Rows* section in this chapter) and export (see Chapter 7).

Editing the Next Row

Starting with version 2.6.1, sequential editing is possible on tables that have a primary key on an integer field. Our `author` table meets the criteria. Let's see what happens when we start editing the row with the `id` value 1:

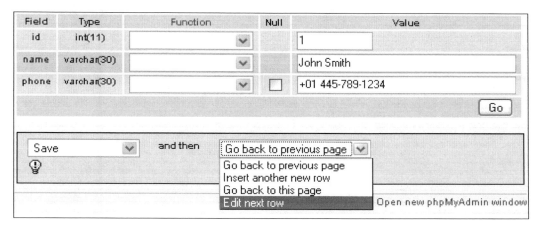

The editing panel appears, and we can edit author number 1. However, in the drop-down menu, the **Edit next row** choice is available. If chosen, the next author—the first one whose primary key value is greater than the current primary key value—will be available to edit.

Deleting Data

phpMyAdmin's interface enables us to delete the following:

- Single rows of data
- Multiple rows of a table
- All the rows in a table
- All the rows in multiple tables

Deleting a Single Row

We can use the small X-shaped icon beside each row to delete the row. If the value of $cfg['Confirm']$ is set to TRUE, every MySQL DELETE statement has to be confirmed before execution. This is the default, because it might not be prudent to allow a row to be deleted with just one click!

The form of the confirmation varies depending on the browser's ability to execute JavaScript. A JavaScript-based confirmation popup would look like the following screenshot:

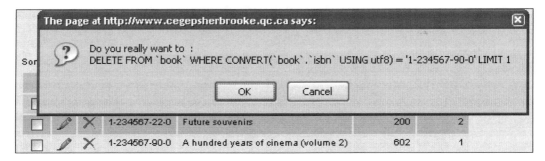

If JavaScript has been disabled in our browser, a distinct panel appears:

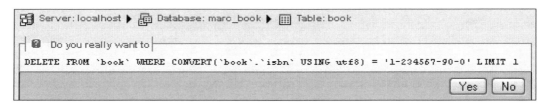

The actual DELETE statement will use whatever information is best to ensure the deletion of only the intended row. In our case, a primary key had been defined and was used in the WHERE clause. In the absence of a primary key, a longer WHERE clause will be generated based on the value of each field. The WHERE clause might even prevent the correct execution of the DELETE operation, especially if there are TEXT or BLOB fields, because the HTTP transaction used to send the query to the web server may be limited in length by the browser or the server.

Deleting Many Rows

A feature added to phpMyAdmin in version 2.5.4 is the multi-row delete. Let's say we examine a page of rows and decide that some rows have to be destroyed. Instead of deleting them one by one with the **Delete** link or icon—and because sometimes the decision to delete must be made while examining a group of rows—there are checkboxes beside rows in Table view mode:

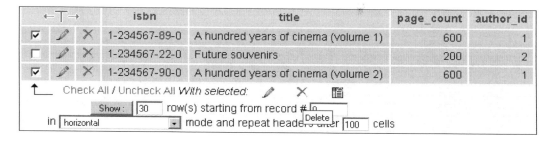

These are used with the **With selected** X-shaped icon. A confirmation screen appears listing all the rows that are about to be deleted. It is also possible to click anywhere on the row's data to activate the corresponding checkbox.

Deleting All the Rows in a Table

To completely erase all the rows in a table (leaving its structure intact), we go to the Database view and click on the database name in the left panel. We then click on the trash can icon located on the same line as the table we want to empty:

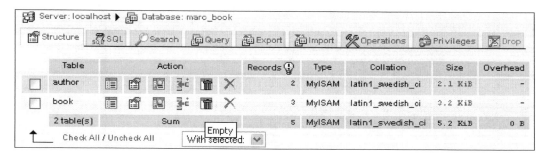

We get a message confirming the TRUNCATE statement (the MySQL statement used to quickly empty a table). For our exercise, we won't delete this precious data!

Emptying a table can also be done in Table view with the **Empty** link located on the top menu:

Deleting data, either row-by-row or by emptying a table, is a permanent action. No recovery is then possible except by using a backup.

Deleting All Rows in Many Tables

The screen before last shows a checkbox to the left of each table name. We can choose some tables, then in the **With selected** menu, choose the **Empty** operation, as shown in the following screen:

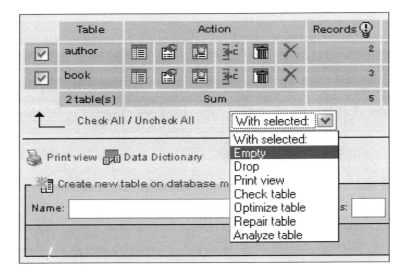

Of course, this decision must not be taken lightly!

Deleting Tables

Deleting a table erases the data *and* the table's structure. We can delete tables using the **Drop** link in Table view:

In the Database view, we can delete a specific table by using the X-shaped icon for that table. The same mechanism also exists for deleting more that one table (with the drop-down menu and the **Drop** action).

The **Empty** and **Drop** actions are marked in red to better indicate the inherent danger of these actions on data.

Deleting Databases

We can delete a whole database—including all its tables—using the **Drop** link in Database view:

By default, $cfg['AllowUserDropDatabase']$ is set to FALSE, so this link is hidden to unprivileged users until this setting is manually changed to TRUE.

To help us think twice, a special message appears before a database is deleted: **You are about to DESTROY a complete database!**

 The database **mysql** containing all user and privilege definitions is so important that the Drop button is deactivated for this database, even for administrators.

Summary

In this chapter, we examined concepts like editing data, including the null field and using the *Tab* key, applying a function to a value, duplicating rows of data, and deleting data, tables, and databases.

6
Changing Table Structures

This chapter explores editing table definitions and using special column types. When developing an application, requirements often change because of new or modified needs. Developers must accommodate these changes through judicious table-structure editing.

Adding a Field

Suppose that we need a new field to store a book's language and, that by default, the books on which we keep data are written in English. We decide that the field will be called **language** and will contain a code composed of two characters (**en** by default).

In the **Structure** sub-page of the Table view for the **book** table, we can find the **Add field** dialog. Here, we specify how many new fields we want and where they will go.

The positions of the new fields in the table only matter from a developer's point of view; we usually group the fields logically so that we can find them more easily in the list of fields. The exact position of the fields will not play a role in the intended results (output from the queries), because these results can be adjusted regardless of the table structure. Usually, the most important fields (including the keys) are located at the beginning of the table, but this is a matter of personal preference.

We choose to put the new field **At End of Table**, so we check the corresponding radio button and click on **Go**:

Other possible choices would be **At Beginning of Table** and **After** (where we would have to choose from the drop-down menu the field after which the new field must go).

We see the familiar panel for the new fields, repeated for the number of fields asked for. We fill it in, and this time, we enter a default value, **en**. We then click on **Save**.

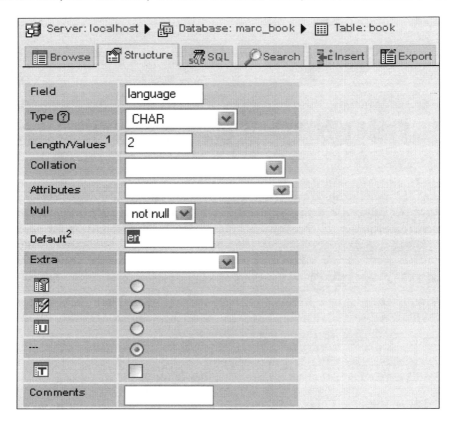

Vertical Mode

The previous panel appeared in vertical mode because the default for $cfg['DefaultPropDisplay']$ is 3, which means that for three columns or less, the vertical mode is used and for more than three, horizontal mode would be automatically selected. We can use here a number of our choosing.

If we set $cfg['DefaultPropDisplay']$ to 'vertical', the panel to add new fields (along with the panel to edit a field's structure) will be always presented in vertical order. The advantages of working in vertical mode become obvious especially when there are more choices for each field, as explained in Chapter 16, *MIME-Based Transformations*.

Horizontal Mode

The $cfg['DefaultPropDisplay']$ parameter can also take a value of 'horizontal'. Let's see how the panel appears in this mode when we ask for three new fields:

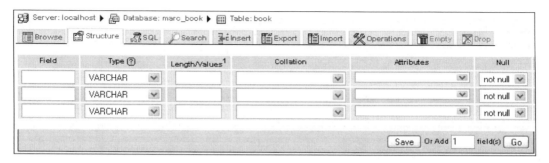

Editing Field Attributes

On the **Structure** sub-page, we can make further changes to our table. For this example, we have set $cfg['PropertiesIconic']$ to 'both' to see the icons along with their text explanation:

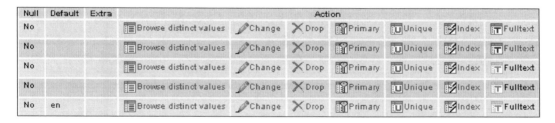

This panel does not allow every possible change to fields. It specifically allows:

- Changing one field structure, using the **Change** link on a specific field
- Removing a field: **Drop**
- Adding a field to an existing **Primary** key
- Setting a non-unique **Index** or a **Unique** index on a field
- Setting a **Fulltext** index (offered only if the field type allows it)

These are quick links that may be useful in some situations, but they do not replace the full index management panel, both of which are explained in this chapter.

We can also use the checkboxes to choose fields and, with the appropriate **With selected** icons, edit the fields or do a multiple field deletion with **Drop**. The **Check All / Uncheck All** option permits us to easily check or uncheck all boxes.

TEXT

We will now explore how to use the **TEXT** field type and the relevant configuration values to adjust for the best possible phpMyAdmin behavior.

First we add to the **book** table a **TEXT** field called **description**:

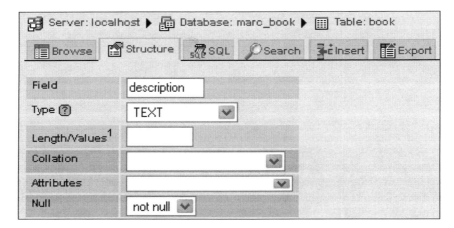

There are three parameters that control the layout of the text area that will be displayed in Insert or Edit mode for the **TEXT** fields. First, the number of columns and rows for each field is defined by:

```
$cfg['TextareaCols']        = 40;
$cfg['TextareaRows']        = 7;
```

This gives (by default) the following space to work on a **TEXT** field:

The settings impose only a visual limit on the text area, and a vertical scroll bar is created by the browser if necessary.

Although **MEDIUMTEXT**, **TEXT**, and **LONGTEXT** columns can accommodate more than 32K of data, some browsers cannot always edit them with the mechanism offered by HTML: a text area. In fact, experimentation has convinced the phpMyAdmin development team to have the product display a warning message, if the contents are larger than 32K, telling users that it might not be editable.

The last parameter has an impact for **LONGTEXT** fields. Setting `$cfg['LongtextDoubleTextarea']` to TRUE doubles the available editing space.

BLOB (Binary Large Object) Fields

BLOB fields are usually used to hold binary data (such as images and sounds), even though the MySQL documentation implies that **TEXT** fields could be used for this purpose. The MySQL 5.1 manual says "In some cases, it may be desirable to store binary data such as media files in **BLOB** or **TEXT** columns" but another phrase, "**BLOB** columns are treated as binary strings (byte strings)" seems to indicate that binary data should really be stored in **BLOB** fields. Thus, phpMyAdmin's intention is to work with **BLOB** fields to hold all binary data.

We will see in Chapter 16, *MIME-Based Transformations* that there are special mechanisms available to go further with **BLOB** fields, including being able to view some images directly from within phpMyAdmin.

First we add a **BLOB** field, **cover_photo**, to our **book** table:

If we now browse the table, we can see the field length information, **[BLOB – 0 B]**, for each **BLOB** field:

isbn	title	page_count	author_id	language	description	cover_photo
1-234567-89-0	A hundred years of cinema (volume 1)	600	1	en		[BLOB - 0 B]
1-234567-22-0	Future souvenirs	200	2	en		[BLOB - 0 B]
1-234567-90-0	A hundred years of cinema (volume 2)	602	1	en		[BLOB - 0 B]

This is because the `$cfg['ShowBlob']` configuration directive is set to FALSE by default, thus blocking the display of **BLOB** contents in Browse and Edit modes (and showing a **Binary - do not edit** warning). This behavior is intentional — usually we cannot do anything with binary data represented in plain text.

Binary Contents Uploads

If we now edit one row, we see the warning and a **Browse...** button. The exact caption on this button depends on the browser. Even though editing is not allowed, we can easily upload a text or binary file's contents into this **BLOB** column.

Let's choose an image file using the **Browse** button — for example, the `logo_left.png` file in a test copy of the `phpMyAdmin/themes/original/img` directory located on our client workstation — and click **Go**.

We need to keep in mind some limits for the upload size. Firstly, the **BLOB** field size is limited to 64K, so phpMyAdmin reminds us of this limit with the **Max: 65,536 Bytes** warning. Also, there could be limits inherent to PHP itself – see Chapter 8, *Importing Structure and Data* – which would be also taken into account in this maximum size value. We have now uploaded an image inside this field for a specific row:

isbn	title	page_count	author_id	language	description	cover_photo
1-234567-89-0	A hundred years of cinema (volume 1)	600	1	en		[BLOB - 6.7 KiB]

If `$cfg['ShowBlob']` is set to TRUE, we see the following in the **BLOB** field:

 To really *see* the image from within phpMyAdmin, refer to Chapter 16, *MIME-Based Transformations.*

The `$cfg['ProtectBinary']` parameter controls what can be done while editing binary fields (**BLOB**s and any other field with the `binary` attribute). The default value `'blob'` protects against the editing of **BLOB** fields but allows us to edit other fields marked as `binary` by MySQL. A value of `'all'` would protect against editing even `binary` fields. A value of FALSE would protect nothing, thus allowing us to edit all fields. If we try the last choice, we see the following in the **Edit** panel for this row:

Chances are this is not our favorite image editor! In fact, data corruption may result even if we save this row without touching the **BLOB** field. But the setting to remove `ProtectBinary` exists because some users put text in their **BLOB** fields and they need to be able to modify this text.

MySQL **BLOB** data types are actually similar to their corresponding **TEXT** data types, but we should keep in mind that a **BLOB** has no character set, whereas a **TEXT** column has a character set that impacts sorting and comparison. This is why phpMyAdmin can be configured to allow editing of **BLOB** fields.

ENUM and SET

Both these field types are intended to represent a list of possible values; the difference is that the user can choose only one value from a defined list of values with **ENUM**, and more than one value with **SET**. With **SET**, the multiple values all go into one cell; multiple values do not imply the creation of more than one row of data.

We add a field named **genre** to the `book` table and define it as an **ENUM**. For now, we choose to put short codes in the value list and make one of them, **'F'**, into the default value:

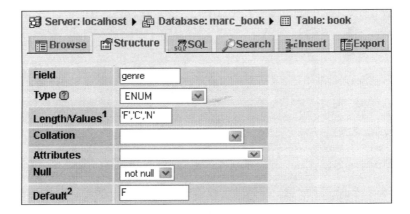

In the value list, we have to enclose each value within single quotes, unlike in the default value field. In our design, we know that these values stand for *Fantasy*, *Child*, and *Novel*, but for now we want to see the interface's behavior with short codes. In the **Insert** panel, we now see a radio box interface:

If we decide to have more self-describing codes, we can go back to **Structure** mode and change the definition for the **genre** field. In the following example, we do not see the complete value list because the field is not large enough, but what we entered was **'Fantasy','Child','Novel'**. We also have to change the default value to one of the possible values, to avoid getting an error message while trying to save this file structure modification.

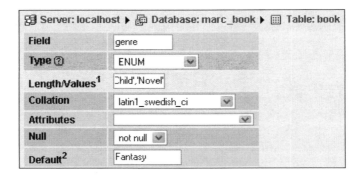

With the modified value list, the **Insert** panel now looks as follows:

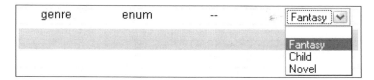

Observe that the radio buttons have been replaced by a drop-down list because the possible values are longer.

If we want more than one possible value selected, we have to change the field type to **SET**. The same value list may be used, but now, using our browser's multiple value selector (control-click on a Windows or Linux desktop, command-click on a Mac), we can select more that one value:

 For the previous example, we would store only the **genre** codes in the **book** table, in a normalized data structure and would rely on another table to store the description for each code. We would not be using **SET** or **ENUM** in this case.

DATE, DATETIME, and TIMESTAMP

We could use a normal character field to store date or time information, but **DATE**, **DATETIME**, and **TIMESTAMP** are more efficient for this purpose. MySQL checks the contents to ensure valid date and time information, and offers special functions to work on these fields.

Calendar Popup

As an added benefit, phpMyAdmin offers a calendar popup for easy data entry.

We will start by adding a **DATE** field, **date_published**, to our **book** table. If we go into Insert mode, we should now see the new field where we could type a date. A **Calendar** icon is also available:

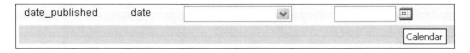

This icon brings a popup window, synchronized to this **DATE** field: if there is already a value in the field, the popup displays accordingly. In our case, there is no value in the field, so the calendar shows the current date:

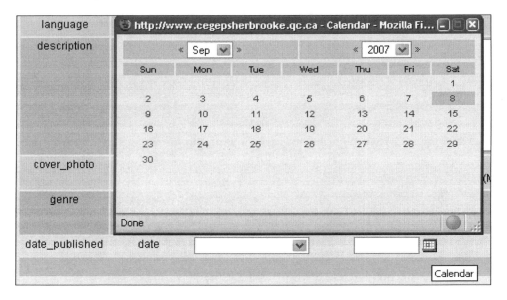

Small symbols on each side of the month and year headers permit easy scrolling through months and years, and a simple click on the date we want transports it to our **date_published** field.

For a **DATETIME** or **TIMESTAMP** field, the popup offers to edit the time part:

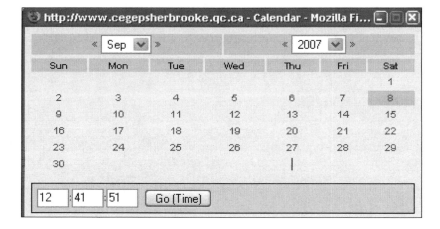

TIMESTAMP Options

Starting with MySQL 4.1.2, there are more options that can affect a **TIMESTAMP** column. Let's add to our **book** table a column named **stamp** of type **TIMESTAMP**. As soon as we choose **TIMESTAMP** from the **Type** drop-down list—provided that JavaScript has been activated in our browser—we see a new checkbox under the **Default** column: **CURRENT_TIMESTAMP**. Note that in the **Attributes** column, we can choose **ON UPDATE CURRENT_TIMESTAMP**.

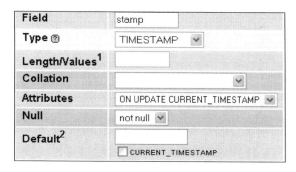

Bit

MySQL 5.0.3 introduced true bit-field values. These take the same amount of space in the database as the number of bits in their definition. Let's say we have three pieces of information about each book, and each piece can only be true (1) or false (0):

- Book is hard cover
- Book contains a CD-ROM
- Book available only in electronic format

We'll use a single `BIT` field to store these three pieces of information. Therefore we add a field to the `book` table:

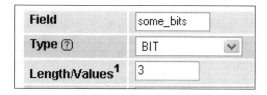

To construct and subsequently interpret the values we store into this field, we have to think in binary, respecting the position of each bit within the field. To indicate that a book is not hard cover, contains a CD-ROM and is available only in electronic format, we would use a value of `011`.

Since version 2.11.0, phpMyAdmin handles BIT fields in a binary way. For example, if we edit one row and set a value of 011 to the some_bits column, the following query is sent at save time:

```
UPDATE `marc_book`.`book` SET `stamp` = NOW( ),
`some_bits` = b '011'

WHERE CONVERT( `book`.`isbn` USING utf8 ) = '1-234567-89-0' LIMIT 1;
```

The highlighted line of this query shows that the column really receives a binary value. At browse time, the exact field value (which is 3, a meaningless value for our purposes) is redisplayed in its binary form 011, which helps to interpret each discrete bit value.

Index Management

phpMyAdmin has a number of index management options, which we will cover in this section.

Single-Field Indexes

We have already seen how the **Structure** panel offers a quick way to create an index on a single field, thanks to some quick links like **Primary**, **Index**, and **Unique**. Under the field list, there is a section of the interface used to manage indexes:

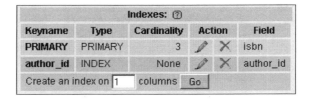

This section has links to edit or delete every index. Here, the **Field** part lists only one field per index, and we can see that the whole field participates in the index because there is no size information after each field name—contrary to what will be seen in our next example.

We will now add an index on the title. However, we want to restrict the length of this index to reduce the space used by the on-disk index structure. The **Create an index on 1 columns** option is appropriate, so we click **Go**. In the next screen, we specify the index details as shown in the following screen:

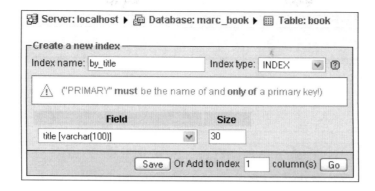

Here is how to fill in this panel:

- **Index name**: A name we invent
- **Index type**: We can choose **INDEX** or **UNIQUE**
- **Field**: We select the field that is used as the index, which is the **title** field
- **Size**: We enter **30** instead of **100** (the complete length of the field) to save space

After saving this panel, we can confirm from the following screenshot that the index is created and does not cover the whole length of the title field:

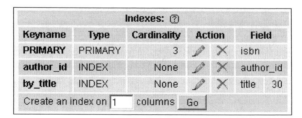

Multi-Field Indexes and Index Editing

In the next example, we assume that in a future application we will need to find the books written by a specific author in a specific language. It makes sense to expand our **author_id** index, adding the **language** field to it.

We click the **Edit** link (small pencil) on the line containing the **author_id** index; this brings us to the following panel, which shows the current state of this index:

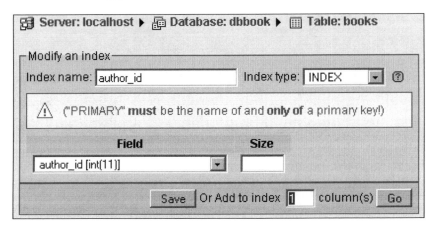

Next, we choose **Add to index 1 column(s)**; we then click **Go**. We select the **language** field on the next panel. This time we do not have to enter a size since the whole field will be used in the index:

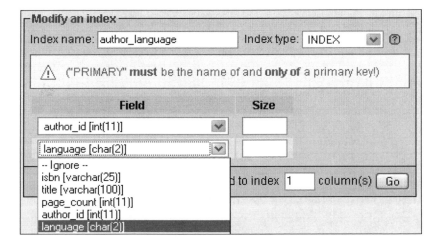

For better documentation, we can change the **Index name** (author_language is appropriate). We save this index modification and we are back to:

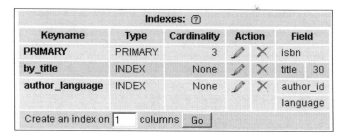

FULLTEXT Indexes

This special type of index allows for full-text searches. It is supported only on MyISAM tables for **VARCHAR** and **TEXT** fields. We can use the **Fulltext** quick link in the fields list or go to the index management panel and choose **Fulltext** in the drop-down menu:

We want a **FULLTEXT** index on the **description** field so that we are able to locate a book from words present in its description. After the index has been created, it looks like:

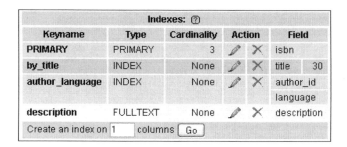

Depending on the MySQL version, we might see **1** as the field length for the newly created index. In fact, MySQL does not support the idea of an index length for **FULLTEXT** indexes: the index is always on the whole field, but this **1** would be the value reported by MySQL.

Table Optimization: Explaining a Query

In this section, we want to get some information about the index that MySQL uses for a specific query, and the performance impact of not having defined an index.

Let's assume we want to use the following query:

```
SELECT   *
FROM `book`
WHERE author_id = 2 AND language = 'es'
```

We want to know which books written by author **2** are in the **es** language, our code for Spanish.

To enter this query, we use the **SQL** link from the database or the table menu, or the SQL query window (see Chapter 12). We enter this query in the query box and click **Go**. Whether the query finds any results is not important right now.

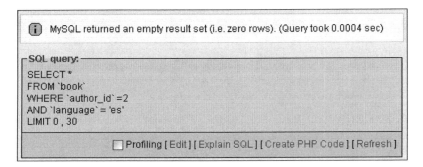

Let's look at the links: **[Edit] [Explain SQL] [Create PHP Code] [Refresh]**

We will now use the **[Explain SQL]** link to get information about which index (if any) has been used for this query:

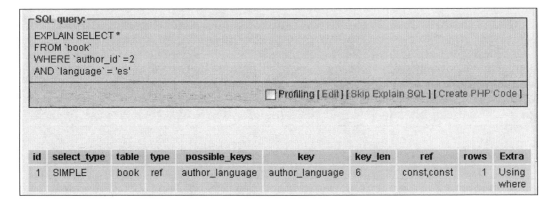

id	select_type	table	type	possible_keys	key	key_len	ref	rows	Extra
1	SIMPLE	book	ref	author_language	author_language	6	const,const	1	Using where

We can see that the **EXPLAIN** command has been passed to MySQL, telling us that the **possible_keys** used is **author_language**. Thus, we know that this index will be used for this type of query. If this index had not existed, the result would have been quite different:

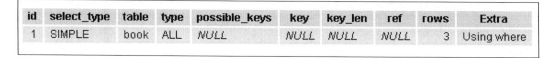

id	select_type	table	type	possible_keys	key	key_len	ref	rows	Extra
1	SIMPLE	book	ALL	NULL	NULL	NULL	NULL	3	Using where

Here, **possible_keys (NULL)** and the **type (ALL)** mean that no index would be used and that all rows would need to be examined to find the desired data. Depending on the total number of rows, this could have a serious impact on the performance. We can ascertain the exact impact by examining the query timing that phpMyAdmin displays on each results page and comparing with or without the index:

Showing rows 0 - 2 (3 total, Query took 0.0003 sec)

However, the difference in time can be minimal if we only have limited test data compared to a real table in production.

Detection of Index Problems

Since version 2.6.1, phpMyAdmin tries to detect some common index problems. For example, let's access the **book** table and add an index on the **isbn** column. When we display this table's structure, we get a warning:

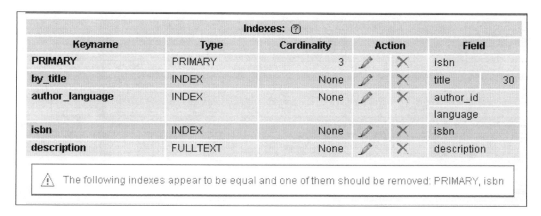

Keyname	Type	Cardinality	Action	Field	
PRIMARY	PRIMARY	3	✏ ✕	isbn	
by_title	INDEX	None	✏ ✕	title	30
author_language	INDEX	None	✏ ✕	author_id	
				language	
isbn	INDEX	None	✏ ✕	isbn	
description	FULLTEXT	None	✏ ✕	description	

⚠ The following indexes appear to be equal and one of them should be removed: PRIMARY, isbn

The intention here is to warn us about an inefficient index structure when considering the whole table. We don't need to have two indexes on the same column.

We should consider this feature as work in progress.

Summary

In this chapter, we saw how to add fields, including special field types like TEXT, BLOB, ENUM, and SET, how to use a calendar popup for DATE, DATETIME, and TIMESTAMP fields, and how to upload binary data into a BLOB field. We also learned how to manage indexes (multi-field and full-text) and get feedback from MySQL about which indexes are used in a specific query.

Exporting Structure and Data

7

Keeping good backups is crucial to a project. Backups consist of up-to-date backups and intermediary snapshots taken during development and production phases. The export feature of phpMyAdmin can generate backups and can also be used to send data to other applications.

Dumps, Backups, and Exports

Let's first clarify some vocabulary. In MySQL documentation, you will encounter the term **dump** and in other applications, the term **backup** or **export**. All these terms have the same meaning in the phpMyAdmin context.

MySQL includes **mysqldump**, a command-line utility that can be used to generate export files, but the shell access needed for command-line utilities is not offered by every host provider. Also, access to the export feature from within the Web interface is more convenient. This is why phpMyAdmin (since version 1.2.0) offers the **Export** feature with more export formats than mysqldump. This chapter will focus on phpMyAdmin's export features.

Before starting an export, we must have a clear picture of the intended goal of the export, and the following questions may help:

- Do we need the complete database or just some tables?
- Do we need just the structure, just the data, or both?
- Which utility will be used to **import** back the data? (Not every export format can be imported by phpMyAdmin.)
- Do we want only a subset of the data?
- What is the size of the intended export, and of the link speed between us and the server?

Scope of the Export

When we click an **Export** link from phpMyAdmin, we can be in one of these views or contexts: Database view, Table view or Server view (more on this latter one in Chapter 19, *MySQL Server Administration*). According to the current context, the resulting export's scope will be a complete database, a single table or even, in the case of Server view, a multi-database export. We will first explain database exports and all the relevant export types, and then we'll go on with table and multi-database exports, underlining the difference for these modes of exporting.

Database Exports

In Database view, click the **Export** link. The default export panel looks like this:

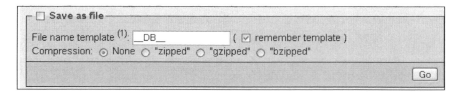

The default values selected here depend on `config.inc.php`, more specially specifically on the `$cfg['Export']` array of parameters. For example, the `$cfg['Export']['format']` parameter is set to `'sql'` so that the **SQL** export mode is chosen by default.

The export panel has three sub-panels. The top panel **Export** and the bottom panel **Save as file** are always there, and the third panel varies (using dynamic menu techniques) so as to show the options for the export mode chosen (which is SQL here).

The Export Sub-Panel

This sub-panel contains a table selector, where we choose the tables and the format that we want. The SQL format is useful, for our needs, since it creates standard SQL commands that would work on any SQL server. Other possible formats include **LaTeX, PDF, Microsoft Excel 2000, Microsoft Word 2000, Comma-Separated Values (CSV), YAML, Open Document Spreadsheet, Open Document Text,** and **XML.** Another format, **Native MS Excel,** is available after further software installation and configuration. (See the section *Native MS Excel* in this chapter.)

 Even if we can export from phpMyAdmin into all these formats, only the SQL and CSV formats can be imported back using the current phpMyAdmin version. *Use only these two formats for backup.*

We shall now discuss the formats (and the options available once they have been chosen) that can be selected with the **Export** sub-panel.

SQL

We will start by clicking **Select All**; we want all the tables. We know that the tables are small, so the on-screen export will not be too large. For the moment, let's deselect the **Extended inserts** checkbox. We then click **Go**, which produces the following output:

```
-- phpMyAdmin SQL Dump
-- version 2.11.0
-- http://www.phpmyadmin.net
--
-- Host: localhost
-- Generation Time: Sep 16, 2007 at 12:55 PM
-- Server version: 5.0.45
-- PHP Version: 5.2.4
SET SQL_MODE="NO_AUTO_VALUE_ON_ZERO";
--
-- Database: `marc_book`
--
```

```
------------------------------------------------------------
--
-- Table structure for table `author`
--
CREATE TABLE IF NOT EXISTS `author` (
  `id` int(11) NOT NULL,
  `name` varchar(30) NOT NULL,
  `phone` varchar(30) default NULL,
  PRIMARY KEY  (`id`)
) ENGINE=MyISAM DEFAULT CHARSET=latin1;
--
-- Dumping data for table `author`
--
INSERT INTO `author` (`id`, `name`, `phone`) VALUES(1, 'John Smith', '+01
445-789-1234');
INSERT INTO `author` (`id`, `name`, `phone`) VALUES(2, 'Maria Sunshine',
'333-3333');
-- ------------------------------------------------------
--
-- Table structure for table `book`
--
CREATE TABLE IF NOT EXISTS `book` (
  `isbn` varchar(25) NOT NULL,
  `title` varchar(100) NOT NULL,
  `page_count` int(11) NOT NULL,
  `author_id` int(11) NOT NULL,
  `language` char(2) NOT NULL default 'en',
  `description` text NOT NULL,
  `cover_photo` blob NOT NULL,
  `genre` set('Fantasy','Child','Novel') NOT NULL default 'Fantasy',
  `date_published` datetime NOT NULL,
  `stamp` timestamp NOT NULL default '0000-00-00 00:00:00' on update
CURRENT_TIMESTAMP,
  `some_bits` bit(3) NOT NULL,
  PRIMARY KEY  (`isbn`),
  KEY `by_title` (`title`(30)),
  KEY `author_language` (`author_id`,`language`),
  KEY `isbn` (`isbn`),
  FULLTEXT KEY `description` (`description`)
) ENGINE=MyISAM DEFAULT CHARSET=latin1;
--
-- Dumping data for table `book`
--
INSERT INTO `book` (`isbn`, `title`, `page_count`, `author_id`,
`language`, `description`, `cover_photo`, `genre`, `date_published`,
`stamp`, `some_bits`) VALUES('1-234567-89-0', 'A hundred years of cinema
(volume 1)', 600, 1, 'en', '', 0x89504e470d0a1a0a0000000d494844, '',
'0000-00-00 00:00:00', '2007-09-08 14:14:35', '_');
```

```
INSERT INTO `book` (`isbn`, `title`, `page_count`, `author_id`,
`language`, `description`, `cover_photo`, `genre`, `date_published`,
`stamp`, `some_bits`) VALUES('1-234567-22-0', 'Future souvenirs', 200, 2,
'en', '', '', '', '0000-00-00 00:00:00', '0000-00-00 00:00:00', '\0');
INSERT INTO `book` (`isbn`, `title`, `page_count`, `author_id`,
`language`, `description`, `cover_photo`, `genre`, `date_published`,
`stamp`, `some_bits`) VALUES('1-234567-90-0', 'A hundred years of cinema
(volume 2)', 602, 1, 'en', '', '', '', '0000-00-00 00:00:00', '0000-00-00
00:00:00', '\0');
```

In this export example, the data for one of the books (starting with 0x8950) has been truncated for brevity. In fact, it would contain the full hexadecimal representation of the cover_photo field of this book.

The first part of the export comprises comments (starting with the characters, --) that detail the utility (and version) that created the file, the date, and other environment information. We then see the CREATE and INSERT queries for each table.

Starting with version 2.6.0, phpMyAdmin generates ANSI-compatible comments in the export file. These comments start with --. They help with importing the file back on other ANSI SQL-compatible systems. In previous versions, the MySQL-specific character, '#', was used.

SQL Options

SQL options are used to define exactly what information the export will contain. We may want to see the structure, the data, or both. Selecting **Structure** generates the section with CREATE queries, and selecting **Data** produces INSERT queries:

```
┌─ Options ────────────────────────────────────────────────────┐
│  Add custom comment into header (\n splits lines)  ┌────────┐ │
│                                                    └────────┘ │
│    ☐ Enclose export in a transaction                          │
│    ☐ Disable foreign key checks                               │
│  SQL compatibility mode                              NONE  ▼   │
│  ⑦                                                            │
│    ┌─ ☑ Structure ─────────────────────────────────────────┐ │
│    │   ☐ Add DROP TABLE / DROP VIEW                         │ │
│    │   ☑ Add IF NOT EXISTS                                  │ │
│    │   ☑ Add AUTO_INCREMENT value                           │ │
│    │   ☑ Enclose table and field names with backquotes      │ │
│    │   ☐ Add CREATE PROCEDURE / FUNCTION                    │ │
│    │   ┌─ Add into comments ──────────────────────────────┐ │ │
│    │   │   ☐ Creation/Update/Check dates                  │ │ │
│    │   └──────────────────────────────────────────────────┘ │ │
│    └────────────────────────────────────────────────────────┘ │
└───────────────────────────────────────────────────────────────┘
```

The general SQL options are:

- **Add custom comment into header**: We can add our own comments for this export (for example, 'Monthly backup') which will show in the export headers (after the PHP version number). If the comment has more than one line, we must use the special character \n to separate each line.

- **Enclose export in a transaction**: Starting with MySQL 4.0.11, we can use the START TRANSACTION statement. This command, combined with SET AUTOCOMMIT=0 at the beginning and COMMIT at the end, asks MySQL to execute the import (when we will re-import this file) in one transaction, ensuring that all the changes are done as a whole.

- **Disable foreign key checks**: In the export file, we can add DROP TABLE statements. However, normally a table cannot be dropped if it is referenced in a foreign key constraint. This option overrides the verification by adding SET FOREIGN_KEY_CHECKS=0 to the export file.

- **SQL compatibility mode:** This lets us choose the flavor of SQL that we export. We must know about the system on which we intend to import this file. Among the choices are **MySQL 3.23**, **MySQL 4.0**, **Oracle,** and **ANSI**.

The options in **Structure** section are:

- **Add DROP TABLE / DROP VIEW**: Adds a DROP TABLE IF EXISTS statement before each CREATE TABLE statement, for example: DROP TABLE IF EXISTS 'author'. This way, we can ensure that the export file can be executed on a database in which the same table already exists, updating its structure, but destroying previous table contents. A DROP VIEW is used for views.

- **Add IF NOT EXISTS**: Adds the IF NOT EXISTS modifier to CREATE TABLE statements, avoiding an error during import if the table already exists.

- **Add AUTO_INCREMENT value**: Puts auto-increment information on the tables into the export, ensuring that the inserted rows in the tables will receive the correct next auto-increment ID value.

- **Enclose table and field names with backquotes**: Backquotes are the normal way of protecting table and field names that may contain special characters. In most cases it is useful to have them, but not if the target server (where the export file will be imported) is running a MySQL version older than 3.23.6, which does not support backquotes.

- **Add CREATE PROCEDURE/FUNCTION**: This includes in the export all procedures and functions found in this database.

- **Add into comments**: This adds information (in the form of SQL comments), which cannot be directly imported, but which nonetheless is valuable and human-readable table information. The amount of information here varies depending on the relational system settings, (see Chapter 11). In fact, with an activated relational system, we would get the following choices:

Selecting **Relations** and **MIME type** would produce an additional section in the structure export:

```
--
-- COMMENTS FOR TABLE 'book':
--     'isbn'
--         'book number'
--     'page_count'
--         'approximate'
--     'author_id'
--         'see author table'
--
--
-- MIME TYPES FOR TABLE 'book':
--     'cover_photo'
--         'image_jpeg'
--     'date_released'
--         'text_plain'
--     'description'
--         'text_plain'
--
-- RELATIONS FOR TABLE 'book':
--     'author_id'
--         'author' -> 'id'
--
```

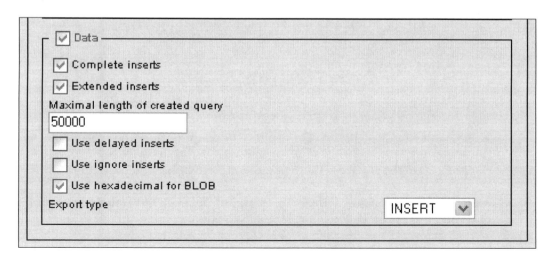

The options available in the **Data** section are:

- **Complete inserts**: Generates the following export for the **author** table:

```
INSERT INTO 'author' ('id', 'name', 'phone')
VALUES (1, 'John Smith', '+01 445 789-1234');
INSERT INTO 'author' ('id', 'name', 'phone')
VALUES (2, 'Maria Sunshine', '+01 455 444-5683');
```

    Notice that every column name is present in every statement. The resulting file is bigger, but will prove more portable on various SQL systems, with the added benefit of being better documented.

- **Extended inserts**: Packs the whole table data into a single INSERT statement:

```
INSERT INTO 'author' VALUES (1, 'John Smith',
  '+01 445 789-1234'), (2, 'Maria Sunshine', '+01 455 444-5683');
```

    This method of inserting data is faster than using multiple INSERT statements, but is less convenient because it makes reading the resultant file harder. **Extended inserts** also produces a smaller file, but each line of this file is not executable in itself because each line does not have an INSERT statement. If you cannot import the complete file in one operation, you cannot split the file with a text editor and import it chunk by chunk.

- **Maximal length of created query**: The single INSERT statement generated for **Extended inserts** might become too big and could cause problems, this is why we can set a limit here—in number of characters—for the length of this statement.

- **Use delayed inserts**: Adds the DELAYED modifier to INSERT statements. This accelerates the INSERT operation because it is queued to the server, which will execute it when the table is not in use. Please note that this is a MySQL non-standard extension, and it's only available for MyISAM, ISAM, MEMORY and ARCHIVE tables.

- **Use ignore inserts**: Normally, at import time, we cannot insert duplicate values for unique keys—this would abort the insert operation. This option adds the IGNORE modifier to INSERT and UPDATE statements, thus skipping the rows which generate duplicate key errors.

- **Use hexadecimal for BLOB**: This option makes phpMyAdmin encode the contents of BLOB fields in 0x format. Such a format is useful because, depending on the software that will be used to manipulate the export file (for example a text editor or mail program), handling a file containing 8-bit data can be problematic. However, using this option will produce an export of the BLOB that can be twice the size or even more.

- **Export type**: The choices are **INSERT**, **UPDATE**, and **REPLACE**. The most well-known of these types is the default **INSERT** — using INSERT statements to import back our data. At import time, however, we could be in a situation where a table already exists and contains valuable data, and we just want to update the fields that are in the current table we are exporting. **UPDATE** generates statements like UPDATE 'author' SET 'id' = 1, 'name' = 'John Smith', 'phone' = '111-1111' WHERE 'id' = '1'; updating a row when the same primary or unique key is found. The third possibility, **REPLACE**, produces statements like REPLACE INTO 'author' VALUES (1, 'John Smith', '111-1111'); which act like an INSERT statement for new rows and updates existing rows, based on primary or unique keys.

The Save as file Sub-Panel

In the previous examples, the results of the export operation were displayed on-screen, and of course, no compression was made on the data. We can choose to transmit the export file via HTTP by checking the **Save as file** checkbox. This triggers a **Save** dialog into the browser, which ultimately saves the file on our local station:

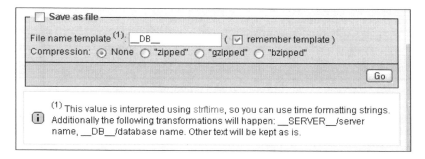

File Name Template

The name of the proposed file will obey the **File name template**. In this template, we can use the special **__SERVER__**, **__DB__** and **__TABLE__** placeholders, which will be replaced by the current server, database or table name (for a single-table export).

Note that there are *two* underscore characters before and after the words. We can also use any special character from the PHP strftime function; this is useful for generating an export file based on the current date or hour. Finally, we can put any other string of characters (not part of the strftime special characters), which will be used literally. The file extension is generated according to the type of export. In this case, it will be .sql. Here are some examples for the template:

- **__DB__** would generate **marc_book.sql**
- **__DB__**-%Y%m%d gives **marc_book-20071206.sql**

The **remember template** option, when activated, stores the entered template settings into cookies (for database, table, or server exports) and brings them back the next time we use the same kind of export.

The default templates are configurable, via the following parameters:

```
$cfg['Export']['file_template_table']      = '__TABLE__';
$cfg['Export']['file_template_database']   = '__DB__';
$cfg['Export']['file_template_server']     = '__SERVER__';
```

Compression

To save transmission time and get a smaller export file, phpMyAdmin can compress to zip, gzip, or bzip2 formats. phpMyAdmin has native support for the zip format, but the gzip and bzip2 formats work only if the PHP server has been compiled with the --with-zlib or --with-bz2 configuration option, respectively. The following parameters control which compression choices are presented in the panel:

```
$cfg['ZipDump']       = TRUE;
$cfg['GZipDump']      = TRUE;
$cfg['BZipDump']      = TRUE;
```

A system administrator installing phpMyAdmin for a number of users could choose to set all these parameters to FALSE so as to avoid the potential overhead incurred by a lot of users compressing their exports at the same time. This situation usually causes more overhead than if all users were transmitting their uncompressed files at the same time.

In older phpMyAdmin versions, the compression file was built in the web server memory. Some problems caused by this were:

- File generation depended on the memory limits assigned to running PHP scripts.
- During the time the file was generated and compressed, no transmission occurred, so users were inclined to think that the operation was not working and that something had crashed.
- Compression of large databases was impossible to achieve.

The $cfg['CompressOnFly'] parameter (set to TRUE by default) was added to generate (for gzip and bzip2 formats) a compressed file containing more headers. Now, the transmission starts almost immediately. The file is sent in smaller chunks so that the whole process consumes much less memory.

Choice of Character Set

Chapter 17 of this book will cover the subject of character sets in more detail. However, it's appropriate at this point to explain a little known feature—the possibility of choosing the exact character set for our exported file.

This feature is activated by setting $cfg['AllowAnywhereRecoding'] to TRUE. We can see here the effect on the interface:

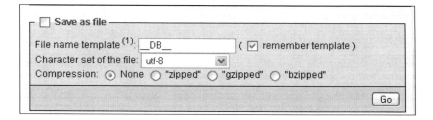

CSV

This format is understood by a lot of programs, and you may find it useful for exchanging data. Note that it is a data-only format—there is no SQL structure here.

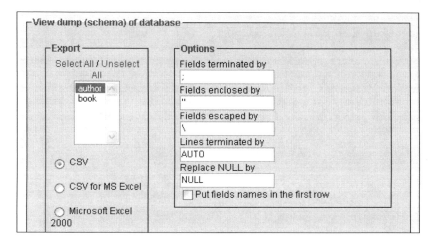

The available options are:

- **Fields terminated by**: We put a comma here, which means that a comma will be placed after each field.

- **Fields enclosed by**: We place an enclosing character here (like the quote) to ensure that a field containing the terminating character (comma) is not taken for two fields.

- **Fields escaped by**: If the export generator finds the **Fields enclosed by** character inside a field, the **Fields escaped by** character will be placed before it in order to protect it. For example, `"John \"The Great\" Smith"`.

- **Lines terminated by**: This decides the character that ends each line. We should use the proper line delimiter here depending on the operating system on which we will manipulate the resulting export file. The default value of this option comes from the `$cfg['Export']['csv_terminated']` parameter which contains `'AUTO'` by default. The `'AUTO'` value produces a value of `\r\n` if the browser's OS is Windows and `\n` otherwise, but this might not be the best choice if the export file is intended for a machine with a different OS.

- **Replace NULL by**: This determines which string takes the place in the export file of any NULL value found in a field.

- **Put fields names in the first row**: This gets some information about the meaning of each field. Some programs will use this information to name the column.

Finally, we select the **author** table.

The result is:

```
"id","name","phone"
"1","John Smith","+01 445 789-1234"
"2","Maria Sunshine","+01 455 444-5683"
```

CSV for MS Excel

This export mode produces a CSV file intended for Microsoft Excel. We can select the exact Microsoft Excel edition.

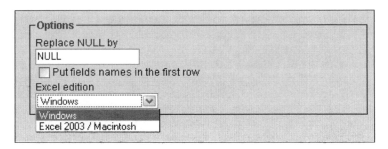

PDF

Since version 2.8.0, it's possible to create a PDF report of a table by exporting in PDF. This feature works on only one table at a time, and we must click the **Save as file** checkbox for normal operation. We can add a title for this report, and it also gets automatically paginated. In versions 2.8.0 to 2.8.2, this export format does not support non-textual (BLOB) data as in the book table; if we try it in this table, it will produce the wrong results.

Here we test it on the **author** table.

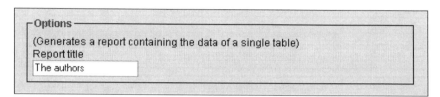

PDF is interesting because of its vectorial inherent nature: the results can be zoomed. Let's have a look at the generated report, as seen from Acrobat Reader:

Microsoft Excel 2000

This export format directly produces an .xls file suitable for all software that understands the Excel 2000 format. We can specify which string should replace any NULL value. The **Put field names in the first row** option, when activated, generates the table's column names as the first line of the spreadsheet. Again, the **Save as file** checkbox should be checked. This produces a file where each table's column becomes a spreadsheet column.

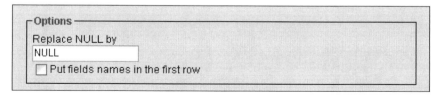

Microsoft Word 2000

This export format directly produces a .doc file suitable for all software that understands the Word 2000 format. We find options similar to those in the Microsoft Excel 2000 export, and a few more. We can independently export the table's **Structure** and **Data**.

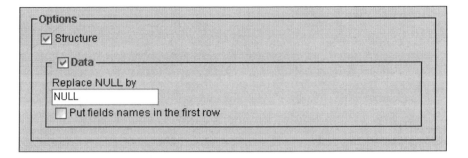

Note that, for this format and the Excel format, we can choose many tables for one export, but unpleasant results happen if one of these tables has non-textual data. Here are the results for the **author** table.

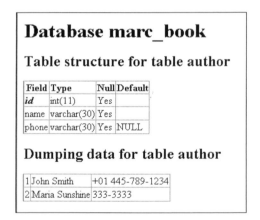

LaTeX

LaTeX is a typesetting language. phpMyAdmin can generate a .tex file that represents the table's structure and/or data in sideways tabular format. Note that this file is not directly viewable, and must be further processed or converted for the intended final media.

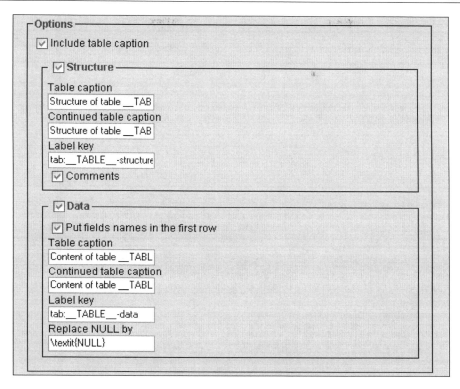

The available options are:

- **Include table caption**: Display captions to the tabular output
- **Structure** and **Data**: The familiar choice to request structure, data, or both
- **Table caption**: The caption to go on the first page
- **Continued Table caption**: The caption to go on pages after page one
- **Relations**, **Comments**, **MIME-type**: Other structure information we want to be output. These choices are available if the relational infrastructure is in place (see Chapter 11).

XML

This format is very popular nowadays for data exchange. Choosing **XML** in the **Export** interface yields no choice for options. What follows is the output for the **author** table:

```
<?xml version="1.0" encoding="utf-8" ?>
<!--
-
```

```
-  phpMyAdmin XML Dump
-  version 2.11.0
-  http://www.phpmyadmin.net
-
-  Host: localhost
-  Generation Time: Sep 16, 2007 at 01:13 PM
-  Server version: 5.0.45
-  PHP Version: 5.2.4
-->
<!--
-  Database: 'marc_book'
-->
<marc_book>
  <!-- Table author -->
    <author>
        <id>1</id>
        <name>John Smith</name>
        <phone>+01 445-789-1234</phone>
    </author>
    <author>
        <id>2</id>
        <name>Maria Sunshine</name>
        <phone>333-3333</phone>
    </author>
</marc_book>
```

Native MS Excel (pre-Excel 2000)

Starting with version 2.6.0, phpMyAdmin offers an experimental module to export directly in .xls format, the native spreadsheet format understood by **MS Excel** and **OpenOffice Calc**. When this support is activated (more on this in a moment), we see a new export choice, **Native MS Excel**, and the following options:

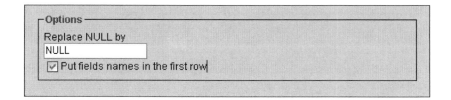

We can optionally put our field names in the first row of the spreadsheet, with **Put fields names in the first row**.

This functionality relies on the PEAR module `Spreadsheet_Excel_Writer`, which is currently at version 0.9.1 and generates Excel 5.0 format files. This module is documented at `http://pear.php.net/package/Spreadsheet_Excel_Writer`, but the complete installation in phpMyAdmin's context is documented here:

1. Ensure that the PHP server has PEAR support. (The `pear` command will fail if we do not have PEAR support.) PEAR itself is documented at `http://pear.php.net`.

2. If we are running PHP in safe mode, we have to ensure that we are allowed to include the PEAR modules. Assuming the modules are located under; `/usr/local/share/pear`, we should have the line `safe_mode_include_dir = /usr/local/share/pear` in `php.ini`.

3. We then install the module with: `pear -d preferred_state=beta install -a Spreadsheet_Excel_Writer` (because the module is currently in beta state). This command fetches the necessary modules over the Internet and installs them into our PEAR infrastructure.

4. We need a temporary directory—under the main phpMyAdmin directory—for the `.xls` generation. It can be created on a Linux system with: `mkdir tmp ; chmod o+rwx tmp`.

5. We set the `$cfg['TempDir']` parameter in `config.inc.php` to `'./tmp'`.

We should now be able to see the new **Native MS Excel data** export choice.

Open Document Spreadsheet

This spreadsheet format is a subset of the Open Document (`http://en.wikipedia.org/wiki/OpenDocument`), which was made popular with the OpenOffice.org office suite. We need to choose only one table to be exported in order to have a coherent spreadsheet. Here is our author table, exported into a file named `author.ods` subsequently looked at from OpenOffice:

Open Document Text

This is another subset of the Open Document standard, this time oriented towards text processing. The available options are:

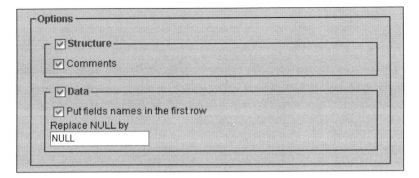

Our `author` table is now exported and viewed from OpenOffice:

Database marc_book

Table structure for table author

Field	Type	Null	Default	Comments
id	int(11)	Yes		
name	varchar(30)	Yes		
phone	varchar(30)	Yes	NULL	

Dumping data for table author

id	name	phone
1	John Smith	+01 445-789-1234
2	Maria Sunshine	333-3333

YAML

This acronym stands for "YAML Ain't Markup Language". YAML is a human-readable data serialization format; its official site is http://www.yaml.org. This format has no option that we can choose from within phpMyAdmin. Here is the YAML export for the author table:

```
1:
  id: 1
  name: John Smith
  phone: +01 445-789-1234
```

```
2:
  id: 2
  name: Maria Sunshine
  phone: 333-3333
```

Table Exports

The **Export** link in the Table view brings up the export sub-panel for a specific table. It is similar to the database export panel, but there is no table selector. However, there is an additional section for split exports before the **Save as file** sub-panel.

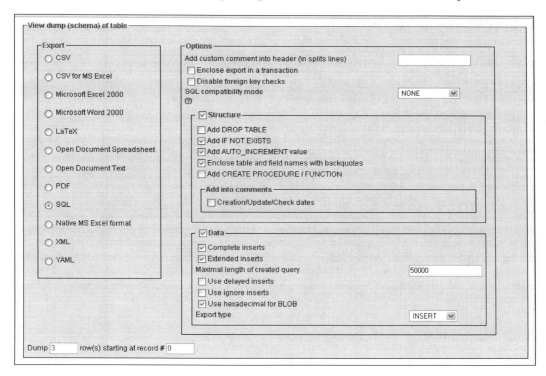

Split-File Exports

The **Dump 3 row(s) starting at record # 0** dialog enables us to split the file into chunks. Depending on the exact row size, we can experiment with various values for the number of rows to find how many rows can be put in a single export file before the memory or execution time limits are hit in the web server. We could then use names like `book00.sql` and `book01.sql` for our export files.

Selective Exports

At various places in phpMyAdmin's interface, we can export the results that we see, or we can select the rows that we want to export.

Exporting Partial Query Results

When results are displayed from phpMyAdmin—here the results of a query asking for the books from **author_id 2**—an **Export** link appears at the bottom of the page:

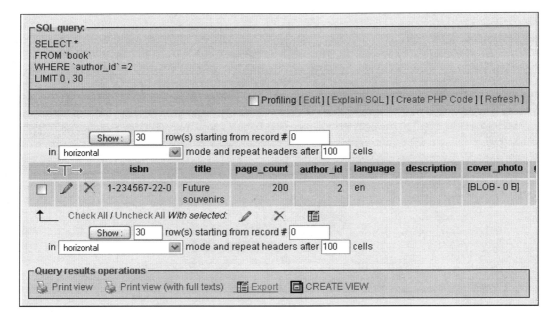

Clicking on this link brings up a special export panel containing the query on the top along with the other table export options:

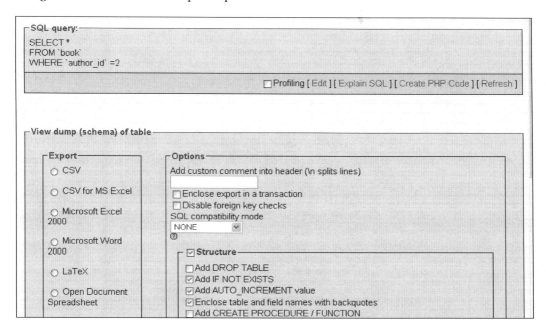

 The results of single-table queries can be exported in all the available formats, while the results of multi-table queries can be exported only in CSV, XML, and LaTeX formats.

Exporting and Checkboxes

Anytime we see results (when browsing or searching, for example), we can check the boxes beside the rows that we want, and use the **With selected: export** icon to generate a partial export file with just those rows.

←T→			isbn	title	page_count	author_id
☑	✎	✗	1-234567-89-0	A hundred years of cinema (volume 1)	600	1
☐	✎	✗	1-234567-22-0	Future souvenirs	200	2
☑	✎	✗	1-234567-90-0	A hundred years of cinema (volume 2)	602	1

↑ Check All / Uncheck All *With selected*: ✎ ✗ 🗎

Show: 30 row(s) starting from record # 0 [Export]

in horizontal ▼ mode and repeat headers after 100 cells

Multi-Database Exports

Any user can export the databases to which he or she has access, in one operation.

On the **Home** page, the **Export** link brings us to the screen shown on the following page, which has the same structure as the other export pages, except for the databases list:

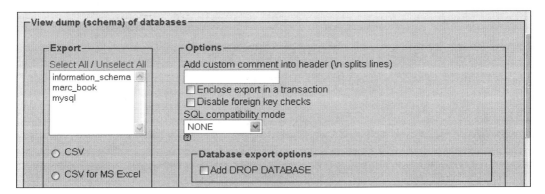

 Exporting large databases may or may not work: this depends on their size, the options chosen, and the web server's PHP component settings (especially memory size and execution time).

Saving the Export File on the Server

Instead of transmitting the export file over the network with HTTP, it is possible to save it directly on the file system of the web server. This could be quicker and less sensitive to execution time limits, because the whole transfer from server to client browser is bypassed. Eventually, a file transfer protocol like FTP or SFTP can be used to retrieve the file, because leaving it on the same machine would not provide good backup protection.

A special directory has to be created on the web server before saving an export file on it. Usually, this is a subdirectory of the main phpMyAdmin directory. We will use save_dir as an example. This directory must have special permissions. First, the web server must have write permissions for this directory. Also, if the web server's PHP component is running in safe mode, the owner of the phpMyAdmin scripts must be the same as the owner of save_dir.

On a Linux system, assuming that the web server is running as group **apache** and the scripts are owned by user **marc**, the following commands would do the trick:

```
# mkdir save_dir
# chown marc.apache save_dir
# chmod g=rwx save_dir
```

> The proper ownership and permissions mask highly depend on the chosen web server and the SAPI (see http://en.wikipedia.org/ wiki/Server_Application_Programming_Interface) used, which influences how directories and files are created and accessed—PHP could be using the scripts' owner as the accessing user, or the web server's user/group itself.

We also have to define the './save_dir' directory name in $cfg['SaveDir']. We are using a path relative to the phpMyAdmin directory here, but an absolute path would work just as well.

The **Save as file** section will appear with a new **Save on server** section:

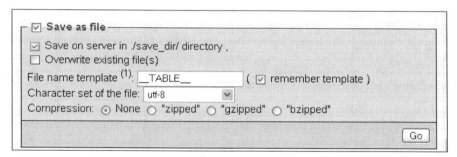

After clicking **Go**, we will get a confirmation message or an error message (if the web server does not have the required permissions to save the file).

> For saving a file again using the same file name, check the **Overwrite existing file(s)** box.

User-Specific Save Directories

We can use the special string, `%u`, in the `$cfg['SaveDir']` parameter. This string will be replaced by the logged-in user name. For example, using:

```
$cfg['SaveDir'] = './save_dir/%u';
```

would give us the on-screen choice **Save on server in ./save_dir/marc/ directory**. These directories (one per potential user) must exist and must bear the proper permissions, as seen in the previous section.

Memory Limits

Generating an export file uses a certain amount of memory, depending on the size of the tables and on the chosen options. The `$cfg['MemoryLimit']` parameter can contain a limit—in bytes—for the amount of memory used by the PHP script that is running. By default, the parameter is set to 0, meaning that there is no limit. Note that, if PHP has its safe mode activated, this memory limit has no effect.

Summary

In this chapter, we examined the various ways to trigger an export: from the Database view, the Table view, or a results page. We also listed the various available export formats, their options, the possibility of compressing the export file, and the various places it might be sent.

Importing Structure and Data

In this chapter, we will learn how to bring back exported data that we might have created for backup or transfer purposes. Exported data may also come from authors of other applications, and could contain the whole foundation structure of these applications and some sample data.

The current phpMyAdmin version (2.11) can directly import files containing MySQL statements (usually having a .sql suffix, but not necessarily so) and CSV files (comma-separated values, although the separator is not necessarily a comma). Future versions might be able to import files in more formats. There is also an interface to the MySQL LOAD DATA INFILE statement, enabling us to load text files containing data, also called CSV. The binary field upload covered in Chapter 6 can be said to belong to the import family.

[Importing and uploading are synonyms in this context.]

Since phpMyAdmin version 2.7.0, there is an **Import** menu in the Database view and in the Table view that regroups import dialogs, and an **Import files** menu available inside the **Query window** (as explained in Chapter 12).

Another feature was added in version 2.11.0: an import file may contain the DELIMITER keyword; this enables phpMyAdmin to mimic the **mysql** command-line interpreter. The DELIMITER feature is used to delineate the part of the file containing a stored procedure, because these procedures can themselves contain semicolons.

The default values for the Import interface are defined in $cfg['Import'].

Before examining the actual import dialog, let's look at some limits issues.

Limits for the Transfer

When we import, the source file is usually on our client machine, so it must travel to the server via HTTP. This transfer takes time and uses resources that may be limited in the web server's PHP configuration.

Instead of using HTTP, we can upload our file to the server using a protocol like FTP, as described in the *Web Server Upload Directories* section. This method circumvents the web server's PHP upload limits.

Time Limits

First, let's consider the time limit. In `config.inc.php`, the `$cfg['ExecTimeLimit']` configuration directive assigns, by default, a maximum execution time of 300 seconds (five minutes) for *any* phpMyAdmin script, including the scripts that process data after the file has been uploaded. A value of `0` removes the limit and in theory gives us infinite time to complete the import operation. If the PHP server is running in safe mode, modifying `$cfg['ExecTimeLimit']` will have no effect, because the limits set in `php.ini` or in user-related web server configuration file (such as `.htaccess` or virtual host configuration files) take precedence over this parameter.

Of course, the time it effectively takes depends on two key factors:

- Web server load
- MySQL server load

 The time taken by the file as it travels between the client and the server does not count as execution time, because the PHP script only starts to execute after the file has been received on the server. So the `$cfg['ExecTimeLimit']` parameter has an impact only on the time used to process data (like decompression or sending it to the MySQL server).

Other Limits

The system administrator can use the `php.ini` file or the web server's virtual host configuration file to control uploads on the server.

The `upload_max_filesize` parameter specifies the upper limit or the maximum file size that can be uploaded via HTTP. This one is obvious, but another less obvious parameter is `post_max_size`. Because HTTP uploading is done via the POST method, this parameter may limit our transfers. For more details about the POST method, please refer to `http://en.wikipedia.org/wiki/Http#Request_methods`.

The memory_limit parameter is provided to avoid web server child processes from grabbing too much of the server memory — phpMyAdmin also runs as a child process. Thus, the handling of normal file uploads, especially compressed dumps, can be compromised by giving this parameter a small value. Here, no preferred value can be recommended — it depends on the size of uploaded data. The memory limit can also be tuned via the $cfg['MemoryLimit'] parameter in config.inc.php, as seen in Chapter 7.

Finally, file uploads must be allowed by setting file_uploads to On. Otherwise, phpMyAdmin won't even show the **Location of the textfile** dialog. It would be useless to display this dialog, because the connection would be refused later by the PHP component of the web server.

Partial Imports

If the file is too big, there are ways in which we can resolve the situation. If we still have access to the original data, we could use phpMyAdmin to generate smaller CSV export files, choosing the **Dump n rows starting at record # n** dialog. If this is not possible, we will have to use a text editor to split the file into smaller sections. Another possibility is to use the upload directory mechanism, which accesses the directory defined in $cfg['UploadDir']. This feature is explained later in the present chapter.

In recent phpMyAdmin versions, the **Partial import** feature can also solve this file size problem. By selecting the **Allow interrupt...** checkbox, the import process will interrupt itself if it detects it is close to the time limit. We can also specify a number of queries to skip from the start, in case we successfully imported a number of rows and wish to continue from that point.

Temporary Directory

On some servers, a security feature called open_basedir can be set up in a way that impedes the upload mechanism. In this case, or for any other reason when uploads are problematic, the $cfg['TempDir'] parameter can be set with the value of a temporary directory — probably a subdirectory of phpMyAdmin's main directory — into which the web server is allowed to put the uploaded file.

Importing SQL Files

Any file containing MySQL statements can be imported via this mechanism. The dialog is available in the Database view or the Table view, via the **Import** sub-page, or in the **Query** window.

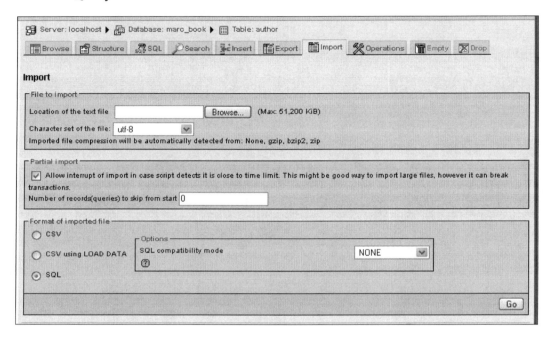

There is no relation between the currently selected table (here **author**) and the actual contents of the SQL file that will be imported. All the contents of the SQL file will be imported, and it is these contents that determine which tables or databases are affected. However, if the imported file does not contain any SQL statements to select a database, all statements in the imported file will be executed on the currently selected database.

Let's try an import exercise. First we make sure that we have a current SQL export of the **book** table (as explained in Chapter 7). This export file must contain the structure and data. Then we drop the **book** table (Yes, really!). We could also simply rename it. (See Chapter 10 for the procedure.)

Now it is time to import the file back. We should be on the **Import** sub-page, where we can see the **Location of the text file** dialog. We just have to hit the **Browse** button and choose our file.

phpMyAdmin is able to detect which compression method (if any) has been applied to the file. The formats that the program can decompress vary depending on the phpMyAdmin version and which extensions are available in the PHP component of the web server.

However, to import successfully, phpMyAdmin must be informed of the character set of the file to be imported. The default value is **utf8**, but if we know that the import file was created with another character set, we should specify it here.

Since version 2.9, there is a **SQL compatibility mode** selector available at import time. This mode should be adjusted to match the actual data that we are about to import, according to the type of server where the data was previously exported.

To start the import, we click **Go**:

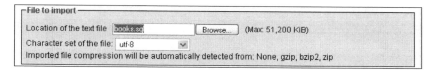

The importation proceeds and we receive a message: **Import has been successfully finished, 2 queries executed**. We can browse our newly created tables to confirm the success of the import operation.

The file could be imported in a different database or even a MySQL server for testing.

Importing CSV Files

In this section, we will examine how to import CSV files. There are two possible methods: **CSV** and **CSV using LOAD DATA**. The first method is implemented internally by phpMyAdmin and is the recommended one for its simplicity. With the second method, phpMyAdmin receives the file and passes it to MySQL to be loaded; in theory, this method should be faster, but it has more requirements due to MySQL itself.

Differences between SQL and CSV Formats

There are some differences between these two formats. The CSV file format contains data only, so we must already have an existing table in place. This table does not need to have the same structure as the original table (from which the data comes); the **Column names** dialog enables us to choose which columns are affected in the target table.

Because the table must exist prior to the import, the CSV import dialog is available only from the **Import** sub-page in the Table view, not in the Database view.

Exporting a Test File

Before trying an import, let's generate an `author.csv` export file from the **author** table. We use the default values in the **CSV export** options. We can then **Empty** the **author** table—we should avoid dropping this table because we still need the table structure.

CSV

From the **author** table menu, we select **Import**, and then **CSV**.

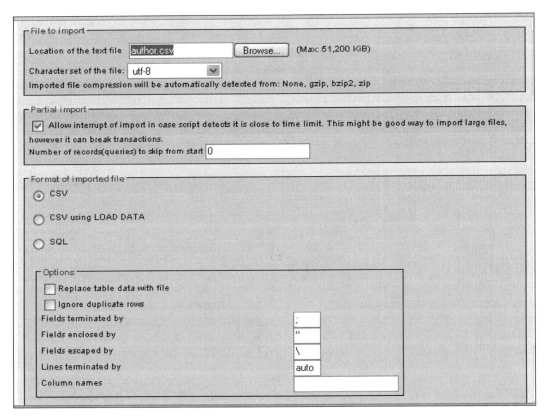

We can influence the behavior of the import in a number of ways. By default, importing does not modify existing data (based on primary or unique keys), but the **Replace table data with file** option instructs phpMyAdmin to use REPLACE statements instead of INSERT; statement so that existing rows are replaced with the imported data.

With **Ignore duplicate rows**, INSERT IGNORE statements are generated. These cause MySQL to ignore any duplicate key problems during insertion. A duplicate key from the import file does not replace existing data, and the procedure continues for the next line of CSV data.

We can then specify the character that terminates each field, the character that encloses data, and the character that escapes the enclosing character. Usually this is ****. For example, for a double quote enclosing character, if the data field contains a double quote, it must be expressed as **"some data \" some other data"**.

For **Lines terminated by**, recent versions of phpMyAdmin offer the **auto** choice, which should be tried first as it automatically detects the end-of-line character. We can also specify manually what characters terminate the lines. The usual choice is **\n** for UNIX-based systems, **\r\n** for DOS or Windows systems, and **\r** for Mac-based systems (up to Mac OS 9). If in doubt, we can use a hexadecimal file editor on our client computer (not part of phpMyAdmin) to examine the exact codes.

By default, phpMyAdmin expects a CSV file with the same number of fields and the same field order as the target table, but this can be changed by entering a comma-separated list of column names in **Column names**, respecting the source file format. For example, let's say our source file only contains the author ID and author name information:

```
"1","John Smith"
"2","Maria Sunshine"
```

We'd have to put **id, name** in **Column names** to match the source file.

When we click **Go**, the import is executed and we get a confirmation. We might also see the actual INSERT queries generated if the total size of the file is not too big.

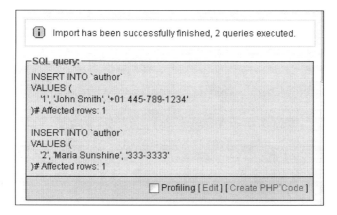

CSV Using LOAD DATA

With this method, phpMyAdmin relies on the server's LOAD DATA INFILE or LOAD DATA LOCAL INFILE mechanisms to do the actual import, instead of processing the data internally. These statements are the fastest way for importing text in MySQL. They cause MySQL to start a read operation from a file located on the MySQL server (LOAD DATA INFILE) or from another place (LOAD DATA LOCAL INFILE), which in this context, is always the web server's file system. If the MySQL server is located on a computer other than the web server, we won't be able to use the LOAD DATA INFILE mechanism.

Requirements

Relying on the MySQL server has some consequences. Using LOAD DATA INFILE requires that the logged-in user possess a global FILE privilege. Also, the file itself must be readable by the MySQL server's process.

[Chapter 19 explains phpMyAdmin's interface to privileges management for system administrators.]

Using the LOCAL modifier in LOAD DATA LOCAL INFILE must be allowed by the MySQL server and MySQL's client library used by PHP.

Both the LOAD methods are available from the phpMyAdmin LOAD interface, which tries to choose the best possible default option.

Using the LOAD DATA Interface

We select **Import** from the **author** table menu. Choosing **CSV using LOAD DATA** brings up the following dialog:

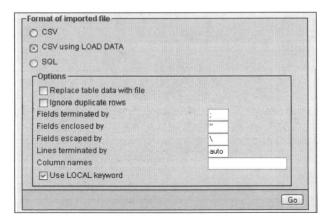

The available options have already been covered in the *CSV* section.

In the familiar **Location of the text file** question, we choose our `author.csv` file.

Finally, we can choose the LOAD method, as discussed earlier, by selecting the **Use LOCAL keyword** option. We then click **Go**.

If all goes well, we see the confirmation screen:

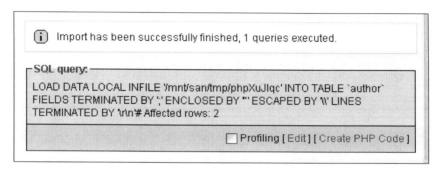

This screen shows the exact LOAD DATA LOCAL INFILE statement used. Here is what has just happened in detail:

- We chose **author.csv**.
- The contents of this file were transferred over HTTP and received by the web server.
- The PHP component inside the web server saved this file in a work directory (here `/mnt/san/tmp/`) and gave it a temporary name.
- phpMyAdmin informed of the location of this working file, built a LOAD DATA LOCAL INFILE command and sent it to MySQL.
- The MySQL server read and loaded the contents of the file into our target table; it then returned the number of affected rows (2), which phpMyAdmin displayed in the results page.

Web Server Upload Directories

To get around cases where uploads are completely disabled by a web server's PHP configuration or where upload limits are too small, phpMyAdmin can read upload files from a special directory located on the web server's file system. This mechanism is applicable for SQL and CSV imports.

We first specify the directory name of our choice in the $cfg['UploadDir']
parameter; for example, './upload'. We can also use the %u string, as described in
Chapter 7, to represent the user's name.

Now, let's go back to the **Import** sub-page and see what happens:

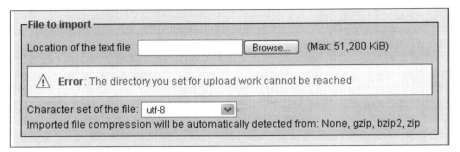

This error message is expected, as the directory does not exist. It is supposed
to have been created inside the current phpMyAdmin installation directory. The
message might also indicate that the directory exists, but can't be read by the
web server. (In PHP safe mode, the owner of the directory and the owner of the
phpMyAdmin-installed scripts must be the same.)

Using an SFTP or FTP client, we create the necessary directory and can upload a file
there (for example book.sql) bypassing any PHP timeouts or upload maximum
limits. Note that the file itself must have permissions that allow the web server to
read it. In most cases, the easiest way is to allow everyone to read the file.

Refreshing the **Import** sub-page brings up the following:

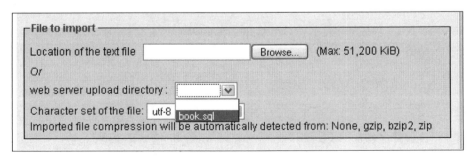

Clicking **Go** should execute the file.

Automatic decompression is also available for the files located in the upload directory. The file names should have extensions like `.bz2`, `.gz`, `.sql.bz2`, or `.sql.gz`.

 Using the double extensions (`.sql.bz2`) is a better way to indicate that a `.sql` file was produced and then compressed, since we see all the steps used to generate this file.

Summary

In this chapter, we learned the various options in phpMyAdmin that allow us to import data, the different mechanisms involved in importing SQL and CSV files, the limits that we might hit when trying a transfer, and ways to bypass these limits.

9
Searching Data

Here we present mechanisms that can be used to find the data we are looking for instead of just browsing tables page-by-page and sorting them. This chapter covers single-table and whole database searches. Chapter 13 is a complement to this chapter and presents multi-table query by example.

Single-Table Searches

This section describes the **Search** sub-page where single-table search is available.

Daily Usage of phpMyAdmin

The main use for the tool for some users is with the **Search** mode, for finding and updating data. For this, the phpMyAdmin team has made it possible to define which sub-page is the starting page in Table view, with the $cfg['DefaultTabTable'] parameter. Setting it to 'tbl_select.php' defines the default sub-page to search.

With this mode, application developers can look for data in ways not expected by the interface they are building, adjusting and sometimes repairing data.

Entering the Search Sub-Page

The **Search** sub-page can be accessed by clicking the **Search** link in the Table view. This has been done here for the **book** table:

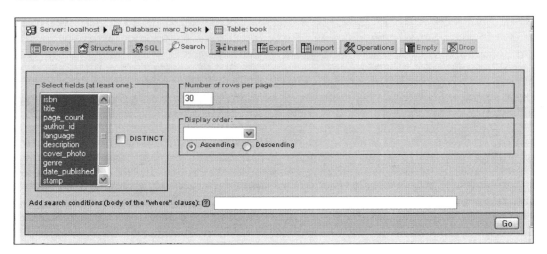

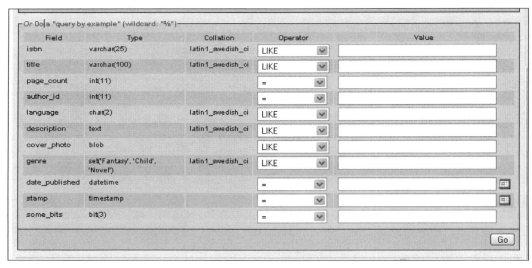

Selection of Display Fields

The first panel facilitates a selection of the fields to be displayed in the results:

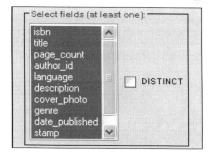

All fields are selected by default, but we can control-click other fields to make the necessary selections. Mac users would use command-click to select / unselect the fields.

Here are the fields of interest to us in this example:

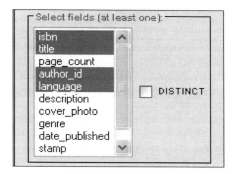

We can also specify the number of rows per page in the textbox just next to the field selection. The **Add search conditions** box will be explained in the *Applying a WHERE Clause* section later in this chapter.

Ordering the Results

The **Display order** dialog permits to specify an initial sorting order for the results to come. In this dialog, a drop-down menu contains all the table's columns; it's up to us to select the one on which we want to sort. By default, the sorting will be in **Ascending** order, but a choice of **Descending** order is available.

It should be noted that on the results page, we can change the sort order using the techniques explained in Chapter 4, *First Steps*.

Search Criteria by Field: Query by Example

The main usage of the **Search** panel is to enter criteria for some fields so as to retrieve only the data in which we are interested. This is called **Query by example** because we give an example of what we are looking for. Our first retrieval will concern finding the book with ISBN **1-234567-89-0**. We simply enter this value in the **isbn** box and choose the = operator:

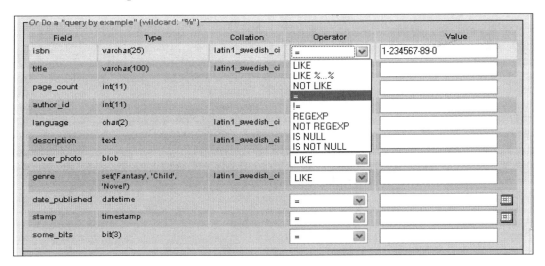

Clicking on **Go** gives the results shown in the following screenshot. The four fields displayed are those selected in the **Select fields** dialog:

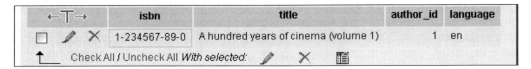

This is a standard results page. If the results ran in pages, we could navigate through them, and edit and delete data for the subset we chose during the process. Another feature of phpMyAdmin is that the fields used as the criteria are highlighted by changing the border color of the columns to better reflect their importance on the results page. It isn't necessary to specify that the **isbn** column be displayed. We could have selected only the **title** column for *display* and selected the **isbn** column as a *criterion*.

Print View

We see the **Print view** and **Print view (with full texts)** links on the results page. These links produce a more formal report of the results (without the navigation interface) directly to the printer. In our case, using **Print view** would produce the following:

SQL result

Host: localhost
Database: marc_book
Generation Time: Sep 21, 2007 at 01:57 PM
Generated by: phpMyAdmin 2.11.0 / MySQL 5.0.45-standard
SQL query: SELECT `isbn` , `title` , `author_id` , `language` FROM `book`
WHERE `isbn` = CONVERT(_utf8 '1-234567-89-0' USING latin1)
COLLATE latin1_swedish_ci LIMIT 0, 30 ;
Rows: 1

isbn	title	author_id	language
1-234567-89-0	A hundred years of cinema (volume 1)	1	en

This report contains information about the server, database, time of generation, version of phpMyAdmin, version of MySQL, and SQL query used. The other link, **Print view (with full texts)** would print the contents of **TEXT** fields in its entirety.

Wildcard Searching

Let's assume we are looking for something less precise: all books with 'cinema' in their title. First, we go back to the search page. For this type of search, we will use SQL's LIKE operator. This operator accepts wildcard characters: the % character (which matches any number of characters) and the underscore (_) character (which matches a single character). Thus we can use **%cinema%** to let phpMyAdmin find any substring that matches the word 'cinema'. If we left out both wildcard characters, we will get exact matches with only that single word.

Since phpMyAdmin 2.6.0, this substring matching has been made easier to access, by adding it to the **Operator** drop-down list. We only have to enter the word **cinema** and use the operator **LIKE %...%** to perform that match. We should avoid using this form of the **LIKE** operator on big tables (thousands of rows), because MySQL does not use an index for data retrieval in this case, leading to wait time that could add up to half an hour (or more). This is why this operator is not the default one in the drop-down list, even though this method of searching is commonly used on smaller tables.

In versions prior to phpMyAdmin 2.6.0, we need to manually insert the % characters to obtain '%cinema%', and use the **LIKE** operator from the drop-down list.

We also specify that the results be sorted (in ascending order) by title. In the search interface, only one sorting field is possible. Here is a screenshot showing how we ask for a search on **cinema** with the operator **LIKE %...%**:

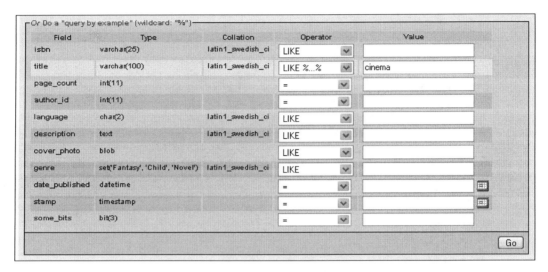

 The **LIKE** operator can be used for other types of wildcard searching, for example **History%** — which would search for this word at the beginning of a title. This form of the **LIKE** query also has the benefit of using an index, if MySQL finds one that speeds up data retrieval.

Using either of these methods of doing the query gives the following results:

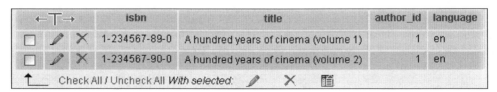

Wildcard characters available are the % character (which matches any number of characters) and the underscore (_) character (which matches a single character).

Combining Criteria

We can use multiple criteria for the same query (for example, to find all English books of more than 300 pages). We see here that there are more comparison choices because of the **page_count** field being numeric:

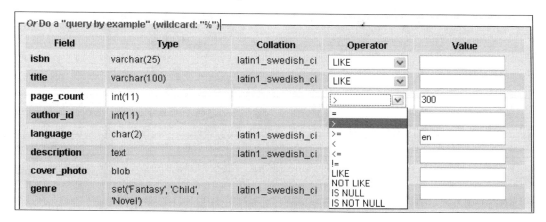

Applying a WHERE Clause

Sometimes we may want to enter a search condition that is *not* offered in the **Function** list of the **Query by example** section; the list cannot contain every possible variation available in the language. Let's say we want to find all English or French books. For this, we can use the **Add search conditions** section:

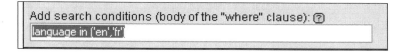

 The complete search expression is generated by combining the search conditions, a logical AND, and the other criteria entered in the **Query by example** lines.

We could have a more complex list of search conditions that would be entered in the same textbox, possibly with brackets and operators like AND or OR.

A **Documentation** link points to the MySQL manual, where we can see a huge choice of available functions. (Each function is applicable to a specific field type.)

Obtaining Distinct Results

Sometimes we want to avoid getting the same results more than once. For example, if we want to know in which cities we have clients, displaying each city name once is enough. Here we want to know in which languages our books are written. In the **Select Fields** dialog, we choose just the **language** field, and we check **DISTINCT**:

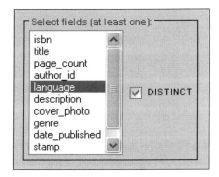

Clicking on **Go** produces the following:

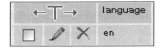

 Using **DISTINCT**, we only see each language once. Without this option, the row containing '**en**' would have appeared three times.

Complete Database Search

In the previous examples, searching was limited to one table. This assumes knowledge of the exact table (and columns) where the necessary information might be stored.

When the data is hidden somewhere in the database or when the same data can be in various columns (for example, a **title** column or a **description** column), it is easier to use the database-search method.

We enter the **Search** page in the Database view for the `marc_book` database:

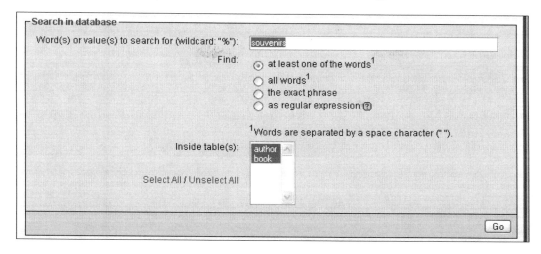

In the **Word(s) or value(s)** section, we enter what we want to find. The % wildcard character can prove useful here. We enter **souvenirs**.

In the **Find** section, we specify how to treat the values entered: we might need to find **at least one of the words** entered, **all words** (in no particular order), or **the exact phrase** (words in the same order, somewhere in a column). Another choice is to use a **regular expression**, which is a more complex way of doing pattern matching. We will keep the default value, **at least one of the words**.

We can choose the tables to restrict the search or select all tables. As we only have two (small) tables, we select them both.

 As the search will be done on each row of every table selected, we might hit some time limits if the number of rows or tables is too big. Thus, this feature can be deactivated by setting `$cfg['UseDbSearch']` to FALSE. (It is set to TRUE by default).

Clicking **Go** finds the following for us:

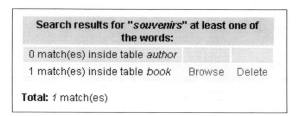

This is an overview of the number of matches and the relevant tables. We might get some matches in tables in which we are not interested. However, for the matches that look promising, we can **Browse** the results page, or we can **Delete** the unwanted rows.

Summary

In this chapter, we have covered single-table searches with query by example criteria and additional criteria specification, selecting displayed values, and ordering results. We also took a look at wildcard searches and full database search.

10
Table and Database Operations

In the previous chapters, we dealt mostly with table fields. In this chapter, we will learn how to perform some operations that influence tables or databases as a whole. We will cover table attributes and how to modify them, and also discuss multi-table operations.

Various links that enable table operations have been put together on one sub-page of the Table view: **Operations**. Here is an overview of this sub-page:

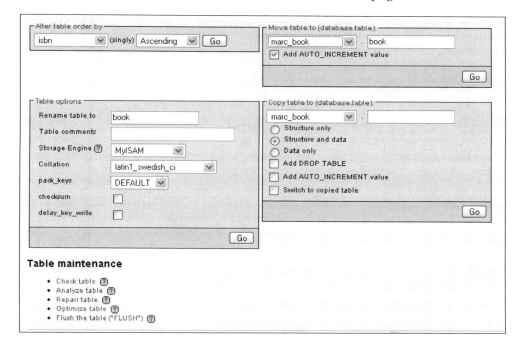

Table Maintenance

During the lifetime of a table, it repeatedly gets modified, and so grows and shrinks. Outages may occur on the server, leaving some tables in a damaged state.

Using the **Operations** sub-page, we can perform various operations, but not every operation is available for every table type:

- **Check table**: Scans all rows to verify that deleted links are correct. Also, a checksum is calculated to verify the integrity of the keys; we should get an 'OK' message if everything is all right.

- **Analyze table**: Analyzes and stores the key distribution; this will be used on subsequent JOIN operations to determine the order in which the tables should be joined.

- **Repair table**: Repairs any corrupted data for tables in the MyISAM and ARCHIVE engines. Note that the table might be so corrupted that we cannot even go into Table view for it! In such a case, refer to the *Multi-Table Operations* section for the procedure to repair it.

- **Optimize table**: This is useful when the table contains overheads. After massive deletions of rows or length changes for VARCHAR fields, lost bytes remain in the table. phpMyAdmin warns us in various places (for example, in the Structure view) if it feels the table should be optimized. This operation is a kind of defragmentation for the table. In MySQL 4.x, this operation works only on tables in the MyISAM, Berkeley (BDB), and InnoDB engines. In MySQL 5.x, it works only on tables in the MyISAM, InnoDB, and ARCHIVE engines.

- **Flush table**: This must be done when there have been lots of connection errors and the MySQL server blocks further connections. Flushing will clear some internal caches and allow normal operations to resume.

- **Defragment table**: Random insertions or deletions in an InnoDB table fragment its index. The table should be periodically defragmented for faster data retrieval.

 The operations are based on the underlying MySQL queries available—phpMyAdmin is only calling those queries.

Changing Table Attributes

Table attributes are the various properties of a table. This section discusses the settings for some of them.

Table Type

The first attribute we can change is called **Table storage engine**:

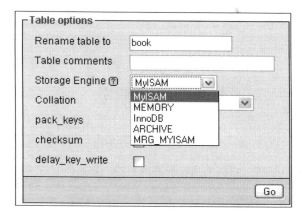

This controls the whole behavior of the table: its location (on-disk or in-memory), the index structure, and whether it supports transactions and foreign keys. The drop-down list may vary depending on the table types supported by our MySQL server.

 Changing the table type may be a long operation if the number of rows is large.

Table Comments

This allows us to enter comments for the table.

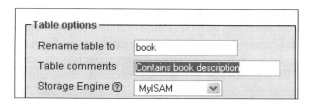

These comments will be shown at appropriate places (for example, in the left panel, next to the table name in the Table view and in the export file). Here is what the left panel looks like when the `$cfg['ShowTooltip']` parameter is set to its default value of TRUE:

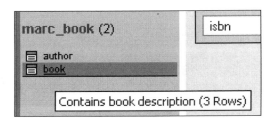

The default value of `$cfg['ShowTooltipAliasDB']` and `$cfg['ShowTooltipAlias TB']` (FALSE) produces the behavior we have seen earlier: the true database and table names are displayed in the left panel and in the Database view for the **Structure** sub-page. Comments appear when the mouse pointer is moved over a table name. If one of these parameters is set to TRUE, the corresponding item (database names for DB and table names for TB) will be shown as the tooltip instead of the names. This time, the mouse-over shows the true name for the item. This is convenient when the real table names are not meaningful.

There is another possibility for `$cfg['ShowTooltipAliasTB']`: the `'nested'` value. Here is what happens if we use this feature:

- The true table name is displayed in the left panel.
- The table comment (for example `project__`) is interpreted as the project name and is displayed as such. (See the *Nested Display of Tables Within a Database* section in Chapter 3).

Table Order

When we **Browse** a table or execute a statement such as SELECT * from book, without specifying a sort order, MySQL uses the order in which the rows are physically stored. This table order can be changed with the **Alter table order by** dialog. We can choose any field, and the table will be reordered once on this field. We choose **author_id** in the example, and after we click **Go**, the table gets sorted on this field.

Reordering is convenient if we know that we will be retrieving rows in this order most of the time. Moreover, if later we use an ORDER BY clause and the table is already physically sorted on this field, the performance should be higher.

This default ordering will last as long as there are no changes in the table (no insertions, deletions, or updates). This is why phpMyAdmin shows the **(singly)** warning.

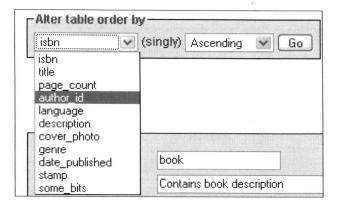

After the sort has been done on **author_id**, books for author **1** will be displayed first, followed by the books for author **2**, and so on. (We are talking about a default browsing of the table without explicit sorting.) We can also specify the sort order: **Ascending** or **Descending**.

If we insert another row, describing a new book from author **1**, and then click **Browse**, the book will not be displayed along with the other books for this author because the sort was done before the insertion.

Table Options

Other attributes that influence the table's behavior may be specified using the **Table options** dialog:

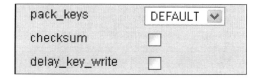

The options are:

- **pack_keys**: Setting this attribute results in a smaller index; this can be read faster but takes more time to update. Available for the MyISAM storage engine.

- **checksum**: This makes MySQL compute a checksum for each row. This results in slower updates, but easier finding of corrupted tables. Available for MyISAM only.

- **delay_key_write**: This instructs MySQL not to write the index updates immediately but to queue them for later, which improves performance. Available for MyISAM only.

- **auto-increment**: This changes the auto-increment value. It is shown only if the table's primary key has the auto-increment attribute.

Renaming, Moving, and Copying Tables

The **Rename** operation is the easiest to understand: the table simply changes its name and stays in the same database.

The **Move** operation (shown in the following screen) can manipulate a table in two ways: change its name and *also* the database in which it is stored:

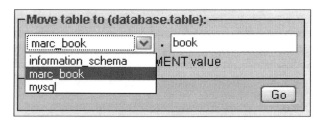

Moving a table is not directly supported by MySQL, so phpMyAdmin has to create the table in the target database, copy the data, and then finally drop the source table.

The **Copy** operation leaves the original table intact and copies its structure or data (or both) to another table, possibly in another database. Here, the **book-copy** table will be an exact copy of the **book** source table. After the copy, we will stay in the Table view for the **book** table unless we selected **Switch to copied table**.

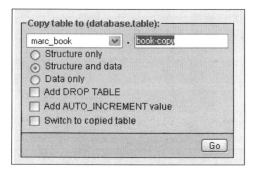

The **Structure only** copy is done to create a test table with the same structure.

Appending Data to a Table

The **Copy** dialog may also be used to append (add) data from one table to another. Both tables must have the same structure. This operation is achieved by entering the table to which we want to copy the data of the current table and choosing **Data only**.

For example, we would want to append data when book data comes from various sources (various publishers), is stored in more than one table, and we want to aggregate all the data to one place. For MyISAM, a similar result can be obtained by using the MERGE storage engine (which is a collection of identical MyISAM tables) but if the table is InnoDB, we need to rely on phpMyAdmin's **Copy** feature.

Multi-Table Operations

In the Database view, there is a checkbox next to each table name and a drop-down menu under the table list. This enables us to quickly choose some tables and perform an operation on all those tables at once. Here we select the **book-copy** and the **book** tables, and choose the **Check** operation for these tables.

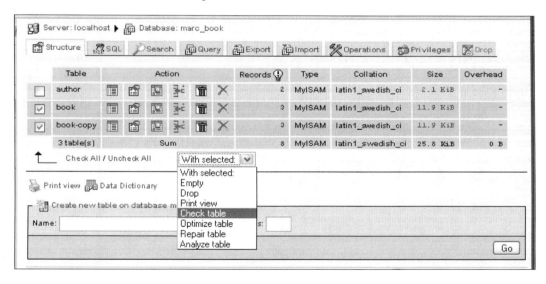

We could also quickly select or deselect all the checkboxes with **Check All / Uncheck All**.

Repairing an "in use" Table

The multi-table mode is the only method (unless we know the exact SQL query to type) for repairing a corrupted table. Such tables may be shown with the **in use** flag in the database list. Users seeking help in the support forums for phpMyAdmin often receive this tip from experienced phpMyAdmin users.

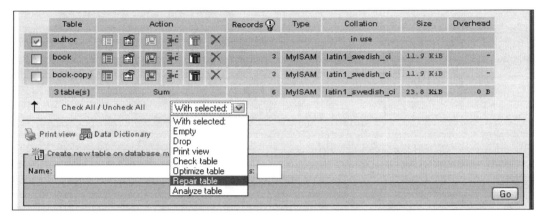

Database Operations

The **Operations** tab in the Database view gives access to a panel that enables us to perform operations on a database taken as a whole.

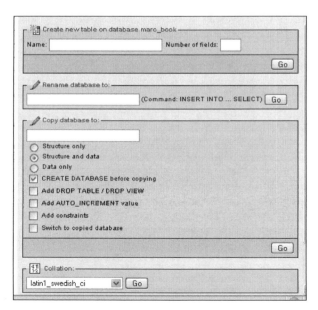

Renaming a Database

Starting with phpMyAdmin 2.6.0, a **Rename database** dialog is available. Although this operation is not directly supported by MySQL, phpMyAdmin does it indirectly by creating a new database, renaming each table (thus sending it to the new database), and dropping the original database.

Copying a Database

Since phpMyAdmin 2.6.1, it is possible to do a complete copy of a database, even if MySQL itself does not support this operation natively.

Copy database to:

marc_book_copy

- ◯ Structure only
- ◉ Structure and data
- ◯ Data only
- ☑ CREATE DATABASE before copying
- ☐ Add DROP TABLE / DROP VIEW
- ☐ Add AUTO_INCREMENT value
- ☐ Add constraints
- ☐ Switch to copied database

Go

Summary

In this chapter, we covered the operations we can perform on whole tables or databases. We also took a look at table maintenance operations for table repair and optimization, changing various table attributes, table movements, including renaming and moving to another database, and multi-table operations.

11
The Relational System

Welcome to the part of the book where we start to cover advanced features. The relational system allows users to do more with phpMyAdmin, as we will see in the following chapters. This chapter explains how to install the linked-tables infrastructure, which is a prerequisite for the advanced features, and explains how to define inter-table relations.

Relational MySQL?

When application developers use PHP and MySQL to build web interfaces or other data manipulation applications, they usually establish relations between tables, using the underlying SQL queries—for example, 'get an invoice and all its items' and 'get all books by an author'.

In the first versions of phpMyAdmin, MySQL was storing information about which table belonged to which database, but the relational data structure (how tables relate to each other) was not stored into MySQL. Relations were temporarily made by the applications to generate meaningful results. In other words, the relations were in our head.

This was considered a shortcoming of MySQL by phpMyAdmin developers and users, and so the team started to build an infrastructure to support relations. The infrastructure evolved to support a growing array of special features. We can describe this infrastructure as **metadata** (data about data).

phpMyAdmin 2.2.0 already had the **bookmarks** feature (being able to recall frequently used queries, as described in Chapter 14), and version 2.3.0 generalized the metadata system. Subsequent versions built on this facility, for example the 2.5.x family with its MIME-based **transformations** (as described in Chapter 16) and the 2.10.x family with a graphical relation builder called **Designer**, described in this chapter.

InnoDB

A new MySQL storage engine **(InnoDB)** became available during phpMyAdmin's development. The InnoDB sub-system has its own web page at `http://www.innodb.com`.

Because the InnoDB sub-system must be made active by a system administrator, it may not be available on every MySQL server. Here are the benefits of using the InnoDB storage engine for a table:

- It supports referential integrity based on foreign keys, which are the keys in a foreign (or reference) table. By contrast, using only phpMyAdmin's internal relations (discussed later) brings no automatic referential integrity verification.
- InnoDB tables exported definitions containing the defined relations, so they are easily imported back for better cross-server interoperability.

InnoDB's foreign key feature can effectively replace (for InnoDB tables only) the part of phpMyAdmin's infrastructure that deals with relations. We will see how phpMyAdmin interfaces to the InnoDB foreign key system.

> The other parts of phpMyAdmin's infrastructure (for example, bookmarks) have no equivalent in InnoDB or MySQL, and thus they are still needed to access the complete phpMyAdmin feature set. However, in MySQL 5, views are supported and have similarities with phpMyAdmin's bookmarks.

Linked-Tables Infrastructure

The relational system's infrastructure is stored in tables that follow a predetermined structure. The data in these tables is generated and maintained by phpMyAdmin on the basis of our actions from the interface.

Goal of the Infrastructure

These metadata tables contain, for all storage engines, information to support the special phpMyAdmin's features like bookmarks and transformations. Moreover, for non-InnoDB tables, relations between tables are kept in this infrastructure.

Location of the Infrastructure

There are two possible places to store these tables:

- In a user's database. Thus every web developer owning a database can benefit from these features.

- In a dedicated database, which we call **pmadb** (phpMyAdmin database). In a multi-user installation (discussed later), this database may be accessible for a number of users while keeping the metadata private.

Because this infrastructure does not exist by default, and because phpMyAdmin's developers want to promote it, the interface displays the following error message for every database when on the **Operations** sub-page in the Database view:

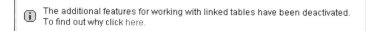

This message can be disabled with the following parameter (which by default, is set to FALSE):

```
$cfg['PmaNoRelation_DisableWarning'] = TRUE;
```

Installing Linked-Tables Infrastructure

The previous error message is displayed even if only part of the infrastructure is lacking. On a fresh installation, of course, all parts are lacking: our database has not yet heard of phpMyAdmin and needs to be outfitted with this infrastructure. Following the **here** link in this message brings up the following explanation:

🗄 **Server: localhost** ▶ 📇 **Database: marc_book**
PMA Database ... not OK [Documentation]
General relation features Disabled

 The message is the same regardless of the current database (here, **marc_book**) because the infrastructure is shared for all our databases and tables (or all users on a multi-user installation).

As the previous screenshot suggests, the **PMA Database** is **not OK**. It's important to realize that the relational system will work only if two conditions are met:

- Proper definitions are present in config.inc.php.
- The corresponding tables (and maybe the database) are created.

To create the necessary structure matching our current version of phpMyAdmin, a command file called `create_tables.sql` is available in the scripts subdirectory of the phpMyAdmin installation directory. However, we should not blindly execute it before understanding the possible choices: multi-user installation or single-user installation.

Multi-User Installation

In this setup, we will have a distinct database (**pmadb**) to store the metadata tables, and our control user will have specific rights to this database. Each user will enter his or her login name and password, which will be used to access his or her databases. However, whenever phpMyAdmin itself accesses **pmadb** to obtain some metadata, it will use the control user's privileges.

We first ensure that the control user `pma` has been created as explained in Chapter 2, and that its definition in `config.inc.php` is appropriate:

```
$cfg['Servers'][$i]['controluser'] = 'pma';
$cfg['Servers'][$i]['controlpass'] = 'bingo';
```

Then we use the `scripts/create_tables.sql` file to create the `phpmyadmin` database, assign proper rights to user `pma`, and populate the database with all the necessary tables. Before using this script, look in the `scripts` directory. There might be other scripts available for different MySQL versions—for example, phpMyAdmin 2.6.0 has `scripts/create_tables_mysql_4_1_2+.sql`, which should be used instead of `create_tables.sql` for MySQL version 4.1.2 and higher.

[Be warned that this script will erase the `phpmyadmin` database, if it exists, destroying all metadata about relations.]

A possible method to execute this script is to use the technique described in Chapter 8 (*Importing Structure and Data*), using the **SQL** sub-page and the file selector. For this to work, we must have the `create_tables.sql` script somewhere on our workstation. After the creation, the left panel looks like this:

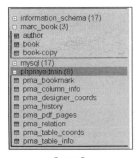

It is now time to adjust all the relational-features related parameters in config.inc.php. Here we use the default values mentioned in the comments inside the file; these database and table names are the ones that have just been created:

```
$cfg['Servers'][$i]['pmadb']           = 'phpmyadmin';
$cfg['Servers'][$i]['bookmarktable']   = 'pma_bookmark';
$cfg['Servers'][$i]['relation']        = 'pma_relation';
$cfg['Servers'][$i]['table_info']      = 'pma_table_info';
$cfg['Servers'][$i]['table_coords']    = 'pma_table_coords';
$cfg['Servers'][$i]['pdf_pages']       = 'pma_pdf_pages';
$cfg['Servers'][$i]['column_info']     = 'pma_column_info';
$cfg['Servers'][$i]['history']         = 'pma_history';
$cfg['Servers'][$i]['designer_coords'] = 'pma_designer_coords';
```

 As table names are case sensitive, we must use the same names as the tables created by the installation script. We are free to change the table names (see the right-hand part of the configuration directives listed) provided we change them accordingly in the database.

Each database or table has a specific function:

- pmadb: Defines which database all the tables are located in.
- bookmarktable: Contains the bookmarks (explained in Chapter 14).
- relation: Defines inter-table relations, as used in many of phpMyAdmin's features.
- table_info: Contains the display field (explained later in this chapter).
- table_coords and pdf_pages: Contain the metadata necessary for drawing a schema of the relations in PDF format (explained in Chapter 15).
- column_info: Used for column-commenting and MIME-based transformations (explained in Chapter 16).
- history: Contains SQL query history information (explained in Chapter 12).
- designer_coords: holds the coordinates used by the Designer feature (explained later in this chapter).

Between each phpMyAdmin version, the infrastructure may be enhanced. (The changes are explained in Documentation.html.) This is why phpMyAdmin has various checks to ascertain the structure of tables. If we know that we are using the latest structure, $cfg['Servers'][$i]['verbose_check'] can be set to FALSE to avoid checks, thereby slightly increasing phpMyAdmin's speed.

The installation is now complete; we will test the features in the coming sections and chapters. We can do a quick check by going back to the **Home** page: the warning message should be gone.

Single-User Installation

Even if we are entitled to only one database by the system administrator, we can still use all the relational features of phpMyAdmin.

In this setup, we will use our normal database (let's assume its name is **marc_book**) to store the metadata tables and will define our own login name (marc) as the control user in config.inc.php:

```
$cfg['Servers'][$i]['controluser']   = 'marc';
$cfg['Servers'][$i]['controlpass']   = 'bingo';
```

The next step is to modify a *local copy* of the scripts/create_tables.sql file to populate our database with all the needed tables. They will have the prefix pma_ to make them easily recognizable. (See also the remark in the *Multi-User Installation* section about other scripts that may be available in the scripts directory.)

 Be warned that this script will erase the special tables, if they exist, destroying all metadata about relations.

If we are using scripts/create_tables.sql, the modification we have to do is to remove the following lines:

```
DROP DATABASE `phpmyadmin`;
CREATE DATABASE `phpmyadmin`;
USE phpmyadmin;
GRANT SELECT, INSERT, DELETE, UPDATE ON `phpmyadmin`.* TO
    'pma'@localhost;
```

This is done because we won't be using the phpmyadmin database or the pma control user.

If we are using scripts/create_tables_mysql_4_1_2+.sql, we have to remove these lines:

```
CREATE DATABASE IF NOT EXISTS `phpmyadmin`
  DEFAULT CHARACTER SET utf8 COLLATE utf8_bin;
USE phpmyadmin;
```

We are now ready to execute the script. There are two ways of doing this:

- As we already have the script in our editor, we can just copy the lines and paste them in the query box of the **SQL** sub-page.
- Another way is to use the technique shown in Chapter 8 (*Importing Structure and Data*), with the **SQL** sub-page and the file selector. We select the create_tables.sql script that we just modified.

After the creation, the left panel shows us the special **pma_** tables along with our normal tables:

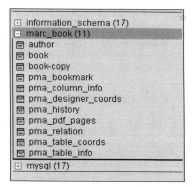

The last step is to adjust all the parameters in `config.inc.php` that relate to relational features. Except for the database name in the `pmadb` parameter, we use the default values mentioned in the comments inside the file:

```
$cfg['Servers'][$i]['pmadb']          = 'marc_book';
```

Defining Relations with the Relation View

After the installation of the linked-tables infrastructure, there are now more options available in the Database view and the Table view. We will now examine a new link in the Table view: **Relation view**. This view is used to:

- Define the relations of the current table to other tables
- Choose the display field

Because our goal here is to create a relation between the **book** table (which contains the author ID) and the **author** table (which describes each author by an ID), we start on the Table view for the **book** table and click the **Relation view** link.

Internal Relations

As the **book** table is in MyISAM format, we see the following screen (otherwise, the display would be different, as explained in the *InnoDB Relations* section later):

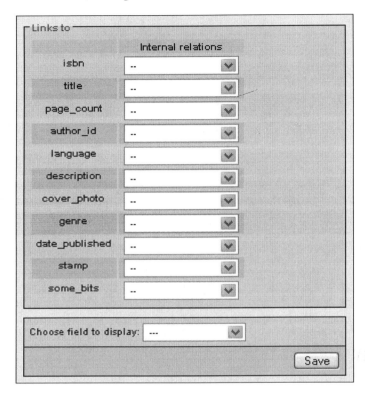

This screen allows us to create **Internal relations** (stored in the **pma_relation** table), because MySQL itself does not have any relational notion for MyISAM tables. The double-dash (**--**) characters indicate that there are *no* relations (links) to any foreign table.

Defining the Relation

We can relate each field of the **book** table to a field in another table (or in the same table, because self-referencing relations are sometimes necessary). The interface finds the unique and non-unique keys in all tables of the same database and presents the keys in drop-down lists. The appropriate choice here is to select for the **author_id** field the corresponding **author_id** field from the **author** table. This is also called *defining the foreign key*.

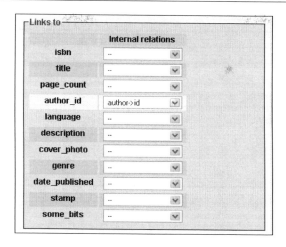

We then click **Save**, and the definition is saved in phpMyAdmin's infrastructure. To remove the relation, we just come back to the screen, select the double-dash choice, and hit **Save**.

Defining the Display Field

The primary key of our **author** table is the **author_id**, which is a unique number that we made up just for key purposes. Another field in our table represents the authors: the name. It would be interesting to see the author's name as an informative description of each row of the **book** table. This is the purpose of the **display field**. We should normally define a display field for each table that participates in a relation as a foreign table.

We will see how this information is displayed in the *Benefits of the Defined Relations* section. We now go to the Relation view for the **author** table (which is the foreign table in this case) and specify the display field. We choose **name** as the display field and click **Save**:

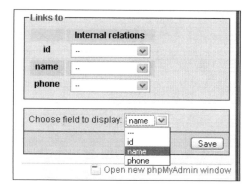

phpMyAdmin offers to define only one display field for a table, and this field is used in all the relations where this table is used as a foreign table.

The definition of this relation is now done. Note that, although we did not relate any of the fields in the **author** table to another table, it can be done. For example, we could have a country code in this table and could create a relation to the country code of a country table.

We will discuss the benefits of having defined this relation in a later section, but first, we will see what happens if our tables are under control of the InnoDB storage engine.

InnoDB Relations

The InnoDB storage engine offers us a foreign key system. To try it, we will first switch our **book** *and* **author** tables to the InnoDB storage engine. We can do this from the **Operations** sub-page in the Table view. We start by doing this for the **author** table:

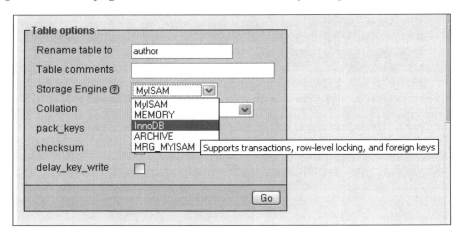

A problem might arise when changing the storage engine of **book** table to InnoDB. We have a full-text index in this table, and some versions of MySQL do not support it for the InnoDB engine. We have to remove the full-text index if we receive the following error message.

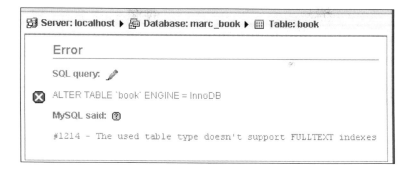

To get rid of this error message, we go back to **Structure** for the **book** table and remove the full-text index on the `description` field. While we are on this screen, let's also remove the combined index we created on `author_id` and `language`. This is because we want to see the consequences of a missing index later in this chapter. At this point, we are able to switch the **book** table to InnoDB.

The foreign key system in InnoDB maintains integrity between the related tables, so we cannot add a non-existent author ID to the **book** table. In addition, actions are programmable when DELETE or UPDATE operations are performed on the master table (in our case, **book**).

Opening the **book** table and entering the **Relation view** now displays a different page:

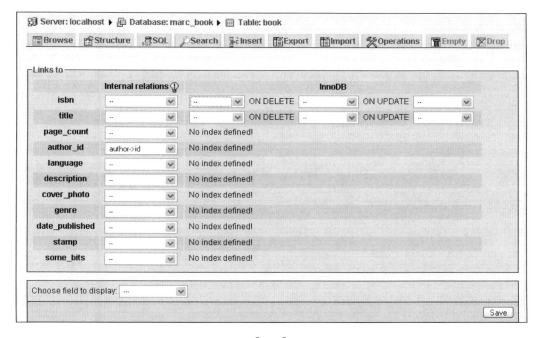

This page tells us that:

- We have an internal relation defined for **author_id** to the **author** table.

- We don't yet have any InnoDB relations defined.

- We will be able to remove the internal relation, when the same relation has been defined in InnoDB. This message can be seen when moving the mouse over the small bulb light. In fact, phpMyAdmin advises us that the internal relation is not necessary when it also exists in InnoDB, so it would be better to remove it.

- **ON DELETE** and **ON UPDATE** options are available for InnoDB relations.

The page might also tell us that our MySQL version is not up to date. (It needs to be 4.0.13 or later.) If we have a version prior to 4.0.13, we won't be able to remove a relation defined in InnoDB, due to a lack of support for the ALTER TABLE ... DROP FOREIGN KEY statement. This is why phpMyAdmin could be giving us this friendly (and crucial!) advice.

In the possible choices for the related key, we see the keys defined in all InnoDB tables of the same database. (Creating a cross-database relation is currently not supported in phpMyAdmin.) We even see the keys defined in the current table, because self-referring relations are possible. We now remove the internal relation for the **author_id** field and hit **Save**. We would like to add an InnoDB-type relation for the **author_id** field, but we cannot—we see the **No index defined!** message on this line. This is because foreign key definitions in InnoDB can be done only if *both* fields are defined as indexes.

 Other conditions regarding constraints are explained in the MySQL manual; please refer to http://dev.mysql.com/doc/refman/5.0/ en/innodb-foreign-key-constraints.html.

Thus, we come back to the **Structure** page for the **book** table and add an ordinary (non-unique) index to the **author_id** field producing:

Keyname	Type	Cardinality	Action		Field	
PRIMARY	PRIMARY	3	🖉	✕	isbn	
by_title	INDEX	3	🖉	✕	title	30
isbn	INDEX	3	🖉	✕	isbn	
author_id	INDEX	3	🖉	✕	author_id	

Indexes: ⓘ

In the **Relation view**, we can again try to add the relation we wanted—it works this time!

We can also set some actions with the **ON DELETE** and **ON UPDATE** options. For example, **ON DELETE CASCADE** would make MySQL automatically delete all rows in the related (foreign) table when the corresponding row is deleted from the parent table. This would be useful, for example, when the parent table is **invoices** and the foreign table is **invoice-items**.

 If we have not done so already, we should define the 'display field' for the **author** table, as explained in the *Internal phpMyAdmin Relations* section.

In phpMyAdmin 2.11.x, we cannot see tables from a different database in order to define a relation to them.

InnoDB Tables without Linked-Tables Infrastructure

Starting with phpMyAdmin 2.6.0, we see the **Relation View** link on the **Structure** page of an InnoDB table even though the linked-tables infrastructure is not installed. This brings us to a screen where we can define the foreign keys—here for the **book** table.

Note that if we choose this way, the 'display field' for the linked table (**author** here) cannot be defined, since it belongs to the phpMyAdmin's infrastructure, so we would lose one of the benefits (seeing the foreign key's associated description).

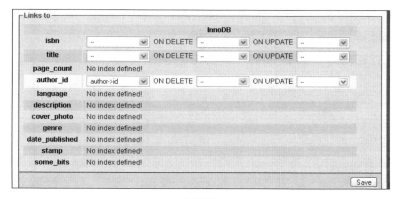

Defining Relations with the Designer

The Ajax-based Designer feature appeared in phpMyAdmin 2.10. It offers a mouse-driven way of managing relations—both internal and InnoDB-based—and of defining the display field for each table. It can also act as:

- A menu to access the structure of existing tables and to access the table creation page.
- A PDF schema manager, if we want a PDF schema encompassing all our tables.

On the Designer workspace, we can work on the relations for all tables on the same panel, whereas the Relation view shows the relations for a single table at a time.

We access this feature from the Database view by clicking the **Designer** menu tab.

 If this menu tab does not appear, it's because we have yet to install the linked-tables infrastructure as described previously in this chapter, especially the `designer_coords` special table.

Interface Overview

The Designer page contains a main workspace where the tables can be seen. This workspace grows and shrinks dynamically, depending on the position of our tables. A top menu contains icons whose description is revealed by hovering on them. Here is a summary of the goal for the top menu's icons:

- **Show/Hide left menu**: For left menu presence.
- **Save position**: Saves the current state of the workspace to the infrastructure.
- **Create table**: Quits the designer and enters a dialog to create a table.
- **Create relation**: Puts the designer in relation creating mode.
- **Choose field to display**: To specify which field represents a table.
- **Reload**: Fetches again the information about tables.
- **Help**: Brings an explanation about selecting the relations.
- **Angular links/Direct links**: Specifies the shape of relation links.
- **Snap to grid**: Influences the behavior of table movements, relative to an imaginary grid.
- **Small/Big All**: Hides or displays the list of columns for every table.
- **Toggle small/big**: Reverses the display mode of columns for every table, because this mode can be chosen table-by-table with its corner icon V/>.

- **Import/Export**: For PDF generation.
- **Move Menu**: The top menu can move to the right and back again.

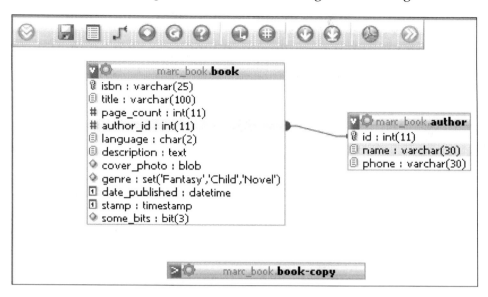

A side menu appears when clicking the **Show/Hide left menu** icon. Its goals are to present the complete list of tables, to decide which table appears on the workspace, and to enable access to the **Structure** page for a specific table. Here we choose to remove the **book-copy** table from the workspace:

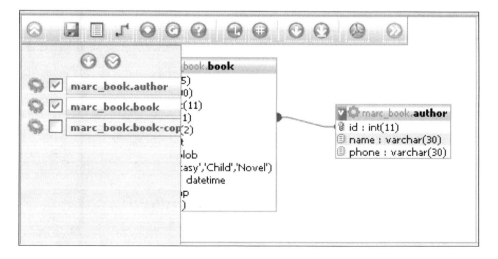

If we want this removal to be permanent, we click on the **Save position** top icon. This icon also saves the current position of our tables on the workspace.

Tables can be moved on the workspace by dragging their title bar, and the list of columns for a table can be made visible/invisible with the upper-left icon of each table. In this list of columns, small icons show us the data type (numeric, text, date) and whether this column is a key.

Defining Relations

Since we already have defined a relation with the Relation view, we'll see first how to remove it. The Designer does not permit to change a relation—only to remove and define it.

The question mark top icon brings us a panel that explains where to click to select a relation for subsequent deletion:

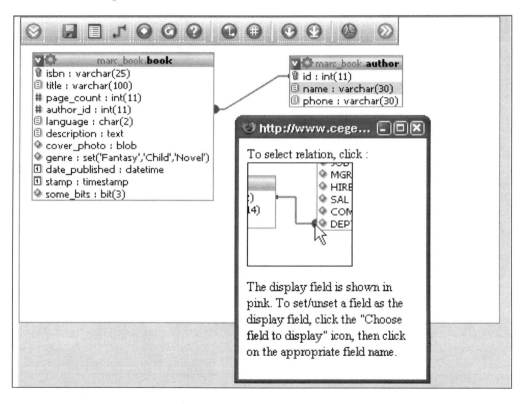

Let's click at the appropriate place to delete this relation. We get a confirmation panel on which we click **Delete**:

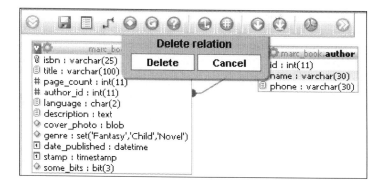

We can then proceed to recreate it. For this, we start by clicking the **Create relation** icon. The cursor then takes the form of a short message saying **Select referenced key**. In our case, the referenced key is the id column of the author table; thus we bring the cursor on this column and click. A validation is done, ensuring that we chose a primary or unique key.

Next, the cursor having changed to **Select foreign key**, we bring it to the author_id column of the book table and click again. We then confirm the relation creation. Currently, the interface does not permit to create compound keys (having more than one column).

InnoDB Relations

To delete or define a relation between InnoDB tables, the procedure is the same as for internal relations, except that at creation time, a different confirmation panel appears, enabling us to specify ON DELETE and ON UPDATE actions.

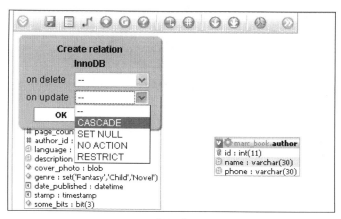

Defining the Display Field

On the workspace, we see in the `author` table that the `name` column has a special background color; this indicates that this column serves as the display field. We can simply click the **Choose field to display** top icon and drag the short message **Choose field to display** onto another column, for example the `phone` column. This changes the display field to this column. If we had dragged the message to an existing display field column, we would have removed this column as a display field for the table.

Exporting for PDF Schema

In Chapter 15 (System Documentation), we'll see how to produce a PDF schema of a subset of our database. If we have used the techniques explained in this latter chapter to create a PDF schema, we can import the coordinates of tables from such a schema into the Designer's workspace and conversely export them to the PDF schema. The **Import/export coordinates** top icon is available for that purpose.

Benefits of the Defined Relations

In this section, we will look at the benefits that we can currently test; other benefits will be described in Chapter 13 (*The Multi-Table Query Generator*) and Chapter 15 (*System Documentation*). Some other benefits of the linked-tables infrastructure will appear in Chapter 14 (*Bookmarks*) and Chapter 16 (*MIME-Based Transformations*).

These benefits are available for both internal and InnoDB relations.

Foreign Key Information

Let's browse the **book** table by entering the **Search** sub-page and choosing to display the first four columns. We see that the related key (**author_id**) is now a link.

←T→			isbn	title	page_count	author_id
☐	✎	✕	1-234567-22-0	Future souvenirs	200	2
☐	✎	✕	1-234567-89-0	A hundred years of cinema (volume 1)	600	1
☐	✎	✕	1-234567-90-0	A hundred years of cinema (volume 2)	602	1

Moving the mouse pointer over any **author_id** value reveals the author's name (as defined by the display field of the **author** table):

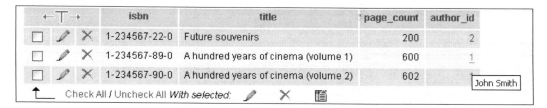

Clicking on the **author_id** brings us to the relevant table, **author**, for this specific author:

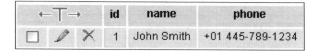

The Drop-Down List of Foreign Keys

Going back to the **book** table, in **Insert** mode (or in **Edit** mode), we now see a drop-down list of the possible keys for each field that has a relation defined. The list contains the keys and the description (display field) in both orders: key to display field, and display field to key. This enables us to use the keyboard and type the first letter of either the key or the display field:

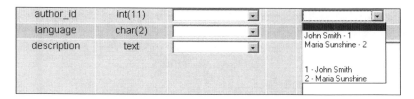

 Only the key (in this case **1**) will be stored in the **book** table. The display field is only there to assist us.

By default, this drop-down list will appear if there are a maximum of 100 rows in the foreign table. This is controlled by the following parameter:

```
$cfg['ForeignKeyMaxLimit'] = 100;
```

For foreign tables bigger than that, a distinct window appears: the browseable foreign-table window.

We might prefer to see information differently in the drop-down list. Here, **John Smith** is the content and **1** is the id. The default display is controlled by:

```
$cfg['ForeignKeyDropdownOrder'] = array( 'content-id', 'id-content');
```

We can use one or both of the strings `content-id` and `id-content` in the defining array, in the order we prefer. Thus, defining `$cfg['ForeignKeyDropdownOrder']` to `array('id-content')` would produce:

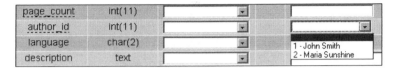

The Browseable Foreign-Table Window

Our current **author** tables have very few entries—two in fact. Thus, to illustrate this mechanism we will set the `$cfg['ForeignKeyMaxLimit']` to an artificially low number, 1. Now in **Insert** mode for the book table, we see a small table-shaped icon for **author_id**, as shown in the screenshot that follows:

This icon opens another window presenting the values of the table **author** and a **Search** input field. On the left, the values are sorted by key value (here, the `author_id` column), and on the right, they are sorted by description. We have added a third author to better see the difference in sorting:

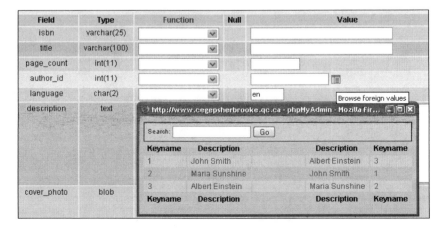

Choosing one of the values (by clicking either a key value or a description) closes this window and brings the value back to the **author_id** column.

Referential Integrity Checks

We discussed the **Operations** sub-page and its **Table maintenance** section in Chapter 10. For this exercise, we suppose that both the book and author tables are not under the control of the InnoDB storage engine. If we have defined an internal relation for the **author** table, a new choice appears for the **book** table: **Check referential integrity**:

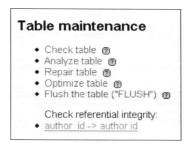

A link (here, **author_id -> author.id**) appears for each defined relation, and clicking it starts a verification. For each row, the presence of the corresponding key in the foreign table is verified, and any errors are reported. If the resulting page reports zero rows, this is good news!

This operation exists, because for non-InnoDB tables, MySQL does not enforce referential integrity, and neither does phpMyAdmin. It is perfectly possible, for example, to import data in the **book** table with invalid values for **author_id**.

Automatic Updates of Metadata

phpMyAdmin keeps the metadata for internal relations synchronized with every change that is made to the tables via phpMyAdmin. For example, renaming a column that is part of a relation would make phpMyAdmin rename it also in the metadata for the relation. The same thing happens when a column or a table is dropped.

 Metadata should be manually maintained in case a change in the structure is done from outside phpMyAdmin.

Column-Commenting

Before MySQL 4.1, the MySQL structure itself does not support adding comments to a column. Thanks to phpMyAdmin's metadata, we can nevertheless comment columns. Since MySQL 4.1, native column commenting is supported. The good news is that for any MySQL version, column commenting via phpMyAdmin is always accessed via the **Structure** page by editing each field's structure. In the following example, we need to comment three columns, so we choose them and click the pencil icon:

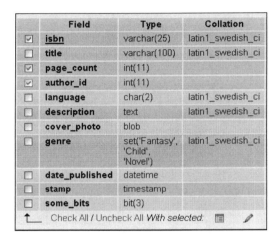

To obtain the next panel as seen here, we are working in vertical mode by setting `$cf g['DefaultPropDisplay']` to `'vertical'`. We enter the following comments:

- isbn: book number
- page_count: approximate
- author_id: cf author table

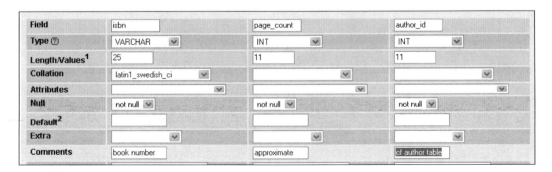

Then we click **Save**.

These comments appear at various places—for example, in the export file (see Chapter 7), on the PDF relational schema (see Chapter 15), and in the **Browse** mode:

If we do not want the comments to appear in **Browse** mode, we can set $cfg['ShowB rowseComments'] to FALSE. (It is TRUE by default.)

Column comments also appear as a tool tip in the **Structure** page, and column names are underlined with dashes. To deactivate this behavior, we can set $cfg['ShowProp ertyComments'] to FALSE. (This one is also TRUE by default.)

Automatic Migration

Whenever phpMyAdmin detects that column comments were stored in its metadata and that we are using MySQL 4.1.2 or a later version, it automatically migrates these column comments to the native MySQL column comments.

Summary

In this chapter, we covered the installation of the necessary infrastructure for keeping special metadata (data about tables), and learned how to define relations between both InnoDB and non-InnoDB tables. We also examined the modified behavior of phpMyAdmin when relations are present, foreign keys, getting information from the table, the Designer feature, and column-commenting.

12
Entering SQL Commands

This chapter explains how we can enter our own SQL commands (queries) into phpMyAdmin and how we can keep a history of those queries.

The SQL Query Box

phpMyAdmin allows us to accomplish many database operations via its graphical interface, but sometimes we have to rely on SQL query input to achieve complex operations. Here are examples of complex queries:

```
SELECT department, AVG(salary) FROM employees GROUP by department
HAVING years_experience > 10;
SELECT FROM_DAYS(TO_DAYS(CURDATE()) +30);
```

The query box is available from a number of places within phpMyAdmin.

The Database View

We encounter our first query box when going to the **SQL** menu available in the Database view.

This box is simple: we type in it some valid (hopefully) MySQL statement and click **Go**. Usually, we don't have to change the standard SQL delimiter, which is a semicolon, but a **Delimiter** dialog exists in case we need to—this is covered in Chapter 18.

For a default query to appear in this box, we can set it with the `$cfg['DefaultQu eryDatabase']` configuration directive, which is empty by default. We could put a query like SHOW TABLES FROM %d in this directive. The %d parameter in this query would be replaced by the current database name, resulting in SHOW TABLES FROM 'marc_book' in the query box.

The Table View

A slightly different box is available in the Table view from the **SQL** menu.

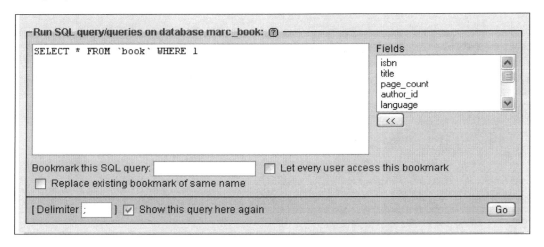

The lower part has bookmark-related choices (explained in Chapter 14). There is also a **Fields** selector and an **Insert** button on the right. The box already has a default query.

This query SELECT * FROM `book` WHERE 1 is generated from the `$cfg['DefaultQue ryTable']` configuration directive, which contains SELECT * FROM %t WHERE 1. Here, the %t is replaced by the current table name. Another placeholder available in `$cfg ['DefaultQueryTable']` is %f, which would be replaced by the complete field list of this table, thus producing the query: SELECT `isbn`, `title`, `page_count`, `author_id`, `language`, `description`, `cover_photo`, `genre`, `date_published`, `stamp`, `some_bits` FROM 'book' WHERE 1.

WHERE 1 is a condition that is always true, so the query can be executed as is. We can replace **1** with the condition we want, or we can type a completely different query.

The Fields Selector

The **Fields** selector is a way to speed up query generation. By choosing a field and clicking on the arrows **<<**, this field name is copied at the current cursor position in the query box. Here we select the **author_id** field, remove the digit **1,** and click **<<**. Then we add the condition **= 2**.

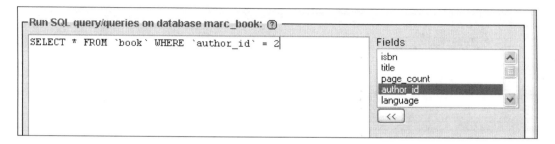

The **Show this query here again** option (checked by default) means that the query will stay in the box after its execution if we are still on the same page. This can be better seen for a query like an UPDATE or DELETE, which affects a table but does not produce a separate results page.

Clicking Into the Query Box

The default value of the $cfg['TextareaAutoSelect']$ configuration directive is TRUE. This is why the first click into this box selects all its contents. (This is a way to quickly copy the contents elsewhere or delete them from the box.) The next click puts the cursor at the click position. If the directive is set to FALSE, the first click does not select all the contents of this text area.

The Query Window

In Chapter 3, we discussed the purpose of this window and the procedure for changing some parameters (like dimension). This window can be easily opened from the left panel using the **SQL** icon or the **Query window** link, and is very convenient for entering a query and testing it:

The following screenshot shows the query window that appears over the right panel:

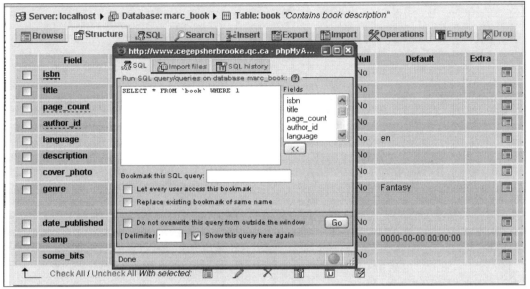

It contains the same **Fields** selector and **<<** button as that used in a Table view context.

This distinct query window only appears if $cfg['QueryFrameJS']$ is set to TRUE; we need to use a JavaScript-enabled browser. If this is set to FALSE, following the **Query window** link will only jump to the normal SQL page with the query box.

Query Window Options

The **SQL** tab is the default active tab in this window. This comes from the configuration directive $cfg['QueryWindowDefTab']$, which contains sql by default.

If we want another tab to be the default active tab, we can replace sql with files or history. Another value, full, shows the contents of all the three tabs at once.

In the query window, we see a checkbox for the **Do not overwrite this query from outside the window** choice. Normally, this is not checked, and the changes we make while navigating generating queries are reflected in the query window. (This is called **synchronization**.) For example, choosing a different database or table from the left or right panel would update the query window accordingly. But if we start to type a query directly in this window, the checkbox will get checked in order to protect its contents and remove synchronization. This way, the query composed here will be locked and protected.

Session-Based SQL History

This feature collects, as session data, all the successful SQL queries we execute and modifies the Query window to make them available. This default type of history is temporary, because $cfg['QueryHistoryDB'] is set to FALSE by default.

Database-Based SQL History (Permanent)

Because we installed the linked-tables infrastructure (see Chapter 11), a more powerful history mechanism is available and is triggered by setting $cfg['QueryHistoryDB'] to TRUE.

After we try some queries from one of the query boxes, a history is built; this history is visible only from the query window:

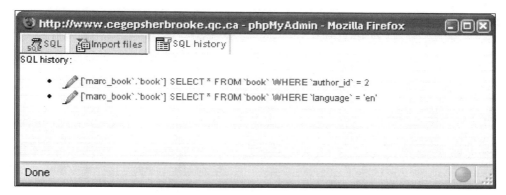

We see (in the reverse order) the last successful queries, and the database on which they were made. Only the queries typed from the query box are kept in this history, not queries generated by phpMyAdmin itself (for example, by clicking on **Browse**).

They are clickable for immediate execution, and the **Edit** icon is available to insert a recorded query into the query box for editing.

The number of queries that will be kept is controlled by $cfg['QueryHistoryMax'], which is set to 25 by default. This limit is not kept for performance reasons but as a practical limit, so as to achieve a visually unencumbered view. Extra queries are eliminated at login time in a process traditionally called **garbage collection**. The queries are stored in the table configured in $cfg['Servers'][$i]['history'].

Editing Queries in the Query Window

On the results page of a successful query, a header containing the executed query appears:

```
┌─SQL query:────────────────────────────────────────────┐
│  SELECT *                                              │
│  FROM `book`                                           │
│  WHERE `author_id` = 2                                 │
│  LIMIT 0 , 30                                          │
│                                                        │
│  ☐ Profiling [ Edit ] [ Explain SQL ] [ Create PHP Code ] [ Refresh ] │
└────────────────────────────────────────────────────────┘
```

Clicking **Edit** opens the Query window's **SQL** tab, with this query ready to be modified. This happens because of the default setting for this parameter:

```
$cfg['EditInWindow']          = TRUE;
```

When it is set to FALSE, a click on **Edit** would not open the query window; instead, the query would appear inside the query box of the **SQL** sub-page.

Multi-Statement Queries

In PHP/MySQL programming, we can only send one query at a time using the `mysql_query()` function call. phpMyAdmin allows for sending many queries in one transmission, using a semicolon as a separator. Suppose we type the following query in the query box:

```
INSERT INTO author VALUES (100,'Paul Smith','111-2222');
INSERT INTO author VALUES (101,'Melanie Smith','222-3333');
UPDATE author SET phone='444-5555' WHERE name LIKE '%Smith%';
```

We will receive the following results screen:

```
┌─SQL query:────────────────────────────────────────────┐
│  INSERT INTO author                                    │
│  VALUES ( 100, 'Paul Smith', '111-2222') ;# Affected rows: 1 │
│  INSERT INTO author                                    │
│  VALUES ( 101, 'Melanie Smith', '222-3333') ;# Affected rows: 1 │
│  UPDATE author SET phone = '444-5555' WHERE name LIKE '%Smith%';# Affected rows: 3 │
│                                                        │
│               ☐ Profiling [ Edit ] [ Create PHP Code ] │
└────────────────────────────────────────────────────────┘
```

We see the number of affected rows through comments because $cfg['VerboseMultiSubmit'] is set to TRUE.

Let's send the same list of queries again and watch the results:

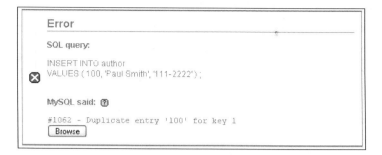

It is normal to receive a **Duplicate entry** error: the value **100** already exists. In version 2.11.0, a **Browse** button permits to display the existing entry; however, this feature was sometimes misbehaving, depending on the key value, so the **Browse** button no longer appears starting from version 2.11.1.

We are seeing the results of the first **INSERT** statement, but what happens to the next one? Execution stops at the first error because $cfg['IgnoreMultiSubmit Errors']$ is set to FALSE, telling phpMyAdmin not to ignore errors in multiple statements. If it is set to TRUE, the program successively tries all the statements, and we get:

This feature would not work as expected if we tried more than one SELECT statement. We would see only the results of the last SELECT statement.

Pretty Printing (Syntax-Highlighting)

By default, phpMyAdmin parses and highlights the various elements of any MySQL statement it processes. This is controlled by $cfg['SQP']['fmtType'], which is set to 'html' by default. This mode uses a specific color for each different element (a reserved word, a variable, a comment, and so on) as described in the $cfg['SQP']['fmtColor'] array located in the theme-specific layout.inc.php file. The default values are:

```
$cfg['SQP']['fmtColor']       = array(
    'comment'                 => '#808000',
    'comment_mysql'           => '',
    'comment_ansi'            => '',
    'comment_c'               => '',
    'digit'                   => '',
    'digit_hex'               => 'teal',
    'digit_integer'           => 'teal',
    'digit_float'             => 'aqua',
    'punct'                   => 'fuchsia',
    'alpha'                   => '',
    'alpha_columnType'        => '#FF9900',
    'alpha_columnAttrib'      => '#0000FF',
    'alpha_reservedWord'      => '#990099',
    'alpha_functionName'      => '#FF0000',
    'alpha_identifier'        => 'black',
    'alpha_variable'          => '#800000',
    'quote'                   => '#008000',
    'quote_double'            => '',
    'quote_single'            => '',
    'quote_backtick'          => ''
);
```

In the previous examples, fmtType was set to 'text' because this mode is more legible in a book. This mode inserts line breaks at logical points inside a MySQL statement, but there is no color involved. With fmtType set to 'html', phpMyAdmin would report the SQL statements as:

```
SQL query:
INSERT INTO author
VALUES ( 100, 'Paul Smith', '111-2222') ; # Error
INSERT INTO author
VALUES ( 101, 'Melanie Smith', '222-3333') ; # Error
UPDATE author SET phone = '444-5555' WHERE name LIKE '%Smith%'; # MySQL returned an empty
result set (i.e. zero rows).
```
☐ Profiling [Edit] [Create PHP Code]

Setting `fmtType` to `'none'` removes every kind of formatting, leaving our syntax intact:

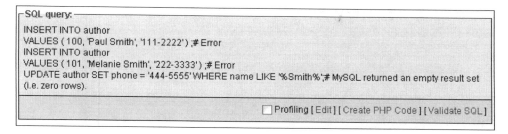

 The multi-dimensional arrays used for holding some parameters in the configuration file reflect a programming style adopted by the phpMyAdmin development team. This avoids having very long parameter names.

The SQL Validator

Each time phpMyAdmin transmits a query, the MySQL server interprets it and provides feedback. The syntax of the query must follow MySQL rules, which are not the same as standard SQL. However, conforming to standard SQL ensures that our queries may be used on other SQL implementations.

A free external service, the Mimer SQL Validator, is offered. It validates our query according to `Core SQL-99` rules and generates a report. The Validator is available directly from phpMyAdmin, and its home page is located at `http://developer.mimer.com/validator/index.htm`.

 This service stores anonymously on their server the queries it receives, for statistical purposes. When storing the queries, it replaces database, table, and columns names with generic names. Strings and numbers that are part of the query are replaced with generic values, so as to protect the original information.

System Requirements

This Validator is available as a SOAP service. Our PHP server must have XML, PCRE, and PEAR support. We need some PEAR modules too. The following command (executed on the server by the system administrator) installs the modules we need:

```
pear install Net_Socket Net_URL HTTP_Request Mail_Mime Net_DIME SOAP
```

If we have problems with this command due to some of the modules being in a beta state, we can execute the following command, which installs SOAP and other dependent modules:

```
pear -d preferred_state=beta install -a SOAP
```

Making the Validator Available

Some parameters must be configured in `config.inc.php`. Setting `$cfg['SQLQuery']['Validate']` to TRUE enables the **Validate SQL** link.

We also have to enable the Validator itself (as other validators might be available on future phpMyAdmin versions). This is done by setting `$cfg['SQLValidator']['use']` to TRUE.

The Validator is accessed with an anonymous Validator account by default, as configured by the following:

```
$cfg['SQLValidator']['username'] = '';
$cfg['SQLValidator']['password'] = '';
```

If the company has provided us with an account, we can instead use that account information here.

Validator Results

There are two kinds of reports returned by the Validator: one if the query conforms to the standard, and another if it does not.

Standard-Conforming Queries

We will try a simple query: SELECT COUNT(*) FROM book. We enter this query in the query box as usual and send it. On the results page, we now see an additional link: **Validate SQL**:

Clicking on **Validate SQL** produces the following report:

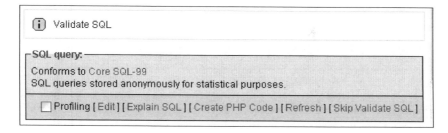

We have the option of clicking **Skip Validate SQL** to see our original query.

Non Standard-Conforming Queries

Let's try this query, which works correctly in MySQL: SELECT * FROM book where language = 'en'. Sending it to the Validator produces the following report:

```
SQL query:
SELECT * FROM book WHERE {error: 1}language = 'en'
{error: 2}LIMIT 0, 30

Errors:

   1.  syntax error: language
       expected: ( + - : ? <ascii identifier> <character set identifier>
              <decimal literal> <delimited identifier> <float literal>
              <hex string literal> <identifier> <integer literal>
              <national string literal> <string literal> ANY ARRAY CASE CAST
              CURRENT_DATE CURRENT_DEFAULT_TRANSFORM_GROUP CURRENT_PATH
              CURRENT_ROLE CURRENT_TIME CURRENT_TIMESTAMP
              CURRENT_TRANSFORM_GROUP_FOR_TYPE CURRENT_USER DATE DEREF EXISTS
              FALSE GROUPING INTERVAL LOCALTIME LOCALTIMESTAMP MODULE NEW NOT
              REPEAT ROW SESSION_USER SOME SYSTEM_USER TIME TIMESTAMP TREAT
              TRUE UNIQUE UNKNOWN USER VALUE
       correction: <identifier>
   2.  syntax error: LIMIT 0 , 30 <end>
       expected: <end> * + - -> / ; [ || <string literal> AND AT COLLATE DAY
              EXCEPT FOR GROUP HAVING HOUR INTERSECT MINUTE MONTH OR ORDER
              SECOND UNION WINDOW YEAR . IS
       correction: <end>

SQL queries stored anonymously for statistical purposes.

   ☐ Profiling [ Edit ] [ Explain SQL ] [ Create PHP Code ] [ Refresh ] [ Skip Validate SQL ]
```

Each time the Validator finds a problem, it adds a message like {**error: 1**} at the point of error and a footnote in the report. This time, the **language** column name is non-standard, so the Validator tells us that it was expecting an identifier at this point. Another error is reported about the use of a LIMIT clause, which was added to the query by phpMyAdmin and is also non-standard.

Another case is that of the backquotes. If we just click on **Browse** for the book table, phpMyAdmin generates select * from `book`, enclosing the table name with backquotes. This is the MySQL way of protecting identifiers, which might contain special characters, like spaces or international characters, or reserved words. However, sending this query to the Validator shows us that the backquotes do not conform to standard SQL. We even get two errors—one for each backquote.

Summary

In this chapter, we took a look at the purpose of query boxes and where they can be found. We also looked at query window options, multi-statement queries, how to use the field selector, how to use the SQL Validator and how to get a history of the typed commands.

13
The Multi-Table Query Generator

The **Search** pages in the Database or Table view are intended for single-table lookups. This chapter covers the multi-table **Query by example (QBE)** feature available in the Database view.

Many phpMyAdmin users work in the Table view, table-by-table, and thus tend to overlook the multi-table query generator, which is a wonderful feature for fine-tuning queries. The query generator is useful not only in multi-table situations but also for a single table. It enables us to specify multiple criteria for a column, a feature that the **Search** page in the Table view does not possess.

 The examples in this chapter assume that a multi-user installation of the linked-tables infrastructure has been made (see Chapter 11) and that the book-copy table created during an exercise of Chapter 10 is still there in the marc_book database.

To open the page for this feature, we go to the Database view for a specific database (the query generator supports working on only one database at a time) and click on **Query**.

The screenshot overleaf shows the initial QBE page. It contains the following elements:

- Criteria columns
- An interface to add criteria rows
- An interface to add criteria columns
- A table selector

- The query area
- Buttons to update or to execute the query

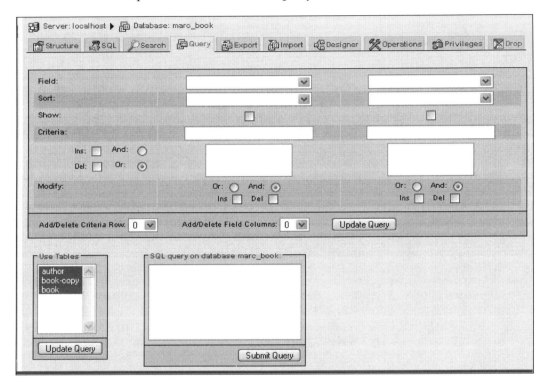

Choosing Tables

The initial selection includes all the tables. In this example, we assume that the linked-table infrastructure has been installed into the **marc_book** database. (See the section, *Single-User Installation*, in Chapter 11.) Consequently, the **Field** selector contains a great number of fields. For our example, we will work only with the **author** and **book** tables:

We then click **Update Query**. This refreshes the screen and reduces the number of fields available in the **Field** selector. We can always change the table choice later, using our browser's mechanism for multiple choices in drop-down menus (usually, control-click).

Column Criteria

Three criteria columns are provided by default. This section discusses the options we have for editing their criteria. These include options for selecting fields, sorting individual columns, entering conditions for individual columns, and so on.

Field Selector: Single-Column or All Columns

The **Field** selector contains all individual columns for the selected tables, plus a special choice ending with an asterisk (*) for each table, which means all the fields are selected:

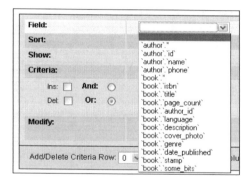

To display all the fields in the **author** table, we choose `author`.* and check the **Show** checkbox, without entering anything in the **Sort** and **Criteria** boxes. In our case, we select `author`.`name`, because we want to enter some criteria for the author's name.

Sorts

For each selected individual column, we can specify a sort (in **Ascending** or **Descending** order) or let this line remain intact (meaning no sort). If we choose more than one sorted column, the sort will be done with a priority from left to right.

[When we ask for a column to be sorted, we normally check the **Show** checkbox, but this is not necessary because we might want to do just the sorting operation without displaying this column.]

Showing a Column

We check the **Show** checkbox so that we can see the column in the results. Sometimes, we may just want to apply a criterion on a column and not include it in the resulting page. Here, we add the phone column, ask for a sort on it, and choose to show both the name and phone number. We also ask for a sort on the name in ascending order. The sort will be done first by name, and then by phone number, if the names are identical. This is because the name is in a column criterion to the left of the phone column, and thus has a higher priority:

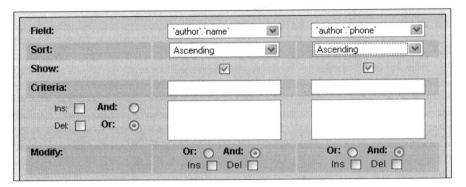

Updating the Query

At any point, we can click the **Update Query** button to see the progress of our generated query. We surely have to click it at least once before executing the query. For now, let's click it and see the query generated in the query area. In the following examples, we will click **Update Query** after each modification:

We have selected two tables, but have not yet chosen any columns from the **book** table, so this table is not mentioned in the generated query.

Criteria

In the **Criteria** box, line, we can enter a condition (respecting the SQL WHERE clause's syntax) for each of the corresponding columns. By default, we have two criteria rows. To find all authors with **Smith** in their name, we use a **LIKE** criterion—LIKE '%SMITH%'—and click **Update Query**:

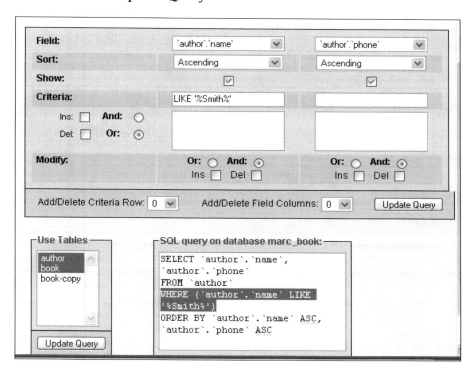

We have another line available to enter an additional criterion. Let's say we want to find the author 'Maria Sunshine' as well. This time, we use an = condition. The two condition rows will be joined by the OR operator selected by default from the left side of the interface:

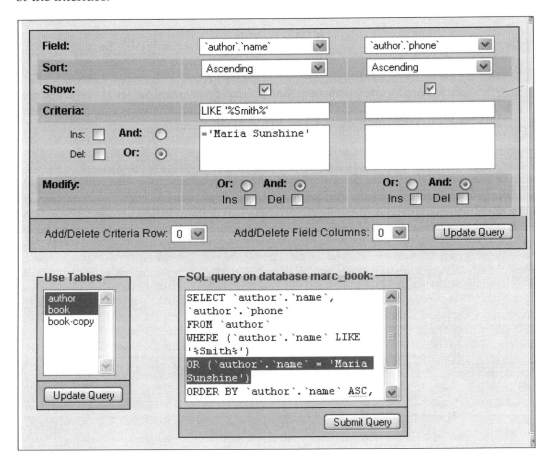

To better demonstrate that the OR operator links both the criteria rows, let's now add a condition, LIKE '%8%', on the phone number:

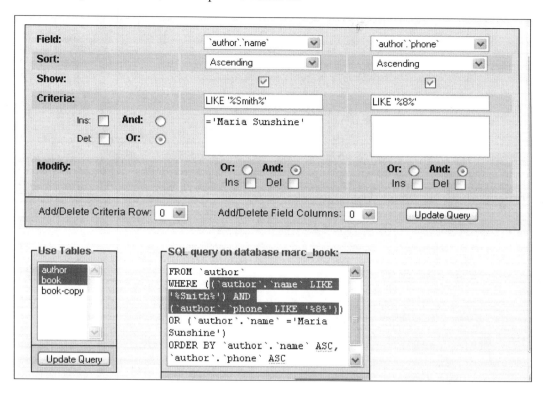

By examining the positioning of the AND and OR operators, we can see that the first conditions are linked by an AND (because AND is chosen under the **name** column) and that the second row of conditions is linked to the rest by the OR operator. The condition we just added (LIKE '%8%') is not meant to find anyone, because in an exercise in Chapter 12, we changed the phone number of all authors with name 'Smith' to '444-5555'.

If we want another criterion on the same column, we just add a criteria row.

Adjusting the Number of Criteria Rows

The number of criteria rows can be changed in two ways. First, we can select the **Ins** checkbox under **Criteria** to add one criteria row (after clicking on **Update Query**):

As this checkbox can only add one criteria row at a time, we'll uncheck it and use instead the **Add/Delete Criteria Row** dialog. Here, we choose to add two rows:

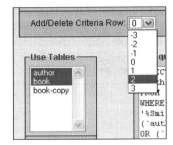

Another click on the **Update Query** button produces the following:

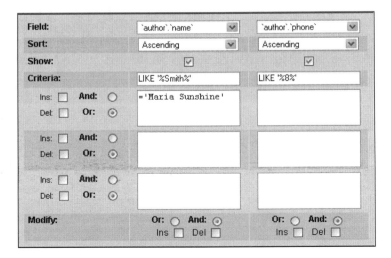

We can also remove criteria rows. This can be done by choosing negative numbers in the **Add/Delete Criteria Row** dialog or by ticking the **Del** checkbox beside the rows we want to remove. Let's remove the two rows we just added because we don't need them now:

The **Update Query** button refreshes the page with the specified adjustment.

Adjusting the Number of Criteria Columns

We can add or delete columns by using a similar mechanism: the **Ins** or **Del** checkboxes under each column, or the **Add/Delete Field Columns** dialog. We already had one unused column (not shown on the previous images to save space). Here, we have added one column using the **Ins** checkbox located under the unused column (this time we will need it):

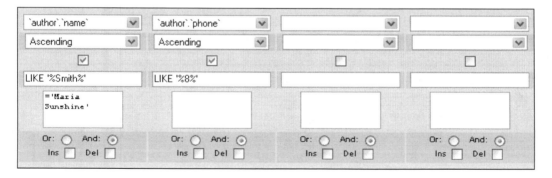

Automatic Joins

phpMyAdmin can generate the joins between tables in the query it builds. Let's now populate our two unused columns with the `title` and `genre` fields from our **book** table and see what happens when we update the query:

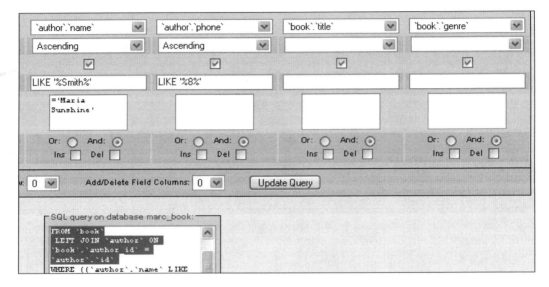

phpMyAdmin used its knowledge of the relations defined between the tables to generate a left join on the **author_id** key field. A shortcoming of the current version is that only the internal relations are examined, not the InnoDB relations.

[There may be more than two tables involved in a join.]

Executing the Query

Clicking the **Submit Query** button sends the query for execution. In phpMyAdmin version 2.11.0, there is no easy way (except by using the browser's **Back** button) to come back to the query generation page after we have submitted our query. The next chapter (*Bookmarks*) discusses how to save the generated query for later execution.

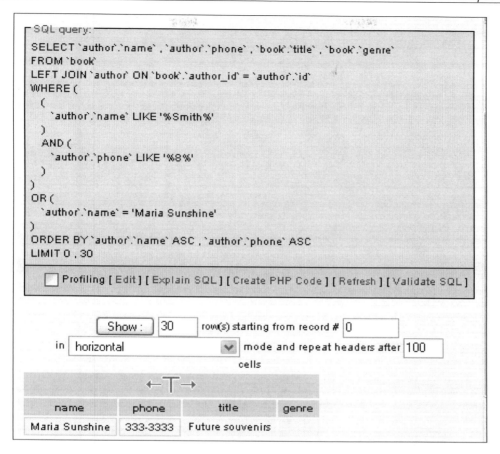

Summary

In this chapter, we have covered various aspects such as opening the query generator, choosing tables, entering column criteria, sorting and showing columns, and altering the number of criteria rows or columns. We also saw how to use the AND and OR operators to define relations between rows and columns, and how to use automatic joins between tables.

14
Bookmarks

This chapter covers one of the linked-tables infrastructure's features: query bookmarks. Being able to label queries and recall them by label can be a real time saver. In Chapter 12, we learned about the SQL history feature, which automatically stores queries (temporarily or permanently).

Bookmarks are queries that are:

- Stored permanently
- Viewable
- Erasable
- Related to one database
- Recorded only as a consequence of a user's wish
- Labeled
- Private by default (only available to the user creating them), but possibly public

A bookmark can also have a variable part, as explained in the *Passing a Parameter Value to a Bookmark* section later in this chapter.

There is no bookmark sub-page to manage bookmarks. Instead, the various actions on bookmarks are available on specific pages such as results pages or query box pages.

Creating a Bookmark after a Successful Query

Initial bookmark creation is made possible by the **Bookmark this SQL-query** button. This button appears only after execution of a query that generates results (when at least one row is found), so this method for creating bookmarks only stores SELECT statements. For example, a complex query produced by the multi-table query generator (as seen in Chapter 13) could be stored as a bookmark in this way, provided it finds some results.

Let's see an example. In the **Search** page for the **book** table, we select the fields that we want in the results, and enter the search values as shown in the following screenshot:

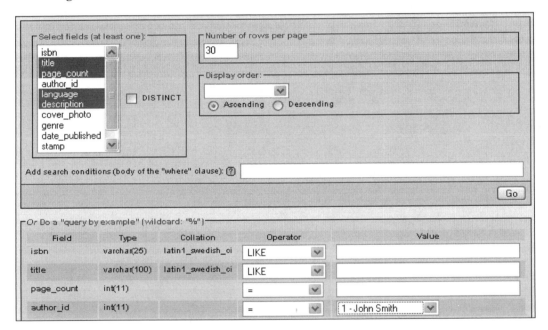

After clicking **Go**, we see that the results page has a bookmark dialog. We have to enter only a label for this bookmark and click **Bookmark this SQL-query** to save this query as a bookmark. Bookmarks are saved in the table defined by `$cfg['Servers'][$i]['bookmarktable']`.

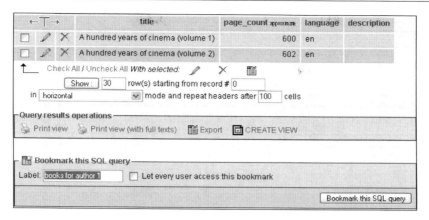

This bookmark dialog can be seen on any page that contains results. As a test, we could just click **Browse** for a table to get results, and then store this query as a bookmark. However, it does not make much sense to store (in a bookmark) a query that can easily be made with one click.

Storing a Bookmark before Sending a Query

Sometimes, we may want to store a bookmark even if a query does not find any results. This may be the case if the matching data is not yet present or if the query is not a SELECT statement. To achieve this, we have the **Bookmark this SQL-query** dialog available in the **SQL** tab of Database view, Table view, and the query window.

We now go to the **SQL** sub-page of the **book** table, enter a query, and directly put the **books in French** bookmark label in the **Bookmark this SQL query** field. If this bookmark label was previously used, a new bookmark *with the same name* will be created, unless we select the **Replace existing bookmark of same name** checkbox. Bookmarks carry an identifying number as well as a user-chosen label.

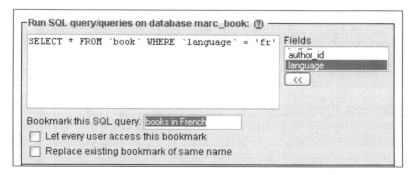

Then we click **Go**, which executes and stores the query as a bookmark. It does not matter if the query finds nothing:

This is how we can generate bookmarks for non-SELECT queries like UPDATE, DELETE, CREATE TABLE, and so on.

 This technique can also be used for a SELECT statement that either returns or does not return results.

Multi-Query Bookmarks

A single bookmark can also store more than one query (separated by semicolon). This is mostly useful for non-SELECT queries. Stacking a lot of SELECT statements would not yield the intended result because we would only see the data fetched by the last SELECT statement.

Recalling from the Bookmarks List

These bookmarks can now be easily found on the following pages:

- The Table view: **SQL** sub-page of any table from **marc_book**
- The query window: the **SQL-History** tab
- While browsing the **pma_bookmark** table (See the *Executing Bookmarks from the pma_bookmark Table* section, later)
- The Database view: **SQL** sub-page of the **marc_book** database

Three choices are available when recalling a bookmark: **Submit**, **View only**, and **Delete** (**Submit** being the default).

Bookmark Execution

Choosing the first bookmark and hitting **Go** executes the stored query and displays its results. The page resulting from a bookmark execution does not have another dialog to create a bookmark, as this would be superfluous.

 The results we get are not necessarily the same as when we created the bookmark. They reflect the current contents of the database. Only the query is stored as a bookmark.

Bookmark Manipulation

Sometimes, we may just want to ascertain the contents of a bookmark. Here, we choose the second bookmark and select **View only**:

The query will only be displayed. We could then click **Edit** and rework its contents. By doing so, we would be editing a copy of the original bookmarked query. To keep this new edited query, we can save it as a bookmark. Again, this will create another bookmark even if we choose the same bookmark label, unless we explicitly ask for the original bookmark to be replaced.

A bookmark can be erased with the **Delete** option. There is *no* confirmation dialog to confirm the deletion of the bookmark. Deletion is followed only by a message stating: **The bookmark has been deleted**.

Public Bookmarks

All bookmarks we create are private by default. When a bookmark is created, the user we are logged in as is stored with the bookmark. Suppose we choose **Let every user access this bookmark** as shown in the following screenshot:

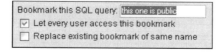

This would have the following effect:

- All users that have access to the same database (the current one) will have access to the bookmark.
- The users' ability to see meaningful results from the bookmark depends on the privileges they have on the tables referenced in the bookmark.
- The users will be able to delete the bookmark.

The Default Initial Query for a Table

In the previous examples, we chose bookmark labels according to our preferences, but by convention, if a bookmark has the same name as a table, it will be executed when **Browse** is clicked for this table. Thus, instead of seeing the normal **Browse** results of this table, we'll see the bookmark's results.

Suppose we are interested in viewing (by default, in the **Browse** mode) the books with a page count lower than 300. We first generate the appropriate query, which can be done easily from the **Search** page, and then we use **book** as a label on the results page:

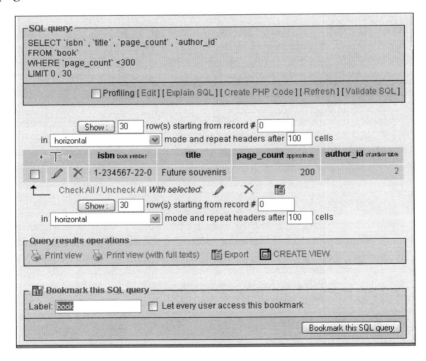

Bookmark Parameters

If we look again at the first bookmark we created (finding all books for **author 1**), we realize that, although useful, it was limited to always finding the same author.

A special query syntax enables the passing of parameters to bookmarks. This syntax uses the fact that SQL comments enclosed within /* and */ are ignored by MySQL. If the /* [VARIABLE] */ construct exists somewhere in the query, it will be expanded at execution time with the value provided when recalling the bookmark.

Creating a Parameterized Bookmark

Let's say we want to find all books for a given author when we don't know the author's name. We first enter the following query:

```
SELECT author.name, author.id, book.title
FROM book, author
WHERE book.author_id = author.id
/* AND author.name LIKE '%[VARIABLE]%' */
```

The part between the comments characters (/* */) will be expanded later, and the tags removed:

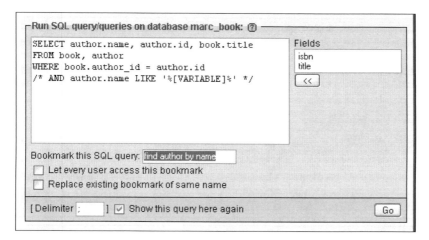

We label it and click **Go**. The first execution of the query just stores the bookmark.

In this example, we have two conditions in the WHERE clause, of which one contains the special syntax. If our only criterion in the WHERE clause needed a parameter, we could use a syntax like WHERE 1 /* and author_id = [VARIABLE] */.

Passing a Parameter Value to a Bookmark

To test the bookmark, we recall it as usual and enter a value in the **Variable** field:

When we click **Go**, we see the expanded query and author Smith's books:

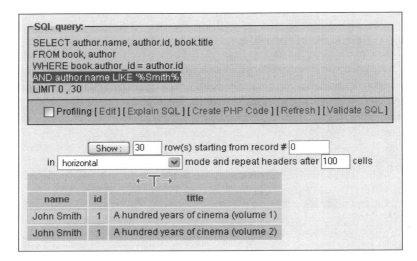

Executing Bookmarks by Browsing the pma_bookmark Table

This feature is only available to users who can directly see the **pma_bookmark** table. This is the default name given when the linked-tables infrastructure is installed. In a multi-user installation, this table is usually located in a database invisible to unprivileged users. Browsing this table displays a new **Execute bookmarked query** button, which triggers the execution of the query:

←T→			id	dbase	user	label	query
☐	✏ 📝	✕	839	marc_book	marc	books for author 1	SELECT `title`, `page_count`, `language`, `descrip...
☐	📝	Execute bookmarked query	ook	marc	books in French	SELECT * FROM `book` WHERE `language` = 'fr'
☐	✏ 📝	✕	843	marc_book	marc	book	SELECT `isbn`, `title`, `page_count`, `author_id` ...
☐	✏ 📝	✕	844	marc_book	marc	find author by name	SELECT author.name, author.id, book.title\r\nFROM bo...

Seeing the text of the query while browsing this table is possible if `$cfg['ShowBlob']` is set to TRUE. Alternatively, we could click the pencil icon to open the **Edit** page for a specific row, so that we can see the query's complete text.

Summary

In this chapter, we saw how to record bookmarks (after or before sending a query), how to manipulate them, and how some bookmarks can be made public. We learned about the default initial query for **Browse** mode. We also covered passing parameters to bookmarks and executing bookmarks directly from the **pma_bookmark** table.

15
System Documentation

Producing and maintaining good documentation about data structure is crucial for a project's success, especially when it's a team project. Fortunately, phpMyAdmin has features that take care of this. When phpMyAdmin generates results, there is always a **Print view** link that can be used to generate a printable report of the data. The **Print view** feature can also be used to produce basic documentation, and this is done in two steps. The first click on **Print view** puts a report on screen, with a **Print** button at the end of the page. This **Print** button generates a report formatted for the printer.

The Database Print View

Clicking **Print view** on the **Structure** sub-page for a database generates a list of tables. This list contains the number of records, storage engine, size, comments, the dates of creation, and last update for each table.

Table	Records	Type	Size	Comments	
author	5	InnoDB	16.0 KiB	InnoDB free: 1410048 kB	
				Creation:	Sep 29, 2007 at 02:06 PM
book	3	InnoDB	64.0 KiB	Contains book description; InnoDB free: 1410048 kB	
				Creation:	Oct 13, 2007 at 09:29 AM
book-copy	3	MyISAM	11.9 KiB	Contains book description	
				Creation:	Sep 21, 2007 at 03:53 PM
				Last update:	Sep 21, 2007 at 03:53 PM
				Last check:	Sep 21, 2007 at 03:53 PM
3 table(s)	11	--	91.9 KiB		

Server: localhost ▶ Database: marc_book

The Selective Database Print View

Sometimes, we prefer to get a report only for certain tables. This can be done from the **Structure** sub-page for a database by selecting the tables we want and choosing **Print view** from the drop-down menu:

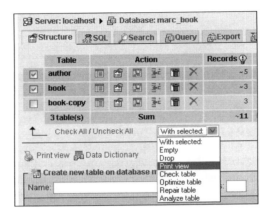

The Table Print View

There is also a **Print view** link on the **Structure** sub-page for each table. Clicking this, produces information about columns, indexes, space usage, and row statistics:

book

Table comments: Contains book description; InnoDB free: 1410048 kB

Field	Type	Null	Default	Links to	Comments	MIME
isbn	varchar(25)	No			book number	
title	varchar(100)	No				
page_count	int(11)	No			approximate	
author_id	int(11)	No		author -> id	cf author table	
language	char(2)	No	en			
description	text	No				
cover_photo	blob	No				
genre	set('Fantasy', 'Child', 'Novel')	No	Fantasy			
date_published	datetime	No				
stamp	timestamp	No	0000-00-00 00:00:00			
some_bits	bit(3)	No				

Indexes:

Keyname	Type	Cardinality	Field	
PRIMARY	PRIMARY	3	isbn	
by_title	INDEX	3	title	30
isbn	INDEX	3	isbn	
author_id	INDEX	3	author_id	

The Data Dictionary

A more complete report about tables and columns for a database is available from the **Structure** sub-page of the Database view. We just have to click **Data dictionary** to get this report, which is partially shown here:

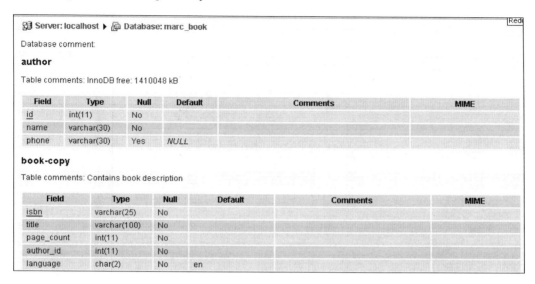

The **MIME** column is empty until we add MIME-related information to some columns. (This is explained in Chapter 16.)

Relational Schema in PDF

In Chapter 11, we defined relations between the **book** and **author** tables. These relations were used for various foreign key functions (for example, getting a list of possible values in **Insert** mode). Now, we will examine a feature that enables us to generate a custom-made relational schema for our tables in a popular format: PDF. This feature requires that the linked-tables infrastructure be properly installed and configured, as explained in Chapter 11.

Adding a Third Table to Our Model

To get a more complete schema, we will now add another table, **country**, to our database. Here is its export file:

```
CREATE TABLE IF NOT EXISTS `country` (
  `code` char(2) NOT NULL,
  `description` varchar(50) NOT NULL,
```

```
    PRIMARY KEY  (`code`)
) ENGINE=MyISAM DEFAULT CHARSET=latin1;

INSERT INTO `country` (`code`, `description`) VALUES
('ca', 'Canada'),
('uk', 'United Kingdom');
```

We will link this table to the **author** table. Firstly, in **Relation view** for the **country** table, we specify the field that we want to display:

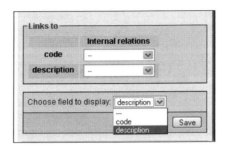

Then, we add a **country_code** column to the **author** table, and in the Relation view, we link it to the newly created **country** table. We must remember to click **Go** for the relation to be recorded. For this example, it is not necessary to enter any country data for an author, as we are interested only in the relational schema.

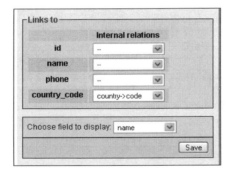

Editing PDF Pages

Each relational schema is called a **page**. We can create or edit a page by clicking **Edit PDF pages** in the **Operations** sub-page of the Database view.

Page Planning

In phpMyAdmin version 2.11.0, a relational schema cannot span multiple databases. But even working with just one database, the number of tables might be large. Representing the various relations between them in a clear way could be a challenge. This is why we may use many pages, each showing some tables and their relations.

We must also take into account the dimensions of the final output. Printing on letter-size paper gives us less space to show all our tables and still have a legible schema.

Creating a New Page

Because there are no existing pages, we need to create one. As our most important table is book, we will also name this page **book**.

We will choose which tables we wish to see in the relational schema. We could choose each table one-by-one, but for a good start, checking the appropriate **Automatic layout** checkbox is recommended. Doing this puts all the related tables from our database onto the list of tables to be included in the schema. It then generates appropriate coordinates so that the tables will appear in a spiral layout, starting from the center of the schema. These coordinates are expressed in millimeters, with (0,0) being located at the upper-left corner. We then click **Go**.

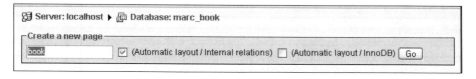

Editing a Page

We now get a page with three different sections. The first one is the master menu, where we choose the page on which we want to work (from the drop-down menu); we can also delete the chosen page. We could also, eventually, create a second schema (page).

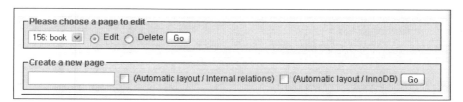

The next section is the table placement part. We now see the benefit of the **Automatic layout** feature: we already have our three tables selected, with the (X,Y) coordinates filled in. We can add a table (on the last line), delete a table (using the checkbox), and change the coordinates (which represent the position of the upper-left corner of each table on the schema):

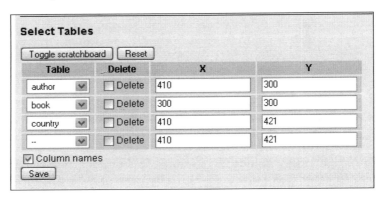

To help set exact coordinates, a visual editor is available for JavaScript-enabled browsers. To control the availability of this editor, the following parameter (which is set to TRUE by default) is available:

```
$cfg['WYSIWYG-PDF']          = TRUE;
```

The editor appears when the **Toggle scratchboard** button is clicked once. It will disappear when this button is clicked again. We can move tables on the scratchboard by dragging and dropping—the coordinates will change, accordingly. The appearance of the tables on the scratchboard provides a rough guide to the final PDF output. Some people prefer to see only the table names (without every column name) on the scratchboard. This can be done by unchecking the **Column names** checkbox and clicking **Save**.

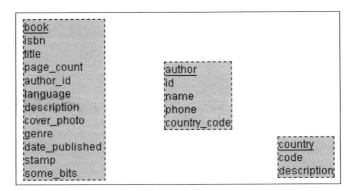

When we are satisfied with the layout, we must click **Save**.

Displaying a Page

The last section of the screen is the PDF report-generation dialog. This is also available from the **Operations** sub-page of the Database view, now that we have created a page:

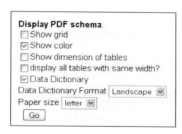

The available options are:

- **Show grid**: The schema will have a grid layer with coordinates displayed.

- **Show color**: The links between tables, table names, and special columns (primary keys and display fields) will be in color.

- **Show dimensions of tables**: The visual dimension of each table in the table title (for example, **32x30**) will be displayed.

- **Display all tables with same width?** All tables will be displayed using the same width. (Normally, the width adjusts itself according to the length of the table and column names.)

- **Data Dictionary**: The data dictionary, which was covered earlier in this chapter, will be included at beginning of the report.

- **Data Dictionary Format**: Here, we choose the printed orientation of the dictionary.

- **Paper size**: Changing this will influence the schema, and the scratchboard dimensions.

In `config.inc.php`, the following parameters define the available paper sizes and the default choice:

```
$cfg['PDFPageSizes']        = array('A3', 'A4', 'A5', 'letter',
'legal');
$cfg['PDFDefaultPageSize']  = 'A4';
```

The following screenshot shows the last page of the generated report (the schema page) in the PDF format. The first four pages contain the data dictionary with an additional feature: on each page, the schema can be reached by clicking the table name, and in the schema, each page in the data dictionary can be reached by clicking the corresponding table.

Arrows point in the direction of the corresponding foreign table. If **Show color** has been selected, primary keys are shown in gray, and display fields in black:

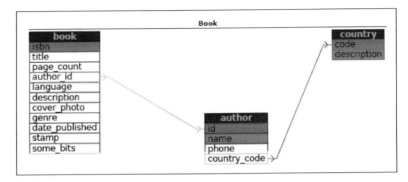

Here is another example generated from the same **book** PDF page definition, this time with the grid but no color:

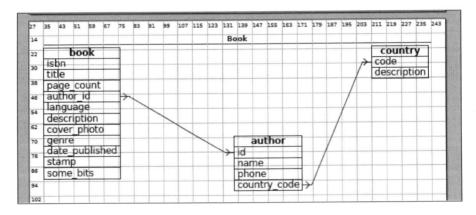

A Note about Fonts Used

All the text we see in the PDF schema is drawn using a specific font. phpMyAdmin 2.11.0 uses the `DejaVuSans` font (`http://dejavu.sourceforge.net`), which covers a wide range of characters.

For actual PDF generation, phpMyAdmin relies on the `tcpdf` library (`http://tcpdf.sourceforge.net`), which is itself an adaptation of the `fpdf` library (`http://www.fpdf.org`). These libraries have two ways of using fonts: **embedded** and **not embedded**. Embedded fonts produce a bigger PDF file, because the whole font is included in the PDF. This is the default option chosen by phpMyAdmin, because the library does not depend on the presence of a specific TrueType font in the client operating system.

The fonts are located in `libraries/tcpdf/font` under the main phpMyAdmin directory.

To use a different font file, we must first add it to the library (tools are present in the original `tcpdf` kit and a tutorial is available on the `http://www.fpdf.org` website), and then modify phpMyAdmin's `pdf_schema.php` source code.

Using the Designer for PDF Layout

The Designer feature, available in Database view, offers a more refined way of moving the tables on-screen because the column links follow the table movements. Therefore, an interface exists between the tables' coordinates, as saved by the Designer, and the coordinates for the PDF schema. Let's enter the Designer and click the small PDF logo:

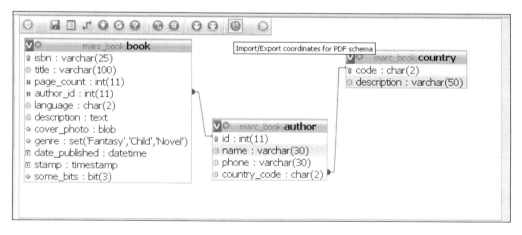

This brings us to a panel where we can choose the (existing) PDF schema name, and the action we want to perform—in our case, we want to export the Designer coordinates to the PDF schema.

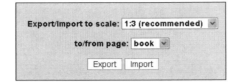

 There is a difference in the span of tables managed by the **Designer** and by the **Edit PDF** feature. The **Designer** manipulates all the tables of a database, whereas the **Edit PDF** panel offers us a choice of tables, so that we can represent a subset of the relations (in the case there are many tables).

Summary

In this chapter, we covered the documentation features offered by phpMyAdmin—the print view for a database or a table, and the data dictionary for a complete column list. We also covered PDF relational schemas. In particular, we saw how to create and modify a PDF schema page, and how to use the visual editor (scratchboard).

16
MIME-Based Transformations

In this chapter, we cover a powerful phpMyAdmin feature: its ability to transform a column's contents according to specific rules, called the transformations. This chapter describes how we can transform the contents that we see in the **Browse** mode for a table. Normally, the exact contents of each row are displayed, except that:

- **TEXT** and **CHARACTER** fields might be truncated, according to $cfg['LimitChars'], and whether we have clicked on the **Full Text** icon.
- **BLOB** fields might be replaced by a message like **[BLOB - 1.5 KB]**.

We will use the term **cell** to indicate a specific column of a specific row. The cell containing the cover photograph for the 'Future souvenirs' book (a **BLOB** column) is currently displayed as cryptic data like **‰PNG\r\n\Z\n\0\0\0\rIHDR\0**, or as a message stating the **BLOB** field's size. It would be interesting to see a thumbnail of the picture directly in phpMyAdmin, and possibly the full-size picture itself.

We define a **transformation** as a mechanism by which all the cells relating to a column are transformed at browse time, using the metadata defined for this column. Only the cells visible on the results page are transformed. The transformation logic itself is coded in PHP scripts, stored in libraries/transformations, and called using a plug-in architecture.

To enable this feature, we must set $cfg['BrowseMIME'] to TRUE in config.inc. php. The linked-tables infrastructure must be in place (see Chapter 11), because the metadata necessary for the transformations is not available in the official MySQL table structure; it is an addition made especially for phpMyAdmin.

In the documentation section on phpMyAdmin's home site, there is a link pointing to additional information for developers who would like to learn the internal structure of the plug-ins in order to code their own transformations.

The MIME Column's Settings

If we go to the Table view of the **Structure** page for the **book** table and click the **Change** link for the **cover_photo**, we see three additional attributes for the fields:

- **MIME type**
- **Browser transformation**
- **Transformation options**

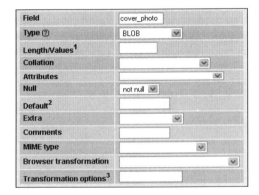

For a specific field, it is possible to indicate only **one** type of transformation. Here, the field is a **BLOB** field, so it can hold any kind of data, but for phpMyAdmin to interpret and act correctly on the data, the transformation system must be informed of the data format and the intended results. Accordingly, we have to ensure that we upload data that always follows the same file format.

We will first learn the purpose of those attributes, and then try some possibilities in the *Examples of Transformation* section.

MIME Types

The MIME specification has been chosen as a metadata attribute to categorize the kind of data a column holds. The current possible values are:

- **image/jpeg**
- **image/png**

- **text/plain**
- **application/octetstream**

The **auto-detect** option in the menu is yet to be implemented, so we do not use it.

The `text/plain` type can be chosen for a column containing any kind of text (for example, XHTML or XML text).

Browser Transformations

This is where we set the exact transformation to be done. More than one transformation may be supported per MIME type. For example, for the **image/jpeg** MIME type, we have two transformations available: **image/jpeg: inline** for a clickable thumbnail of the image, and **image/jpeg: link** to display just a link.

As we can see in the following image, moving the mouse over each choice in the drop-down menu gives a short explanation of the corresponding transformation. A more complete explanation of the transformations and the possible options is available on clicking on the **transformation descriptions** link.

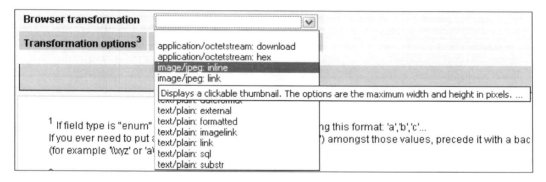

Transformation Options

We will see in the *Examples of Transformations* section that some transformations accept options. For example, a transformation that generates an image will need the width and height in pixels. A comma is used to separate the values in the option list, and some options may need to be enclosed within quotes.

Some options have a default value, and we must be careful to respect the documented order for options. For example, if there are two options and we only want to specify a value for the second option, we can use empty quotes as a placeholder for the first option to let the system use its default value.

Requirements for Image Generation

The normal generation of thumbnails requires that some components exist on the web server and that a parameter in `config.inc.php` be correctly configured.

The GD2 Library

phpMyAdmin uses internally some functions to create the thumbnails. These functions need the GD2 library to be present on our PHP server.

phpMyAdmin can detect the presence of the correct GD2 library, but this detection takes some time, and takes place not once per session, but on almost every action taken in phpMyAdmin.

Setting the `$cfg['GD2Available']` parameter in `config.inc.php` to its default value, `'auto'` indicates that a detection of the library's presence and version is needed.

If we know that the GD2 library is available, setting `$cfg['GD2Available']` to `yes` will make execution quicker. If the GD2 library is not available, you are recommended to set this parameter to `no`.

To find out which GD2 library we have on the server, we can go to phpMyAdmin's **Home** page, and click **Show PHP information**. If this link is not present, we have to set the `$cfg['ShowPhpInfo']` parameter to `true`. We then look for a section titled **gd** and verify which version is `identified`.

gd	
GD Support	enabled
GD Version	bundled (2.0.28 compatible)
GIF Read Support	enabled
GIF Create Support	enabled
JPG Support	enabled
PNG Support	enabled
WBMP Support	enabled
XBM Support	enabled

The JPEG and PNG Libraries

Our PHP server needs to have support for JPEG and PNG images if we or our users want to generate thumbnails for those types of images. For more details, please refer to `http://php.net/manual/en/ref.image.php`.

Memory Limits

On some PHP servers, the default value in `php.ini` for `memory_limit` is 8 MB. This is too low for correct image manipulation. For example, in one test, a value of 11 MB in `memory_limit` was needed to generate the thumbnail from a 300 KB JPEG image.

Examples of Transformations

We will now discuss a few transformation examples. We will start by changing the field type of our **cover_photo** field.

Clickable Thumbnail (.jpeg or .png)

We change our **cover_photo** field type from **BLOB** to **MEDIUMBLOB** to ensure that we can upload photographs that are bigger than 65 KB to it. We then enter the following attributes:

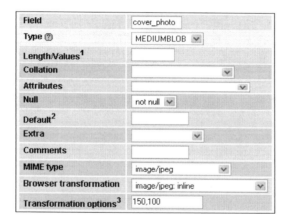

Here, the options are presented as **width,height**. If we omit the options, the default values are **100,100**. The thumbnail generation code preserves the original aspect ratio of the image, so the values entered are the *maximum* width and height of the generated image. We then upload a `.jpeg` file in a cell (using instructions from Chapter 6). As a result, we get the following in **Browse** mode for this table:

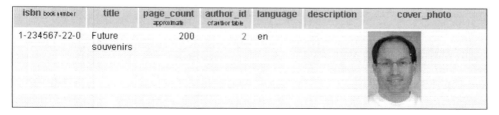

This thumbnail can be clicked to reveal the full-size photograph.

 The thumbnail is not stored anywhere in MySQL, but generated each time we go into **Browse** mode for this set of rows. On a double Xeon 3.2GHz server, we commonly experience a generation rate of 6 JPEG images per second.

For a .png file, we have to use **image/png** as the MIME type, and **image/png: inline** as the transformation.

Another point to note: we have seen in Chapter 6, in section *BLOB (Binary Large Object) Fields* that the $cfg['ShowBlob']$ parameter is normally used to permit or block the display of BLOB contents, but this parameter does not influence the thumbnail's display—it can be set to TRUE or FALSE.

Links to an Image

To get a link without thumbnails, we use the **image/jpeg: link** transformation. There are no transformation options. This link can then be used to view the photograph (by left-clicking on the link), and then possibly download it (by right-clicking on the photograph itself):

isbn book number	title	page_count approximate	author_id creation table	language	description	cover_photo	genre
1-234567-22-0	Future souvenirs	200	2	en		[BLOB]	

Date Formatting

We have a field named **date_published** in our **book** table; let's ensure that its type is **DATETIME**. Then we set its MIME type to **text/plain**, and the browser transformation to **text/plain: dateformat**. The next step is to edit the row for the 'Future souvenirs' book, and enter **2003-01-01 14:56:00** in the **date_published** field. When we browse the table, and see the field formatted. Moving the mouse over the field reveals the unformatted original contents:

This transformation accepts two options. The first is the number of hours that will be added to the original value (by default, this is zero.) Adding the number of hours can be useful if we *store* all the times based on **Universal Coordinated Time (UTC)**, but want to *display* them for a specific zone (UTC+5). The second option is the time format we want to use, made from any PHP `strftime` parameters. So, if we put this in the transformation options, **'0','Year: %Y'**, we will get:

date_published	stamp
Year: 2003	2006-07-22 09:51:50
Year: 19 2003-01-01 14:56:00 00-00 00:00:00	
Year: 1999	0000-00-00 00:00:00

Links from Text

Suppose that we have put a complete URL: `http://domain.com/abc.pdf` — in the **description** field in our **book** table. The text of the link will be displayed while browsing the table, but we would not be able to click it. We'll now see the use of the **text/plain** MIME type in such a situation.

text/plain: link

If we use a MIME type of **text/plain** and a browser transformation of **text/plain: link**, in the scenario just mentioned, we will still see the text for the link, and it will be clickable:

isbn book number	title	page_count approximate	author_id creation table	language	description
1-234567-22-0	Future souvenirs	200	2	en	http://domain.com/abc.pdf
1-234567-89-0	A hundred years of cinema (volume 1)	600	1	en	

If all the documents that we want to point to, are located at a common URL prefix, we can put this prefix (for example, `http://domain.com/`) in the first transformation option, with the enclosing quotes. Then, we would only put the last part of the URL (`abc.pdf`) in each cell.

A second transformation option is available for setting a title. This would be displayed in **Browse** mode instead of the URL contents, but a click would nonetheless bring us to the intended URL.

 If we use only the second transformation option, we have to put quotes where the first option is to be entered, as follows: `''`,`'this is the title'`.

text/plain: imagelink

This transformation is similar to the previous one, except that we place in the cell a URL that points to an image. This image will be fetched and displayed in the cell along with the link text. The image could be anywhere on the Web, including our local server.

The first available option is the common URL prefix (like the one for **text/plain: link**), the second option is the width of the image in pixels (default: 100), and the third is the height (default: 50).

If the text for the link is too long, the transformation does not occur. In this case, we can click the **Full Texts** icon to reveal the complete link. Then, we'll see the image altogether.

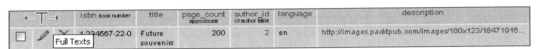

Other transformations like `image/jpeg: inline` and `image/png: inline` specify the exact `MIME` type of the image; in these cases, phpMyAdmin uses GD2 library functions for the thumbnail generation. However, the link contained in a `text/plain: imagelink` transformation may refer to any browser-supported image type, so phpMyAdmin just displays a resized image with an HTML `img` tag and its `width` and `height` attributes, according to the size options defined in the transformation. To see the original image, we can click either the link or the thumbnail.

Preserving the Original Formatting

Normally, when displaying text, phpMyAdmin does some escaping of special characters. For example, if we enter **This book is good** in the description field for one book, we would normally see **This book is good** when browsing the table. However, if we use the transformation **text/plain: formatted** for this field, we get the following while browsing:

←T→			isbn	title	page_count	author_id	language	description	cover_photo
☐	✎	✗	1-234567-22-0	Future souvenirs	200	2	en	This book is **good**	[BLOB]
☐	✎	✗	1-234567-89-0	A hundred years of cinema (volume 1)	600	1	en		[BLOB - 0 Bytes]

In this example, the results are correct. However, other HTML entered in the data field could produce surprising results (including invalid HTML pages). For example, because phpMyAdmin presents results using HTML tables, a non-escaped `</table>` tag in the data field would ruin the output.

Displaying Parts of a Text

The **text/plain: substr** transformation is available to display only a part of the text. Here are the options:

- First: where to start in the text (default: 0)
- Second: how many characters (default: all the remaining text)
- Third: what to display as a suffix to show that truncation has occurred (default: ...)

Remember that `$cfg['LimitChars']` is doing a character truncation for every non-numeric field, so **text/plain: substr** is a mechanism for fine-tuning this, field-by-field.

Download Link

Let's say we want to store a small audio comment about each book, inside MySQL. We add to the **book** table a new field, with name **audio_contents** and type **MEDIUMBLOB**, to the **book** table. We set its **MIME type** to **application/octetstream** and choose the **application/octetstream: download** transformation. In the options, we insert **'comment.wav'**.

MIME type	Browser transformation	Transformation options[3]
application/octetstream ▾	application/octetstream: download ▾	'comment.wav'

This MIME type and extension will inform our browser about the incoming data, and the browser should open the appropriate player. To insert a comment, we first record it in .wav format and then upload the contents of the file into the **audio_contents** field for one of the books. When browsing our table, we can see a link for our audio comment.

Hexadecimal Representation

Characters are stored in MySQL (as in computers in general) as numeric data, and converted into something meaningful for the screen or printer. Users sometimes cut and paste data from one application to phpMyAdmin, leading to unexpected results if the characters are not directly supported by MySQL. A case I remember involved special quotation marks entered in a Microsoft Word document and pasted to phpMyAdmin. It helps to be able to see the exact hexadecimal codes, and this can be done by using the application/octetstream: hex transformation.

In the following example, we have applied this transformation to the **title** field of our **book** table. When browsing the row containing the **Future souvenirs** title, we now see:

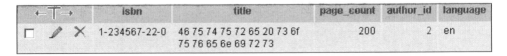

			isbn	title	page_count	author_id	language
☐	✎	✕	1-234567-22-0	46 75 74 75 72 65 20 73 6f 75 76 65 6e 69 72 73	200	2	en

As we know which character set this column is encoded with (see Chapter 17), we can compare its contents with a chart describing each character. For instance, http://en.wikipedia.org/wiki/Latin1 describes the **latin1** character set.

SQL Pretty Printing

Let's say we are using a table to store the text of a course about SQL. In one column, we might have put sample SQL statements. With the **text/plain: sql** transformation, these SQL statements will be displayed in color with syntax highlighting, when browsing this table.

External Applications

The transformations that have been described previously are implemented directly from within phpMyAdmin. However, some transformations are better done via existing external applications.

The **text/plain: external** transformation enables us to send the cell's data to another application that will be started on the web server, capture this application's output, and display it in the cell's position.

This feature is only supported on a Linux or UNIX server (under Microsoft Windows, output and error redirection cannot be easily captured by the PHP process). Furthermore, PHP should not be running in safe mode, so the feature might not be available on hosted servers. A minimum PHP version of 4.3.0 is required for this feature to work.

For security reasons, the exact path and name of the application cannot be set from within phpMyAdmin as a transformation option. The application names are set directly inside one of the phpMyAdmin scripts.

First, in the phpMyAdmin installation directory, we edit the text_plain__external.inc.php file in libraries/transformations/, and find the following section:

```
$allowed_programs = array();
//$allowed_programs[0] = '/usr/local/bin/tidy';
//$allowed_programs[1] = '/usr/local/bin/validate';
```

No external application is configured by default; we have to explicitly add our own.

 The names of the transformation scripts are constructed using the following format: the MIME type, a double underscore, and then a part indicating which transformation occurs.

Each allowed program must be described here, with an index number, starting from 0, and its complete path. Then, we save the modifications to this script and put it back on the server if needed. The remaining setup is completed from the panel where we chose the options for the other browser transformations.

Of course, we choose **text/plain: external** in the transformations menu.

As the first option, we place the application number. (For example, 0 would be for the tidy application.) The second option holds the parameters we need to pass to this application. If we want phpMyAdmin to apply the `htmlspecialchars()` function to the results, we put **1** as the third parameter. (This is done by default.) We could put a **0** there to avoid protecting the output with `htmlspecialchars()`.
If we want to avoid reformatting the cell's lines, we put **1** as the fourth parameter. This will use the NOWRAP modifier, and is done by default.

External Application Example: In-Cell Sort

This example shows how we can sort the text contents of one cell. We start by modifying the `text_plain__external.inc.php` script, as mentioned in the above section, to add the `sort` program:

```
$allowed_programs[0] = '/bin/sort';
```

Note that our new program bears the index number 0.

Then we add a **TEXT** field, **keywords**, to our **book** table and fill in the MIME-related information, entering **'0','-r'** as the transformation options:

MIME type	Browser transformation	Transformation options[3]
text/plain	text/plain: external	'0','-r'

The **'0'** here, refers to the index number for `sort`, and the **'-r'** is a parameter for `sort`, which makes the program sort in reverse order.

Next, we **Edit** the row for the book *A hundred years of cinema (volume 1)*, entering some keywords in no particular order and hitting **Go** to save:

To test the effects of the external program, we browse our table and see the sorted in-cell keywords:

date_published	stamp	keywords
Year: 2003	2006-07-22 10:20:10	
Year: 1999	2006-07-22 10:58:39	sport history cinema

Indeed, the keywords are displayed in reverse sorted order in this cell.

Summary

In this chapter, we saw how we can improve the browsing experience by transforming data using various methods. We can see thumbnail and full-size images of .jpeg and .png **BLOB** fields, generate links, format dates, display only parts of texts, and execute external programs to reformat each cell's contents.

17
Character Sets and Collations

This chapter explains how phpMyAdmin stores and fetches data, and how it deals with the character set and collation features available under MySQL. The program's behavior is highly dependent on the MySQL version used.

A **character set** describes how symbols for a specific language or dialect are encoded. A **collation** contains rules to compare and sort the characters of a character set. (See the *MySQL 4.1.x and Later* section in this chapter.)

The character set used to *store* our data may be different from the one used to *display* it, leading to data discrepancies. Thus, a need to transform the data arises.

Language Files and UTF-8

"Unicode is an industry standard designed to allow text and symbols [...] to be consistently represented and manipulated by computers". See http://en.wikipedia.org/wiki/Unicode and also http://www.unicode.org.

Unicode currently supports more than 600 languages, which is its main advantage over other character sets available with ISO or Windows. This is especially important with a multi-language product like phpMyAdmin.

To represent or encode these Unicode characters, many Unicode Transformation Formats (UTF) exist. A popular transformation format is UTF-8, which uses one to four 8-bit octets per character. For more details, visit http://en.wikipedia.org/wiki/UTF-8.

Note that the browser must support UTF-8 (as most current browsers do). The phpMyAdmin distribution kit includes a UTF-8 version of every language file in the lang subdirectory, and some of them are only available in UTF-8 encoding.

A majority of the language files are also coded using ISO or Windows character sets, with the goal of supporting older browsers. Also, when connecting to a pre-MySQL 4.1 server, a user can still choose a non-UTF-8 character set if his or her web server or phpMyAdmin version are not configured to recode characters. (See the *Data Recoding* section in this chapter.)

The availability of a UTF-8 language file in the **Language** selector depends on both the phpMyAdmin version and the MySQL version. If we are using a phpMyAdmin version before 2.6.0, availability also depends on some of the settings in `config.inc.php`.

Versions of MySQL Prior to 4.1.x

Versions of MySQL before 4.1.x do not transform the data to the desired character set, so the actual recoding is done directly by phpMyAdmin, both before sending data to the MySQL server, and after receiving it.

Data Recoding

Here is the most important configuration parameter for recoding, shown here with its default value:

```
$cfg['AllowAnywhereRecoding'] = FALSE;
```

To activate recoding, we have to set it to TRUE. When this is done, phpMyAdmin verifies that the conditions for recoding are met. For the actual encoding of data, the PHP component of the web server must support the `iconv` or the `recode` module. If this is not the case, and the parameter has been set to TRUE, the following error message will be generated:

Cannot load iconv or recode extension needed for charset conversion, configure php to allow using these extensions or disable charset conversion in phpMyAdmin.

If this message is displayed, consult your system's documentation (PHP or the operating system) for the installation procedures.

Before phpMyAdmin 2.6.0, the default `config.inc.php` file did not make use of UTF-8 encoding, so the `$cfg['AllowAnywhereRecoding']` parameter was set to FALSE, and no UTF-8 languages were offered in the **Language** selector. To enable it, we just changed the parameter to TRUE.

Since phpMyAdmin 2.6.0, the parameter is still set to FALSE by default, but the UTF-8 language choices are nevertheless displayed in the **Language** selector. This may lead to encoding problems. (See the section *The Impact of Switching* letter in this chapter.)

Another parameter, $cfg['RecodingEngine'], specifies the actual recoding engine, the choices being auto, iconv, and recode. If it is set to auto, phpMyAdmin will first try the iconv module, and then the recode module.

Character Sets

When it is connected to a pre-MySQL 4.1.x server, phpMyAdmin has limited support for character set conversion. Currently, we can specify which character set applies to a query and its results. The character set used by default is defined by the following parameter.

```
$cfg['DefaultCharset'] ='iso-8859-1';
```

This is only the default choice; users may always select another character set from the choices listed in this parameter (the actual parameter in config.inc.php contains more):

```
$cfg['AvailableCharsets'] = array(
    'iso-8859-1',
    'iso-8859-2',
    'iso-8859-3',
    'iso-8859-4');
```

These choices are displayed to users in the same order as that defined in the parameter $cfg['AvailableCharsets'], so, we can move the more popular choices to the top. Any character set supported by the iconv or recode recoding engines may be used.

If we are using phpMyAdmin 2.6.0 or newer, and $cfg['AllowAnywhereRecoding'] has been left set to its default value FALSE, we will see the following on the **Home** page:

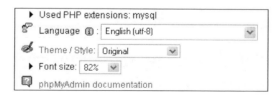

There is no **MySQL Charset** selector. The character set defined in the chosen **Language** (here **English utf-8**) will be used to communicate with MySQL.

Choosing the Effective Character Set

Now, we set $cfg['AllowAnywhereRecoding']$ to TRUE. Then, we choose **English (en-utf-8)** in the **Language** selector. The **Home** page has changed:

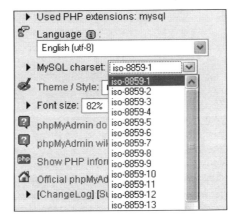

The **MySQL Charset** choice appears only if the current chosen **Language** uses **utf-8** encoding. From now on, every communication that occurs between the web server and the MySQL server will use this MySQL character set.

 The choice of character set is remembered for 30 days using a cookie mechanism. Depending on where the cookies are stored (on the local computer or on a network server), the character set may need to be chosen again if we log into phpMyAdmin from another computer.

The Impact of Switching

When we choose a character set, all the data stored in MySQL will be recoded with this character set. If we subsequently change the character set used by phpMyAdmin, we will get incorrect results when fetching the data. There is no easy way of finding which character set was used to store a particular row of data.

Here is an example with our **author** table. We first create a new author with a character **é** in his name:

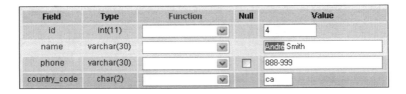

Field	Type	Function	Null	Value
id	int(11)			4
name	varchar(30)			André Smith
phone	varchar(30)		☐	888-999
country_code	char(2)			ca

There is no problem here when inserting, browsing, or searching for this new author, as the chosen character set, iso-8859-1, can deal with the é character.

However, if we switch the MySQL character set to UTF-8 later on, we will have a problem when browsing the **author** table:

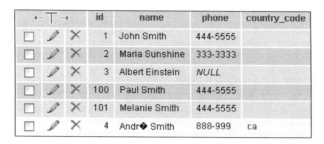

The same problem occurs when we switch from one language to another, if $cfg['AllowAnywhereRecoding'] is set to FALSE, and the two languages are encoded in different character set. It is therefore highly recommended to avoid switching character sets if our system is not configured to do the necessary conversion.

Importing and Exporting with Character Sets

If $cfg['AllowAnywhereRecoding'] is set to TRUE, then the **File to import** section of the **Import** sub-pages is modified, so that we can choose a character set for the file to be imported:

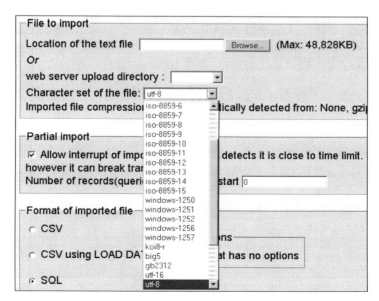

In the **Export** dialog, we can also choose the character set of the file to be created:

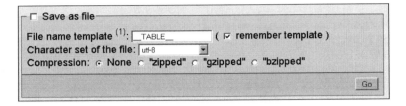

MySQL 4.1.x and Later

Since MySQL 4.1.x, the MySQL server does the character recoding work for us. Also, MySQL enables us to indicate the character set and collation for each database, each table, and even each field. A default character set for a database applies to each of its tables, unless it is overridden at the table level. The same principle applies to every field.

Since phpMyAdmin 2.6.0, support for MySQL 4.1.x character set and collation features is no longer experimental, as it was in previous versions.

The $cfg['AllowAnywhereRecoding'] parameter has no impact for MySQL version 4.1.x and later, except to enable the **Character set of the file** drop-down menu in the **Export** sub-page.

Collations

When strings have to be compared and sorted, precise rules must be followed by the system (MySQL, in this case). For example, is 'A' equivalent to 'a'? Is 'André' equivalent to 'Andre'? A set of these rules is called a **collation**.

A proper choice of collation is important for obtaining the intended results when searching data, for example from phpMyAdmin's **Search** page, and also when sorting data.

For an introduction to collations, see http://dev.mysql.com/doc/mysql/en/ Charset-general.htm, and for a more technical explanation of the algorithms involved, refer to http://www.unicode.org/reports/tr10/.

The Home Page

Here is what the **Home** page looks like, when connecting to a MySQL 4.1.x or later server (the sections that follow detail the changes):

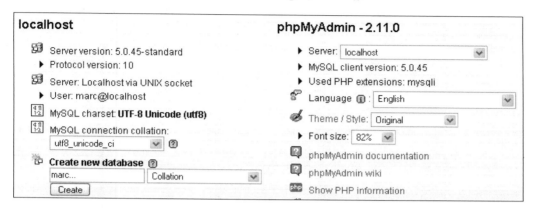

Creating a Database

When creating a database, we can choose its default character set and collation with the **Collation** dialog. This setting can be changed later. (See the section *The Database View*.)

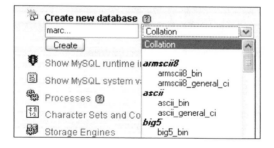

Available Character Sets and Collations

The **Character Sets and Collations** link on the **Home** page opens the Server view for the **Charsets** sub-page, which lists the character sets and collations supported by the MySQL server. The default collation for each character set is shown with a different background color (using the row-marking color defined in `$cfg['BrowseMarkerColor']`):

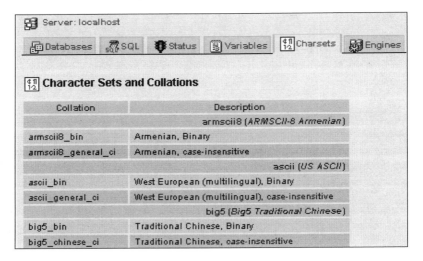

Effective Character Sets and Collations

phpMyAdmin picks the 'effective' character set—the one that best fits our selected language (which obviously is the one we want to see in our browser). For example, we will see the following on the **Home** page:

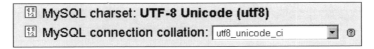

The character set information (as seen here after **MySQL charset**) is passed to the MySQL server. MySQL then transforms the characters that will be sent to our browser into this character set. MySQL also interprets what it receives from the browser according to the character set information. Remember that all tables and fields have a character set information describing how their data is encoded.

We can also choose which character set and collation will be used for our connection to the MySQL server using the **MySQL connection collation** dialog. Normally, the default value should work, but if we are entering some characters using a different character set, we can choose the proper character set in this dialog.

The following parameter defines the default connection collation:

```
$cfg['DefaultConnectionCollation'] = 'utf8_unicode_ci';
```

The Database View

We can also use the Database view's **Operations** sub-page to change the default character set for the database:

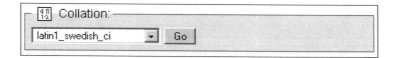

We can see the collation used for each table on the **Structure** page for the database:

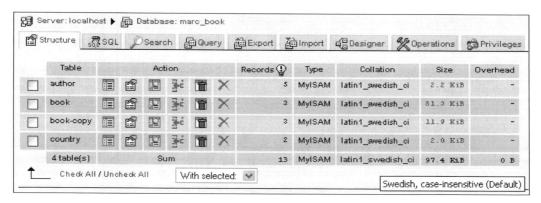

On the **Sum** line, it makes sense to display the total number of records and the total size, but the **Collation** information is not a "total collation"; phpMyAdmin uses this space to display the default collation for the current database, as can be seen by hovering over this collation name.

The Table View

We can use the Table view's **Operations** sub-page to change the default character set and collation information for a table:

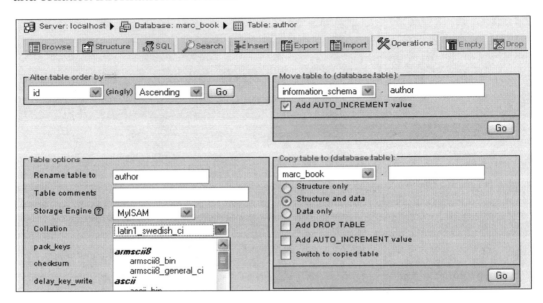

We can also use the Table view's **Structure** sub-page to choose the character set for a column, by clicking the **Change** link for this column:

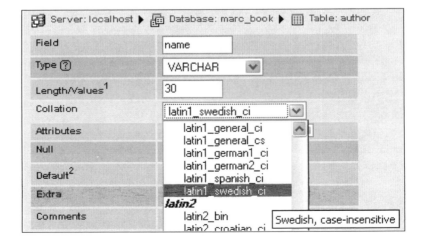

Importing and Exporting with Character Sets

When exporting results, we can see the default character set and collation information for the table and its columns:

```
CREATE TABLE IF NOT EXISTS `author` (
  `id` int(11) NOT NULL,
  `name` varchar(30) character set latin1 collate latin1_general_ci
NOT NULL,
  `phone` varchar(30) default NULL,
  `country_code` char(2) NOT NULL,
  PRIMARY KEY  (`id`)
) ENGINE=MyISAM DEFAULT CHARSET=latin1;
```

Here, we have changed the collation of the name column to latin1_general_ci; therefore, it is shown in the export results—because this collation is different to the table's default collation.

Server View

In the Server view, we can obtain statistics about the databases. (See the *Database Information* section in Chapter 19.) If our server supports character sets and collations, we will see an additional information column, **Collation**, on this page:

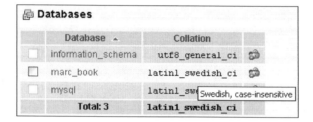

Kanji Support

If phpMyAdmin detects usage of the Japanese language, it checks whether PHP supports the mb_convert_encoding() multi-byte strings function. If it does, additional radio buttons are displayed on the following pages, so that we can choose between the EUC-JP and SJIS Japanese encodings:

- **export**
- **insert text from a file**
- **query box**

Here is an example taken from the **Export** page:

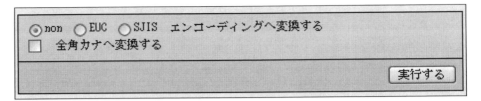

Summary

In this chapter, we covered the use of language files in phpMyAdmin. We looked at UTF-8 and the impact of switching from one character set to another. We also saw how phpMyAdmin has to recode data when the version of MySQL is earlier than 4.1.x, and we looked at the character set and collation features of MySQL version 4.1.x and later.

18
MySQL 5.0 Features

MySQL 5.0 sports a number of new features. The announcement of these features calmed down a number of developers and industry observers who were claiming that MySQL was an inferior product, compared to some competitors who had already implemented these features. Views, stored procedures, triggers, a standard INFORMATION_SCHEMA, and (more recently) a profiling mechanism are now present in the MySQL spectrum.

Observations on the History of MySQL 5.0

In June 2005, I attended LinuxTag in Karlsruhe, Germany with other phpMyAdmin developers, where we demoed our software. At this conference, we participated to a joint celebration of PHP's and MySQL's tenth anniversary, along with the respective fathers of these products, Rasmus and Monty. A few weeks before that, at the MySQL Users Conference in Santa Clara, a presentation was titled "PHP 5 + MySQL 5 = A Perfect 10". Indeed, we were aware of what this anniversary meant in terms of products' maturity.

The MySQL 5.0.x history spans quite a long time. Indeed, the 5.0.0 alpha version became available in December 2003, and started the round of new features with basic support for stored procedures. In the next version (5.0.1), views support was born. Information_schema appeared in version 5.0.2. Later, version 5.0.3 was labeled Beta and released in March 2005, while 5.0.13 was considered a release candidate in September 2005. A production release, 5.0.15, was made available in October 2005.

 You should worry and talk to your system administrator or ISP if they want you to use a pre-5.0.15 version of the 5.0.x family, as this is not considered production-ready.

Another new feature, profiling, was surprisingly added in version 5.0.37, well after the 5.0.x family was branded as production-ready.

Views

MySQL 5.0 introduced support for named, updatable views. A view is a derived table—consider it as a virtual table—whose definition is stored in the database. A SELECT statement done on one or more tables (or even on views) is stored as a view and can itself be queried. Views can be used to:

- Limit the visibility of columns (do not show the salary)
- Limit the visibility of rows (do not show data for specific world regions)
- Hide a changed table structure (so that legacy applications can continue to work)

As a view has itself some permissions attached to it, it is easier to GRANT permissions on the view as a whole, rather than defining cumbersome column-specific privileges on the underlying tables.

To activate views support on a server after an upgrade from a pre-5.0 version, the administrator has to execute the mysql_fix_privileges_tables script, as described in the MySQL manual.

> Each user must have the appropriate SHOW_VIEW or CREATE_VIEW privilege to be able to see or manipulate views. These privileges exist at the global (server), database and table levels.

phpMyAdmin supports two ways of creating a view; we'll explain first the manual method, then go on with a more automatic way.

Manually Creating a View

To manually create a view, we use the query box to enter the appropriate statement. Let's input the following lines and click **Go**:

```
CREATE VIEW book_author AS
SELECT book.isbn, book.title, author.name FROM book
LEFT JOIN author ON author.id = book.author_id
```

> Creating a view implies that the user has privileges on the tables involved, or at least a privilege like SELECT or UPDATE on all the columns mentioned in the view.

At this point, the view has been created and the left panel is updated to reflect this fact. If we refresh our browser's page, and then access the marc_book database, we see:

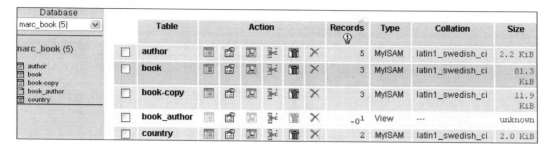

In the left panel, there is a different icon next to the **book_author** view; it can be used to browse this view. In the right panel, we see the newly created view's information. The number of records for the view currently indicates 0 (more on this in the *Performance Hint* section, later in this chapter), and **View** is indicated in the **Type** column. There is no collation or size associated with a view.

This creation step was done manually; other operations on views are handled by phpMyAdmin's interface.

Right Panel and Views

Since a view has similarities compared to a table, its name is available in the navigation panel, among the names of ordinary tables. After clicking on this view's name, a panel similar to the one seen for tables is displayed, but with fewer menu tabs than for a normal table. Indeed, some operations do not make sense on a view, for example, **Import**, because a view does not really contain data, but other actions are perfectly acceptable, such as **Browse**.

Let's browse this view:

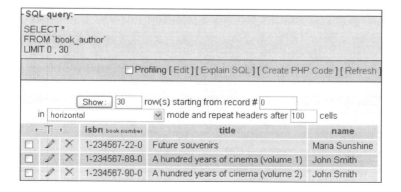

We notice that in the generated SQL query, we do not see our original CREATE VIEW statement. The reason is that we are selecting from the view, and this is done with a SELECT statement, hiding the fact that we are pulling data from a view. However, exporting the view's structure would display how MySQL internally stored our view:

```
CREATE ALGORITHM=UNDEFINED DEFINER='marc'@'%' SQL SECURITY DEFINER
VIEW `book_author` AS
select `book`.`isbn` AS 'isbn',
`book`.`title` AS 'title',
`author`.`name` AS 'name'
from (`book` left join `author` on((`book`.`author_id` = `author`.
`id`)));
```

The right panel's menu may look similar to the one for a table, but when needed, phpMyAdmin generates the appropriate syntax for handling views. For example, a click on **Drop** would produce:

Do you really want to: DROP VIEW 'book_author'

At this point, we can confirm (or not) this view's deletion.

 To perform actions on views, a user needs to have the appropriate privilege at the view level, but not necessarily any privilege on the tables involved in this view. This is how we can achieve column and table hiding.

Creating a View from Results

Creating a complex view might require typing the complete statement into a query box. Another possibility is to take advantage of phpMyAdmin's **Search** (at the table level) or **Query** (at the database level) features to build a rather complex query, execute it, and then easily create a view from the results. We'll see how it is done.

We mentioned that a view can be used to limit the visibility of columns (and in fact, of tables). Let's say that the number of pages in a book is highly classified information. We open the book table, click **Search**, and choose a subset of the columns:

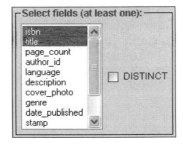

Clicking **Go** produces a results page, on which we see a **CREATE VIEW** link:

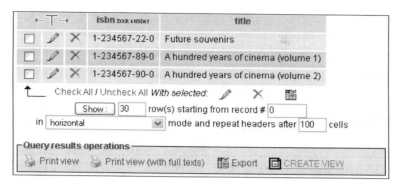

We use this link to bring the view creation panel, which already has the underlying query in the **AS** box. We need to choose a name for this view (here **book_public_info**) and we can optionally set different column names for it (here **number, title**). The other options can influence the view's behavior and are explained in the MySQL manual (`http://dev.mysql.com/doc/refman/5.0/en/create-view.html`).

A click on **Go** generates the view we asked for.

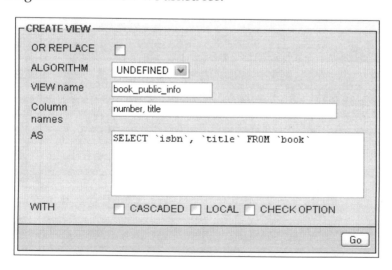

The CHECK OPTION clause influences the behavior of updateable views (this is explained in the MySQL manual at `http://dev.mysql.com/doc/refman/5.0/en/create-view.html`).

Renaming a View

phpMyAdmin 2.11.0 does not support this directly from the interface, however, since MySQL 5.0.14, the RENAME TABLE statement can be used (from a phpMyAdmin's query box) as long as we are renaming inside the same database. For example, RENAME TABLE book_public_info TO book_public_info2.

Performance Hint

Since version 2.10, phpMyAdmin uses a new configuration parameter, $cfg['MaxEx actCountViews'], that acts as a limit for the rows counting phase of phpMyAdmin. Sometimes, a view comprises many huge tables and browsing it would make a large number of virtual rows appear. Therefore, the default value of 0 for this parameter ensures that no row counting happens for views. In this case, we'll see rather strange results when browsing a view: **Showing rows 0 - -1 (0 total, Query took 0.0006 sec)**. But this is more acceptable than slowing down a server.

If we nonetheless prefer to see a more exact row count for views, we can put a larger value in this parameter, which acts as an upper limit for the rows counting phase.

Routines: Stored Procedures and Functions

It took a while before phpMyAdmin started to include support for these features. The reason is that stored procedures and functions are blocks of code (like a subprogram) that are kept as part of the database and phpMyAdmin, being a web interface, is more oriented towards operations that are quickly done with a mouse.

Nonetheless, in version 2.11, there are a few features that permit a developer to create such routines, save them, recall them to make some modifications, and delete them.

Procedures are accessed by a CALL statement, to which we can pass parameters, whereas functions are accessed from SQL statements (for example a SELECT) like other MySQL internal functions returning a value.

 The CREATE ROUTINE and ALTER ROUTINE privileges are needed to be able to create, see, and delete a stored procedure or function. The EXECUTE privilege is needed to run the routine, but it is normally granted automatically to its creator.

Creating a Stored Procedure

We'll create a procedure that has the effect to change the page count for a specific book, adding a specific number of pages. The book's ISBN, and number of pages to add, will be the input parameters to this procedure.

Changing the Delimiter

The standard SQL delimiter is the semicolon, and this character will be used inside our procedure to delimit SQL statements. However, the CREATE PROCEDURE statement is itself a SQL statement, so we must come up with a way to indicate to the MySQL parser where this statement ends. The query box has a **Delimiter** input box that contains a semicolon by default, therefore, we change it to another string, which by convention will be a double slash //.

Entering the Procedure

Then, we enter the procedure's code in the main query box:

```
CREATE PROCEDURE `add_page`(IN param_isbn VARCHAR(25), IN param_pages
INT, OUT param_message VARCHAR(100))
BEGIN
 IF param_pages > 100 THEN
   SET param_message = 'the number of pages is too big';
 ELSE
   UPDATE book SET page_count = page_count + param_pages WHERE
isbn=param_isbn;
   SET param_message = 'success';
 END IF;
END
//
```

After clicking **Go**, if the syntax is correct, we get a success message; if not, well it's time to revise our typing abilities or to debug our syntax; unfortunately, MySQL does not come with a procedure debugger.

Testing the Procedure

Again, in the query box, we test our procedure by entering the following statements—we are using a SQL variable @message that will receive the contents of the OUT parameter param_message.

```
call add_page('1-234567-22-0', 4, @message);
SELECT @message;
```

We can then verify that the page count for this book has been increased. We also need to test the problematic case:

```
call add_page('1-234567-22-0', 101, @message);
SELECT @message;
```

This procedure is now available for calling from PHP, using the mysqli extension.

Manipulation

A procedure is stored inside a database and is not tied to a specific table; therefore, the interface to manipulate procedures and functions can be found at the database level, on the **Structure** page.

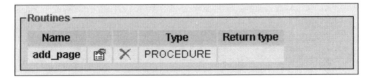

The first icon brings this procedure's text into a query box for editing. The second icon would be used to delete this procedure. When editing the procedure, we notice that the text was somewhat modified:

```
DROP PROCEDURE `add_page`//
CREATE DEFINER=`marc`@`%` PROCEDURE `add_page`(IN param_isbn
VARCHAR(25), IN param_pages INT, OUT param_message VARCHAR(100))
BEGIN
  IF param_pages > 100 THEN
    SET param_message = 'the number of pages is too big';
  ELSE
    UPDATE book SET page_count = page_count + param_pages WHERE
isbn=param_isbn;
    SET param_message = 'success';
  END IF;
END
```

First, a DROP PROCEDURE appears. This is normal because MySQL does not offer a statement that would permit to change the body of a procedure; therefore, we have to delete a procedure each time we want to change it. It's true that the ALTER PROCEDURE statement exists, but it can only change the procedure's characteristics, for example, adding a comment to it. Then, a DEFINER clause is shown; it was generated at create time and indicates who created this procedure.

At this point, we make any changes we need to the code and hit **Go** to save this procedure.

It might be tempting to open the book table on its **Structure** page and look there for a list of procedures that manipulate this table, like our add_page() procedure. However, all procedures are stored at the database level, and there is no direct link between the code itself (UPDATE book) and the place where the procedure is stored.

Manually Creating a Function

Functions are similar to stored procedures. However, a function may return just one value, whereas a stored procedure can have more than one OUT parameter. On the other hand, using a stored function from within a SELECT statement may seem more natural and avoids the need of an intermediate SQL variable to hold the value of an OUT parameter.

What is the goal of functions? As an example, a function can be used to calculate the total cost of an order, including tax and shipping. Putting this logic inside the database, instead of at the application level, helps to document the application-database interface and avoids duplicating business logic in every application that needs to deal with this logic.

We should not confuse MySQL 5.0's functions with UDF (User-Defined Functions), which existed before MySQL 5.0. A UDF is constituted of code written in C or C++, compiled into a shared object, and referenced with a CREATE FUNCTION statement plus the SONAME keyword.

phpMyAdmin's treatment for functions is in many points similar to what we have covered for procedures:

- The query box to input a function
- The use of a delimiter
- The mechanism to manipulate an already-defined function

Let's define a function that retrieves the country name, based on its code. I prefer to use a `param_` prefix to clearly identify parameters inside the function's definition and a `var_` prefix for local variables.

```
CREATE FUNCTION get_country_name(param_country_code CHAR(2))
 RETURNS VARCHAR(50)
BEGIN
  DECLARE var_country_name VARCHAR(50) DEFAULT 'not found';
  SELECT description
    INTO var_country_name
    FROM country
    WHERE code = param_country_code;
  RETURN var_country_name;
END
```

We note that our newly-created function can be seen on the database's `Structure` page, along with its friend the `add_page` procedure:

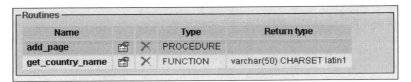

Testing the Function

To test this function, we can try:

```
SELECT CONCAT('ca->', get_country_name('ca'), ', zz->', get_country_
name('zz')) as test;
```

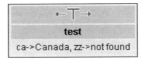

Exporting Stored Procedures and Functions

When exporting a database, procedures and functions do not appear (by default) in an SQL export. A checkbox **Add CREATE PROCEDURE / FUNCTION** exists in the **Structure** dialog of the **Export** page, to include those in the SQL export file. If we try it (with a minimum phpMyAdmin version of 2.11.3 in which a bug was fixed just in time for this exercise), we obtain:

```
DELIMITER $$
--
-- Procedures
```

```
--
CREATE DEFINER=`marc`@`%` PROCEDURE `add_page`(IN param_isbn
VARCHAR(25), IN param_pages INT, OUT param_message VARCHAR(100))
BEGIN
 IF param_pages > 100 THEN
   SET param_message = 'the number of pages is too big';
 ELSE
   UPDATE book SET page_count = page_count + param_pages WHERE
isbn=param_isbn;
   SET param_message = 'success';
 END IF;
END$$
--
-- Functions
--
CREATE DEFINER=`marc`@`%` FUNCTION `get_country_name`(param_country_
code CHAR(2)) RETURNS varchar(50) CHARSET latin1
BEGIN
 DECLARE var_country_name VARCHAR(50) DEFAULT 'not found';
 SELECT description into var_country_name FROM country WHERE code =
param_country_code;
 RETURN var_country_name;
END$$

DELIMITER ;
```

Triggers

Triggers are code that we associate to a table to be executed when certain events occur, for example after a new INSERT in table book. The event does not have to happen from within phpMyAdmin.

Contrary to routines that are related to a whole database and visible on the database's **Structure** page, triggers for each table are accessed from *this specific table's* **Structure** page.

 Prior to MySQL 5.1.6, we needed the SUPER privilege to create and delete triggers. In version 5.1.6, a TRIGGER table-level privilege was added to the privilege system, so a user no longer needs the powerful SUPER privilege for these tasks.

In order to perform the following exercise, we'll need a new column in our `author` table, `total_page_count`.

Field	Type
id	int(11)
name	varchar(30)
phone	varchar(30)
country_code	char(2)
total_page_count	int(11)

The idea here is that every time a new book is created, its page count will be added to the author's total page count. I know that some people may advocate that it would be better to not keep a separate column for the total here and compute the total instead, each time we need it. In fact, a design decision must be made when dealing with this situation in the real world: do we need to retrieve the total page count very quickly, for example for web purposes? And what is the response time to compute this value from a production table with thousands of rows? Anyway, since I need it as an example, the design decision is easy to make here.

Let's not forget that following its addition to the table's structure, the `total_page_count` column should be initially seeded with the correct total, which is not the purpose of our trigger.

Manually Creating a Trigger

The current phpMyAdmin version does not have an interface for trigger creation, therefore, we input in a query box the trigger definition, taking special care of changing the delimiter box:

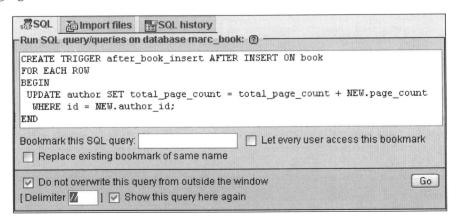

Afterwards, the **Structure** page for our book table reveals a new **Triggers** section, which can be used the same way as for routines to edit or delete a trigger:

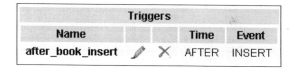

Testing the Trigger

Contrary to testing stored procedures or functions, there is neither a CALL sequence nor a function inside a SELECT statement to execute the trigger. Any time the defined operation (a book INSERT) happens, the code will execute (in our case, after the insertion). Therefore, we just have to insert a new book to see the author.total_page_count column be updated.

Of course, a completely automatic management of this column would involve creating AFTER UPDATE and AFTER DELETE triggers on the book table.

Information_schema

In the SQL:2003 standard, access to the data dictionary (or database metadata) is provided by a structure called information_schema. Beacause this is part of the standard and already exists in other database systems, the decision to implement this feature into MySQL was a very good one.

> MySQL has added some information that is not part of the standard, for example INFORMATION_SCHEMA.COLUMNS.COLUMN_TYPE. Beware of that fact if you plan to use this information in a software project that has to remain portable to other SQL implementations.

A phpMyAdmin user sees information_schema as a normal database containing views that describe many aspects of the structure of the databases hosted on this server. Here is a subset of what can be seen (and in fact, the only possible operation on this database is SELECT).

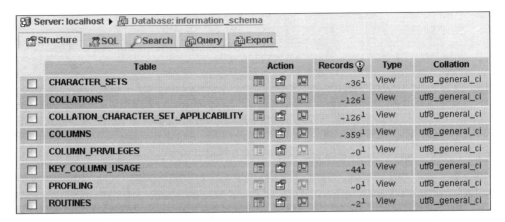

Internally, phpMyAdmin calls information_schema for some of its operations, instead of the corresponding SHOW statements to retrieve metadata. However, phpMyAdmin developers have noticed — and this was confirmed by other developers at the 2007 MySQL Users Conference — that some SELECT operations involving a WHERE clause on information_schema are really slow (many minutes of wait time) when the server hosts hundreds of databases or tables. Therefore, in the current state of MySQL, caution must be exercised about using this feature in our programming projects.

The $cfg['Servers'][$i]['hide_db'] parameter can be used to hide this "database" to users that might be confused by the sudden apparition of a database they know nothing about. It probably depends on their level of expertise in MySQL; on a multi-user installation of phpMyAdmin, we cannot please everyone about this parameter's value.

Profiling

We have previously seen the **Profiling** checkbox appear in query results:

When this box is checked, phpMyAdmin goes in a mode where every query (including the current one) is being analyzed and a report about each MySQL internal operation's execution time is displayed.

Profiling	
Status	**Time**
(initialization)	0.000004
checking permissions	0.000007
Opening tables	0.000105
System lock	0.000009
Table lock	0.00001
init	0.000017
optimizing	0.000006
statistics	0.000008
preparing	0.000008
executing	0.000005
Sending data	0.000432
end	0.000007
query end	0.000005
freeing items	0.000007
closing tables	0.000028
logging slow query	0.000006

Although the profiling system can report additional information about operations (like the CPU time and even the internal server's function names involved), phpMyAdmin currently displays only the name of the operation and its duration.

At time of press, MySQL version 5.1.22 does not have this feature, although it is present since 5.0.37. However, for administrators who are confident about compiling their own MySQL server, Jeremy Cole, this feature's author, maintains patches applicable to a 5.1 server on `http://jcole.us/patches/mysql/5.1`.

Summary

MySQL 5.0's new features helped the product become more standard-compliant. Even though phpMyAdmin has limited support for these features, especially lacking a syntax-oriented editor, it has a basic set of features to work with views, routines, triggers and `information_schema`, and to display profiling information.

MySQL Server Administration

19

This chapter will look at how a system administrator can use the phpMyAdmin server management features for day-to-day user account maintenance, server verification, and server protection. Non-administrators can also obtain server information from phpMyAdmin.

Entering the Server View

The Server view can be accessed from the **Home** page by choosing one of the following links:

- **Show MySQL runtime information**
- **Show MySQL system variables**
- **Processes**
- **Character sets and collations**
- **Storage Engines**
- **Privileges**
- **Databases**
- **Binary log**
- **Import**
- **Export**

The **Privileges** link is visible only if we are logged in as a privileged user. When in the Server view, we see a menu to go to the other server-related sub-pages.

User and Privileges Management

The **Privileges** sub-page in the Server view contains dialogs to manage MySQL user accounts, and their privileges on global, database, and table levels. This sub-page is centered on the user and is hierarchical: for example, when editing a user's privileges, we can see the global privileges as well as the database-specific privileges. Then, we can go deeper to see the table-specific privileges for this database-user combination.

The User Overview

The first page displayed when we enter the **Privileges** sub-page is called **User overview**. This shows all user accounts and a summary of their global privileges:

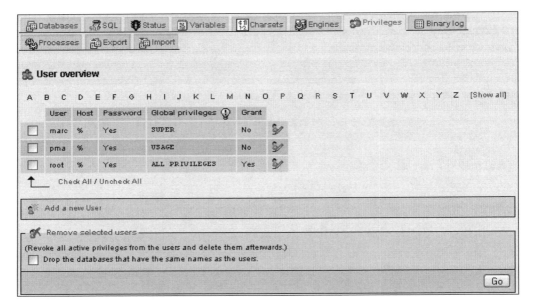

From this page, we can:

- Edit a user's privileges with the **Edit** link on a user's line.
- Use the checkboxes to remove users with the **Remove selected users** dialog.
- Access the page where the **Add a new user** dialog is available.
- Reload the privileges. The effective privileges (the ones against which the server bases its access decisions) are the privileges that are located in the server's memory.

- Modifications to the privileges made from the **User Overview** page are made both in memory and on disk, in the **mysql** database. Modifications made directly on the **mysql** database do not have immediate effect. The **Reload** operation reads the privileges from the database and makes them effective in memory.

The displayed users' list has columns with the following characteristics:

- **User**: Users listed in alphabetical order.
- **Host**: The host for which this user definition applies. This is the machine name or IP address from which this user will be connecting to the MySQL server. A % value here indicates all hosts.
- **Password**: Contains **Yes** if a password is defined and **No** if one isn't. The password itself cannot be seen from phpMyAdmin's interface or by directly looking at the mysql.user table, as it is obfuscated with a one-way hashing algorithm.
- **Global privileges**: Listed for each user.
- **Grant**: Contains **Yes** if the user can grant his or her privileges to others.

Adding a User

The **Add a new user** link brings a dialog for user account creation:

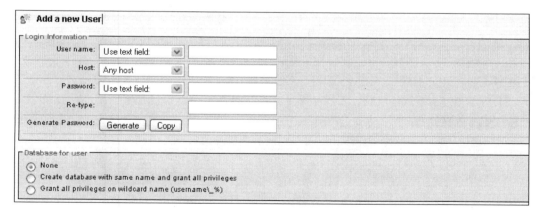

User Name

The **User name** menu offers two choices. We can choose **Use text field** and input a user name in the box, or we can choose **Any user** to create an anonymous user (the blank user). Let's choose **Use text field** and enter **bill**.

Host

By default, this menu is set to **Any host** with % as the host value. The **Local** choice means "localhost". The **Use host table** choice (which creates a blank value in the host field) means to "look in the mysql.hosts table for database-specific privileges". Choosing **Use text field** allows us to input the exact host value we want. Let's choose **Local**.

Password

Even though it's possible to create a user without a password (with the **No password** choice), it's best to have a password. We have to enter it twice (as we cannot see what is entered) to confirm the intended password. Let's input **bingo**.

Some administrators prefer to improve security by having phpMyAdmin generate a password itself. In the **Generate Password** dialog, a click on **Generate** puts a random password (in clear) on-screen. At this point, we should note the password so that we can pass it on to the user. Then a click on **Copy** puts this password in the **Password** and **Re-Type** fields.

Database Creation and Rights

A frequent convention is to assign to a user the rights to a database having the same name as this user. To accomplish this, the **Database for user** section offers the checkbox **Create database with same name and grant all privileges**; clicking this checkbox automates the process by creating both the database and the corresponding rights. Please note that with this method, each user would be limited to one database (user `bill`, database `bill`).

Another possibility is to allow users to create databases that have the same prefix as their user name; therefore the other choice **Grant all privileges on wildcard name (username_%)** performs this function by assigning a wildcard privilege. With this in place, user `bill` could create the databases `bill_test`, `bill_2`, `bill_payroll` and so on; phpMyAdmin does not pre-create the databases in this case.

Global Privileges

Global privileges determine the user's access to all databases, so these privileges are sometimes known as "superuser privileges". A normal user should not have any of these privileges unless there is a good reason.

Of course, if we are really creating a superuser, we will select every global privilege that he or she needs. These privileges are further divided into **Data**, **Structure**, and **Administration** groups.

In our example, **bill** will not have any global privileges.

Resource Limits

We can limit the resources used by this user on this server (for example, the maximum queries per hour). Zero means no limit. We will not impose any resources limits on **bill**.

The following screenshot shows the status of the screen just before hitting **Go** to create this user's definition (with the other fields left set to their default values):

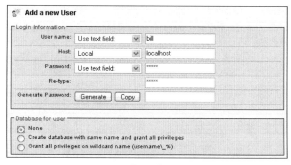

Editing a User

The page used to edit a user appears after a user's creation, or whenever we click **Edit** for a user in the **User overview** page. There are four sections on this page, each with its own **Go** button, so each section is operated independently and has a distinct purpose.

Edit Privileges

The section for editing the user's privileges has the same look as the **Add a new User** dialog, and is used to view and to change global privileges.

Database-Specific Privileges

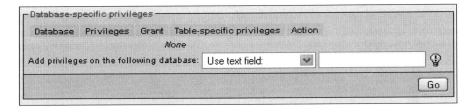

In this section, we define the databases to which our user has access, and his or her exact privileges. Currently, we see *None* because we haven't defined any. There are two ways of defining database privileges. First, we can choose one of the existing databases from the drop-down menu:

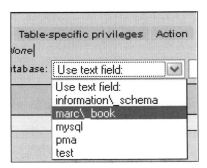

This assigns privileges only for the chosen database. We can also choose **Use text field** and enter a database name. We could insert a non-existent database name here so that this user can create it later (provided we give him or her the CREATE privilege in the next panel), or we could use special characters like the underscore and the percent sign for wildcards.

For example, entering **bill** here would enable him to create a **bill** database, and entering **bill%** would enable him to create a database with any name that starts with **bill**. For our example, we will enter **bill**.

The next screen is used to set **bill**'s privileges on the **bill** database and create table-specific privileges.

To learn more about the meaning of a specific privilege, we can move the mouse over a privilege name (which is always in English) and an explanation about this privilege appears in the current language. We give **SELECT, INSERT, UPDATE, DELETE, CREATE, ALTER, INDEX,** and **DROP** privileges to **bill** on this database, and click **Go**.

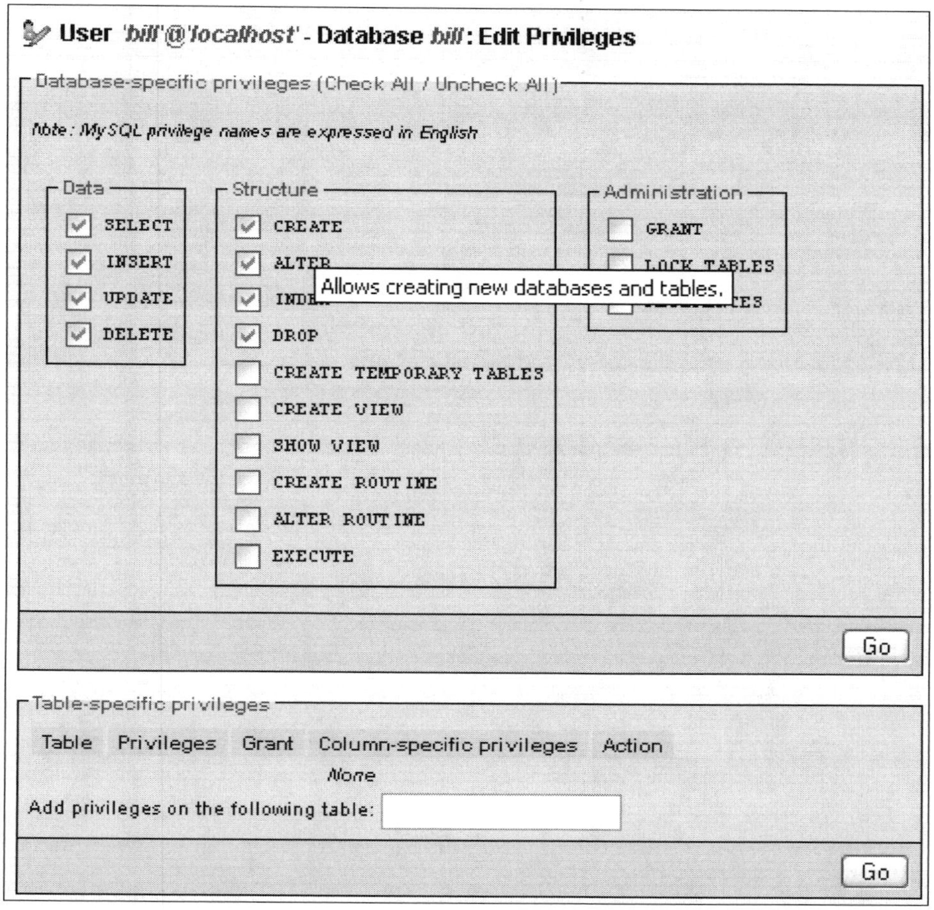

After the privileges have been assigned, the interface stays at the same place so that we can further refine these privileges. We cannot assign table-specific privileges for the moment because the database does not yet exist.

The way to go back to **bill**'s general privileges page is to click the *'bill'@'localhost'* title:

This brings us back to the familiar page, except for a change in one section:

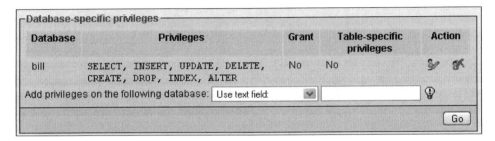

We see the existing privileges on the **bill** database for user **bill** (which we can **Edit** or **Revoke**), and we can add privileges for **bill** on another database. We also see that **bill** has no table-specific privilege on the **bill** database.

Changing the Password

This dialog is part of the **Edit user** page, and we can use it to change **bill's** password or to remove it—enabling **bill** to login without a password:

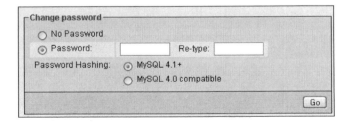

Changing Login Information or Copying a User

This dialog can be used to change the user's login information, or to copy his or her login information to a new user:

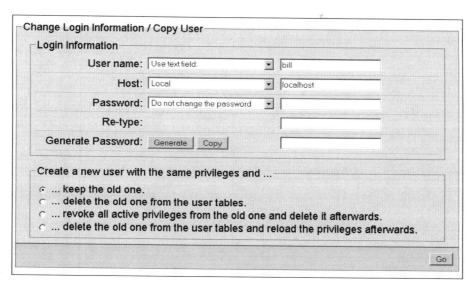

For example, suppose that Bill calls and tells us that he prefers the login name **billy** instead of **bill**. We just have to add a **y** to the user name, choose **Local** as the host, and select **delete the old one from the user tables**:

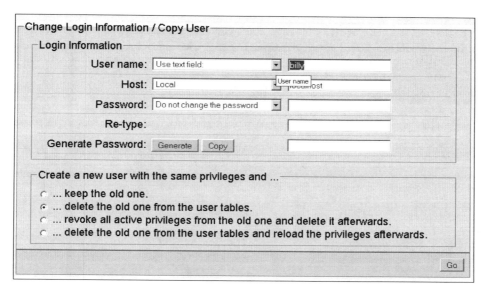

After this operation, **bill** no longer exists in the **mysql** database, and all his privileges, including the privileges on the **bill** database, will have been transferred to the new user, **billy**. But **bill**'s user definition will still exist in memory, so it is still effective. If we had chosen the **delete the old one from the user tables and reload the privileges afterwards** option instead, **bill**'s user definition would immediately have ceased to be valid.

Alternatively, we could have created another user based on **bill** by making use of the **keep the old one** choice. We can transfer the password to the new user by choosing **Do not change the password**, or change it by entering a new password twice. The **revoke all active privileges** option immediately terminates the effective current privileges for this user if he or she is logged in.

Removing a User

This is done from the **User overview** section of the **Privileges** page. We select the user to be removed, and then (in **Removing selected users**) we can choose to drop any databases that have the same name as the users we are deleting. A click on **Go** effectively removes the selected users.

Database Information

When we enter the **Databases** sub-page, we see the list of existing databases:

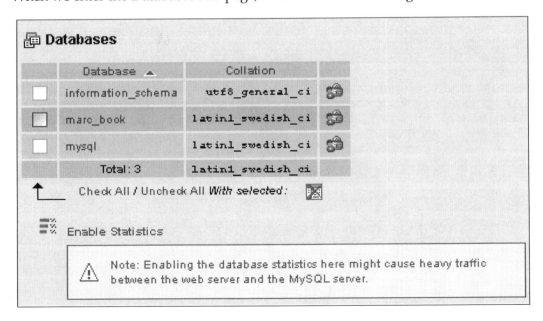

We also see an **Enable Statistics** link. By default, statistics are not enabled because computing the size of data and indexes for all the tables in all the databases may cost valuable MySQL server resources.

Enabling Statistics

If we click the **Enable Statistics** link, a modified page appears:

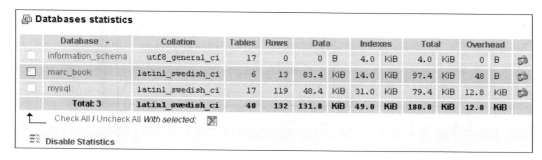

Sorting Statistics

By default, the list is sorted by database name in ascending order. If we need to find the database with the most tables, or the database that takes the most space, a simple click on the **Tables** or **Total** column header sorts them accordingly. A second click reverses the sort order.

Checking the Database Privileges

Clicking the **Check Privileges** icon displays all the privileges on a specific database. A user's global privilege might be shown here because it gives him or her access to this database as well. We can also see the privileges specific to this database. An **Edit** link takes us to another page that is used to edit the user's privileges:

User	Host	Type	Privileges	Grant	Action
admin	%	global	ALL PRIVILEGES	Yes	
marc	%	wildcard: marc%	SELECT, INSERT, UPDATE, DELETE, CREATE, DROP	No	
root	%	global	ALL PRIVILEGES	Yes	

Users having access to "marc_book"

Dropping Selected Databases

This is an operation that should not be taken lightly. To drop one or more databases, we check the boxes next to the names of the databases to be dropped, and click on the **Drop Selected Databases** link. A confirmation screen then appears.

Server Operations

The **Status**, **Variables**, and **Processes** links are available to get information about the MySQL server or to act upon specific processes.

Server Status Verification

These statistics reflect the MySQL server's total activity, including (but not limited to) the activity generated by queries sent from phpMyAdmin.

The General Status Page

Clicking the **Status** link produces runtime information about the server. The page has several sections. First we get information about the elapsed running time and the startup time, and then we get the total and average values for traffic and connections (where ø means average):

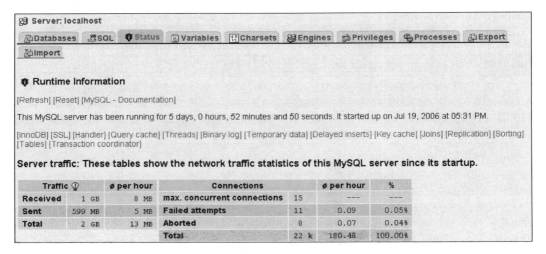

Next, the statistics about queries are displayed (shown partially here). The average number of queries per hour, minute, and second give a good indication of the server load.

This is followed by statistics about each MySQL command, the absolute number of times, hour average, and the number of times as a percentage of the total.

Query statistics: Since its startup, 2,826,620 queries have been sent to the server.			

Total	ø per hour	ø per minute	ø per second
3 M	23.38 k	389.73	6.50

Query type		ø per hour	%	Query type		ø per hour	%
admin commands	0	0.00	0.00%	savepoint	0	0.00	0.00%
alter db	0	0.00	0.00%	select	3 M	21.37 k	92.12%
alter table	34	0.28	0.00%	set option	11 k	91.68	0.40%
analyze	0	0.00	0.00%	show binlog events	0	0.00	0.00%
backup table	0	0.00	0.00%	show binlogs	185	1.53	0.01%
begin	0	0.00	0.00%	show charsets	1 k	10.95	0.05%
change db	31 k	258.80	1.12%	show collations	1 k	10.95	0.05%
change master	0	0.00	0.00%	show column types	0	0.00	0.00%
check	0	0.00	0.00%	show create db	824	6.82	0.03%
checksum	0	0.00	0.00%	show create table	12 k	100.16	0.43%
commit	0	0.00	0.00%	show databases	386	3.19	0.01%

Depending on the MySQL version, many other sections containing server information are displayed.

InnoDB Status

On servers supporting InnoDB, a link appears at the end of the **InnoDB section**. When this link is clicked, information about the InnoDB subsystem is displayed, including information about the last InnoDB error that occurred:

Server Variables

The **Variables** sub-page displays various settings of the MySQL server, which can be defined in, say, the my.cnf MySQL configuration file. These values can't be changed from within phpMyAdmin:

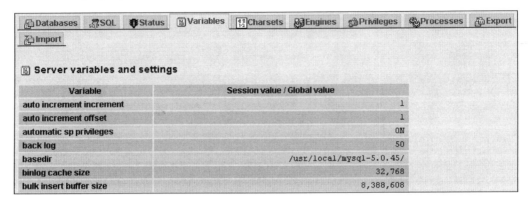

Server Processes

The **Processes** sub-page is available to superusers and normal users. A normal user would see only the processes belonging to him or her, whereas a superuser sees all the processes.

This page lists all active processes on the server, and a **Kill** link that allows us to terminate a specific process.

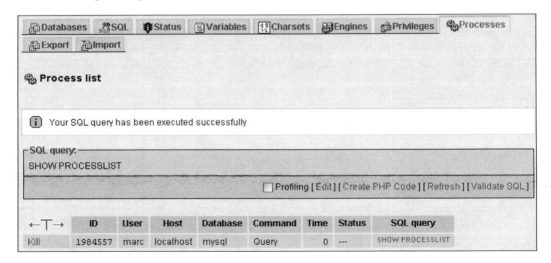

This example has only one running process, the process created by the SHOW PROCESSLIST command itself. This process is not killable because it is no longer running when we get to see the page. We would normally see more processes running on a server.

Storage Engines

Information about the various storage engines is available on a two-level format. First, the **Engines** tab displays an overview of the possible engines for the current MySQL version. The names of the engines that are enabled on this server are clickable:

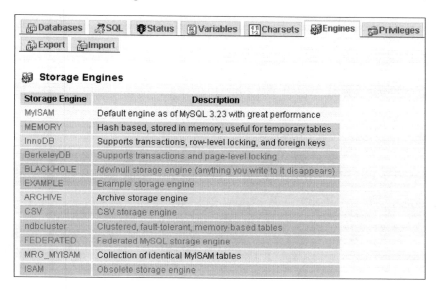

A click on one engine name brings a detailed panel about its settings. Moving the mouse over the light bulbs reveals even more information about a particular setting.

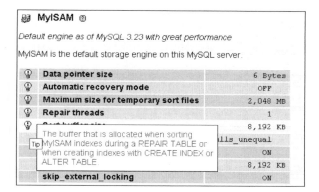

The Binary Log

If MySQL's binary log is active on our server, the menu in the Server view changes so that a **Binary log** tab appears. This tab gives access to an interface to the SHOW BINLOG EVENTS command. This command produces the list of SQL statements that have updated data on our servers. This list could be huge and currently phpMyAdmin does not limit its display, so we should take care.

In the following screen, we choose which binary log we want to examine (unless the server has only one binary log), and the statements are then displayed:

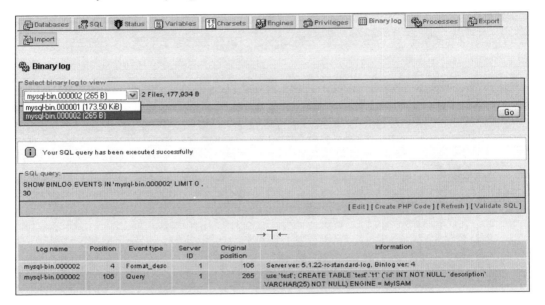

Summary

In this chapter, we have seen various features available to system administrators, such as user account management, privileges management, database privileges checks, and server status verification.

Troubleshooting and Support

20

This chapter proposes guidelines for solving some common problems, and gives hints on how to avoid them. It also explains how to interact with the development team for support, bug reports, and contributions.

System Requirements

A section at the beginning of the `Documentation.html` file (which is included with the downloaded kit) discusses system requirements for the particular phpMyAdmin version we are using. It is crucial that these requirements be met and that the environment be properly configured, so that problems are avoided.

Some problems, such as phpMyAdmin bugs, are in fact caused by the server environment. Sometimes, the web server is not configured to interpret `.php` files correctly, or the PHP component inside the web server does not run with the `mysql` extension. Also, MySQL accounts may be badly configured. This can happen on home servers as well as hosted servers.

When we suspect that something is wrong, we can try a simple PHP script, `test.php`, which contains the following to check if the PHP component answers correctly:

```php
<?php
echo 'hello';
?>
```

We should see the **hello** message. If this works, we can try another script:

```php
<?php
phpinfo();
?>
```

This script displays information about the PHP component, including the available extensions. We should at least see a section about MySQL (proving that the `mysql` extension is available), which gives information about the MySQL **Client API version**.

We can also try other PHP scripts that make a connection to MySQL, to see if the problem is more general than just phpMyAdmin not working. As a general rule, we should be running the latest stable versions of every component.

Base Configuration

We should always double-check the way we made the installation, including proper permissions and ownerships. Typos may occur when modifying `config.inc.php`.

Solving Common Errors

To help solve a problem, we should first pinpoint the origin of the error message. Here are the various components that can generate an error message:

- MySQL server: These messages are relayed by phpMyAdmin, which displays **MySQL said** followed by the message.
- PHP component of the web server: For example, **Parser error**.
- Web server: The error can be seen from the browser, or in the web server's log files.
- Web browser: For example, JavaScript errors.

The *Error Messages* and *Other Problems* sections are mostly based on various messages found on phpMyAdmin's help forum, and in the FAQ section of `Documentation.html`.

Error Messages

This section refers to explicit error messages, as displayed by phpMyAdmin.

Cannot Load MySQL Extension

To connect to a MySQL server, PHP needs the **MySQL extension**, which is a set of MySQL functions. This extension may compiled-in, as part of the PHP server, or it may need to be loaded dynamically, in which case, phpMyAdmin may have tried to load it and failed. This error implies that no other PHP script can make connections to a MySQL server.

The required extension is contained in a file that can be named `mysql.so` on Linux or UNIX, or `mysql.dll` on Windows. If our PHP server comes from a software package, we can find and install another software package, probably called `php-mysql`. (The name is distribution dependent.) Otherwise, we can compile our own PHP server with the appropriate extension, as explained in the PHP documentation. At least one well-known Linux distribution (RedHat 8.0) fails to offer this extension as part of the web server/PHP server installation dialog, although the package is present on installation disk 3.

The `mysqli` extension is designed to work with MySQL 4.1.3 and later versions, and can be distributed in the form of a package named `php-mysqli`.

MySQL Said: Can't Connect to Local MySQL Server

This message indicates that the MySQL server is not running, or cannot be reached from the web server. It can also be a socket (Linux/UNIX) or a named pipe (Windows) configuration problem.

Socket Problem (Linux/UNIX)

The socket configured in `php.ini` (an example of which is given below) does not correspond to the socket of the running MySQL server:

```
mysql.default_socket = /tmp/mysql.sock
```

As a result, PHP cannot reach MySQL. We can change it to:

```
mysql.default_socket = /var/lib/mysql/mysql.sock
```

However, to be sure, we must find the exact location of this socket.

Named Pipe Problem (Windows)

This is a problem similar to the above, but on Windows. It can be solved by adjusting `mysql.default_socket` with the correct named pipe used to connect locally to a MySQL server. For example:

```
mysql.default_socket = MySQL
```

Error # 2003: The Server is not Responding

If the MySQL server is not on the same machine as the web server, and is not answering, phpMyAdmin (starting with version 2.6.0) detects the fact and reports it, accordingly.

MySQL Said: Access Denied

This error can be solved when we understand the relevant login parameters.

When Using http Authentication

We cannot use the web server security mechanism based on a `.htaccess` file and the `http` authentication in `config.inc.php` together. A workaround is to use `cookie` as the authentication type instead of `http`.

When Using http, cookie, or config Authentication

The host parameter in `config.inc.php` must match the host defined in the user access privileges. Sometimes, a system administrator may create an account authorizing user `bill` and host `localhost`. If we try to use `127.0.0.1` host in `config.inc.php`, it will be rejected by MySQL, even though it points to the same machine. The same problem can occur if we try the real name of the machine (`mysql.domain.com`) and the definition has been made for `localhost`.

Access Denied ... "using password: NO"

If the message ends with **using password: NO**, it means that we are not transmitting a password, and MySQL is rejecting this login attempt. The password value may not have been set in `config.inc.php`.

Access Denied ... "using password: YES"

A password is transmitted, but the host/username/password combination has been rejected by MySQL.

Warning: Cannot Add Header Information

This problem is caused by some characters (such as blank lines or spaces) being present in `config.inc.php`, either before the `<?php` tag at the beginning, or after the `?>` tag at the end. We should remove these with an editor that supports `.php` files (as discussed in Chapter 2).

MySQL Said: Error 127, Table Must Be Repaired

In the left panel, we click on the database name. In the right panel, we select the name of the table for which there is an error (using the relevant checkbox). We then choose **Repair** from the lower drop-down list. More details are available in Chapter 10.

BLOB Column Used in Key Specification without a Key Length

MySQL requires that an index set on a **BLOB** column be limited in size. The simple index creation technique available when creating a column does not permit the size to be specified, so we need to create the column without an index. We then come back to the **Structure** page, and use the **Create an index** dialog to choose the **BLOB** column and set a size for the index.

IIS: No Input File Specified

This is a permission problem. **Internet Information Server (IIS)** must be able to read our scripts. As the server is running under the user IUSR_machinename, we have to do the following:

- Right-click on the folder where we installed phpMyAdmin.
- Choose **Properties.**
- Click on **Add** under the **Security** tab, and select the IUSR_machinename user from the list.
- Ensure that this user has read permission to the directory.

A "404: page not found" Error when Modifying a Row

This happens when the $cfg['PmaAbsoluteUri'] parameter in config.inc.php is not set properly. Chapter 2 explains how to take care of this parameter.

Other Problems

Here, we cover solutions to problems that do not show up on screen as a specific error message.

Blank Page or Weird Characters

By default, phpMyAdmin uses output buffering and compression techniques to speed up the transmission of results to the browser. These techniques can interfere with other components of the web server, causing display troubles. We can set $cfg['OBGzip'] to FALSE in config.inc.php. This should solve the problem.

Not Being Able to Create a Database

No privileges appears next to the **Create database** dialog on the **Home** page if phpMyAdmin detects that the account used to log in does not have the permissions to create a database. This situation occurs frequently on hosted servers where the system administrator prefers to create one database for each customer.

If we are not on a hosted server, this message simply reflects the fact that we do not have the global **CREATE** privilege, nor any **CREATE** privilege on a wildcard database specification.

Problems Importing Large Files or Uploading Large BLOB Files

Usually, these problems indicate that we have hit a limit during the transfer. Chapter 8 explains these limits and the recommended course of action. As a last resort solution, we might have to split our large text files. (Search the Internet for **file splitters**.)

MySQL Root Password Lost

The MySQL manual explains the general solution at
`http://www.mysql.com/doc/en/Resetting_permissions.html`.

The solution involves stopping the MySQL server, restarting it with the special option, **skip-grant-tables** (that basically starts the server without security). The way to stop and restart the server depends on the server platform used. Then, we can connect to the server from phpMyAdmin as a superuser (like root), and any password. The next step is to change root's password. (See Chapter 17.) Then we can stop the MySQL server and restart it using normal procedures. (Security will become active again.)

Duplicate Field Names when Creating a Table

Here is a curious symptom: when we try to create a table containing, for example, one field named **FIELD1** of type **VARCHAR(15)**, it looks like phpMyAdmin has sent a command to create two identical fields named **FIELD1**. The problem is not caused by phpMyAdmin, but by the environment. In this case, the Apache web server seems well configured to run PHP scripts, when in fact, it is not. However, this bug only appears for some scripts.

The problem occurs when two different (and conflicting) sets of directives are used in the Apache configuration file:

```
SetOutputFilter PHP
SetInputFilter PHP
```

...and:

```
AddType application/x-httpd-php .php
```

These sets of directives may be in two different Apache configuration files, so they are difficult to notice. The recommended way is to use AddType, so we just have to put comments on the other lines, as shown in the following snippet, and restart Apache:

```
#SetOutputFilter PHP
#SetInputFilter PHP
```

Authentication Window Displayed More Than Once

This problem occurs when we try to start phpMyAdmin with a URL other than the one set in $cfg['PmaAbsoluteUri']. For example, a server may have more than one name, or we may be trying to use the IP address instead of the name.

Column Size Changed by phpMyAdmin

MySQL itself sometimes decides to change the column type and size, for a more efficient column definition. This happens mostly with **CHAR** and **VARCHAR**.

Seeing Many Databases that Are Not Ours

This problem occurs mostly after an upgrade to MySQL 4. The automatic server upgrade procedure gives the global privileges **CREATE TEMPORARY TABLES**, **SHOW DATABASES**, and **LOCK TABLES** to all users. These privileges also enable users to see the names of all the databases (but not their tables) until we upgrade the grant tables, as described in the MySQL manual. If the users do not need these privileges, we can revoke them, and they will only see the databases to which they are entitled.

Not Being Able to Store a Value Greater Than 127

This is normal if we have defined a column of type **TINYINT**, since 127 is the maximum value for this column type. Similar problems may arise with other numeric column types. Changing the type to **INT**, expands the available range of values.

Seeking Support

The starting point for support is the home page `http://www.phpmyadmin.net`, which has sections about documentation and support (feedback). There you will find links to the discussion forums, and to various trackers such as:

- Bugs tracker
- Feature requests tracker
- Translations tracker
- Patches tracker
- Support tracker

FAQs

The `Documentation.html` file, which is part of the product, contains a lengthy FAQ section with numbered questions and answers. It is recommended to peruse this FAQ section as the first source for help.

Help Forums

The development team recommends that you first use the product's forums to search for the problem encountered, and then start a new forum discussion before opening a bug report.

Creating a SourceForge Account

Creating a (free) SourceForge user account and using it for posting on forums is highly recommended. This enables better tracking of questions and answers.

Choosing the Thread Title

It is important to choose the summary title carefully when you start a new forum thread. Titles like "Help me!", "Help a newbie!", "Problem", or "phpMyAdmin error!" are difficult to deal with because answers are threaded to this title, and further reference becomes problematic. Better titles would be "Import with UploadDir", "User can't but root can login" or "Server not responding".

Reading the Answers

As people will read and almost always answer your question, giving feedback in the forum about the answers can really help the person who answered, and others who have the same problem.

Support Tracker

This is another place to ask for support. Also, if we have submitted a bug report, which is in fact a support request, the report will be moved to the support tracker. With your SourceForge user account, you will be notified of this tracker change.

Bug Tracker

In this tracker, we see bugs that have not yet been fixed, plus bugs that have been fixed for the next version. (This is to avoid getting duplicate bug reports.)

Environment Description

As developers will be trying to reproduce the problem mentioned, it helps to describe your environment. This description can be short, but should contain the following items:

- phpMyAdmin version (the team, however, expects that it is the current stable version)
- Web server name and version
- PHP version
- MySQL version
- Browser name and version

Usually, specifying the operating system on which the server or the client are running is not necessary, unless we notice that the bug pertains to only one OS. For example, FAQ 5.1 describes a problem where the user could not create a table having more than 14 fields. This happens only under Windows 98.

Bug Description

We should give a precise description of what happens (including any error message, the expected results, and the effective results we get). Reports are easily managed if they describe only one problem per bug report (unless the problems are clearly linked).

Sometimes, it might help to attach a short export file to the bug report, to help developers reproduce the problem. Screenshots are welcome.

Contributing to the Project

Since 1998, hundreds of people have contributed translations, code for new features, suggestions, and bug fixes.

The Code Base

The development team maintains an evolving code base from which they periodically issue releases. A paragraph in the home page downloads section describes how to use Subversion to get the latest version in development. (This can be also done by downloading the Subversion snapshot.) A contribution (translation update, patch, new feature) will be considered with a higher priority if it refers to the latest code base, and not to an ancient phpMyAdmin version.

Translation Updates

Taking a look at the project's current list of 54 languages, we notice that they are not equally well maintained. The details about translations are available at http://cihar.com/phpMyAdmin/translations/. We can try to join the official translator for a particular language, to propose corrections to/or translations of recently added messages. If this person does not answer, we can send our modifications to the translation tracker, inside a compressed (.zip) file.

Patches

The development team can manage patches more easily if they are submitted in the form of a context diff against the current code base, with an explanation of the problem solved or the new feature achieved. Contributors are officially credited in Documentation.html.

Future phpMyAdmin Versions

Here are the points that the development team is considering for the next versions:

- Improved support of MySQL's new features
- User preferences in permanent storage
- Internal code improvements

In particular, version 3 will most likely support these minimum versions: PHP 5.2 and MySQL 5. Also, this version will remove the support of non-UTF-8 language files.

Summary

In this chapter, we saw how to prevent problems with a properly configured server, and where to ask for help. We also explained some common errors and suggested solutions. Moreover, the *Contributing to the Project* section explained how to help in order to improve phpMyAdmin.

Index

A

authentication, phpMyAdmin
  about 33
  authentication types 33
  control user 33
  cookie authentication 35, 36
  HTTP authentication 34
  logout 34
  password storage, cookie authentication 35
  signon 36

B

BLOB fields
  about 101
  binary contents upload 102
bookmarks
  creating 220, 221
  default initial query 224
  executing 223
  features 219
  from pma_bookmark, executing 226
  manipulating 223
  multi-query bookmarks 222
  parameterized bookmarks, creating 225
  parameters 225
  parameter value, passing to bookmark 226
  public bookmarks 223, 224
  retrieving 222
  storing 221, 222
browse mode
  about 75
  color-marking rows 81
  column length, limiting 81, 82
  customizing 83

  data, sorting 80
  distinct values, browsing 82
  navigation bar 77-79
  query results, operations 80
  query results, sorting 80
  row background color, changing 81
  SQL query links 76
bug tracker, phpMyAdmin
  about 305
  bug description 305
  bug tracker 305
  environment description 305

C

cell 239
character set
  about 253
  choosing, MySQL version prior to 4.1.x 256
  effective character set, MySQL version 4.1.x 260
  exporting 263
  importing and exporting 257
  MySQL version, prior to 4.1.x 255
  switching, MySQL version prior to 4.1.x 256
collation
  about 253
  MySQL version 4.1.x 258
column-commenting
  about 192, 193
  automatic migration 193
column criteria, multi-table query generator
  columns in result, displaying 210
  criteria columns, adjusting 215
  criteria rows, adjusting 214

right panels 267, 268
uses 266

W

Web 7
Web applications 7
Web server
upload directory 147, 148

X

XML format, database export 129

Y

YAML format, database export 132

Thank you for buying
Mastering phpMyAdmin 2.11 for Effective MySQL Management

Packt Open Source Project Royalties

When we sell a book written on an Open Source project, we pay a royalty directly to that project. Therefore by purchasing Mastering phpMyAdmin 2.11 for Effective MySQL Management, Packt will have given some of the money received to the phpMyAdmin Project.

In the long term, we see ourselves and you — customers and readers of our books — as part of the Open Source ecosystem, providing sustainable revenue for the projects we publish on. Our aim at Packt is to establish publishing royalties as an essential part of the service and support a business model that sustains Open Source.

If you're working with an Open Source project that you would like us to publish on, and subsequently pay royalties to, please get in touch with us.

Writing for Packt

We welcome all inquiries from people who are interested in authoring. Book proposals should be sent to authors@packtpub.com. If your book idea is still at an early stage and you would like to discuss it first before writing a formal book proposal, contact us; one of our commissioning editors will get in touch with you.

We're not just looking for published authors; if you have strong technical skills but no writing experience, our experienced editors can help you develop a writing career, or simply get some additional reward for your expertise.

About Packt Publishing

Packt, pronounced 'packed', published its first book "Mastering phpMyAdmin for Effective MySQL Management" in April 2004 and subsequently continued to specialize in publishing highly focused books on specific technologies and solutions.

Our books and publications share the experiences of your fellow IT professionals in adapting and customizing today's systems, applications, and frameworks. Our solution-based books give you the knowledge and power to customize the software and technologies you're using to get the job done. Packt books are more specific and less general than the IT books you have seen in the past. Our unique business model allows us to bring you more focused information, giving you more of what you need to know, and less of what you don't.

Packt is a modern, yet unique publishing company, which focuses on producing quality, cutting-edge books for communities of developers, administrators, and newbies alike. For more information, please visit our website: www.PacktPub.com.

Drupal 5 Themes

ISBN: 978-1-847191-82-3   Paperback: 250 pages

Create a new theme for your Drupal website with a clean layout and powerful CSS styling

1. Learn to create new Drupal 5 Themes

2. No experience of Drupal 5 theming required

3. Set up and configure themes

4. Understand Drupal 5's themeable functions

Mastering Joomla! 1.5 Extension and Framework Development

ISBN: 978-1-847192-82-0   Paperback: 380 pages

The Professional Guide to Programming Joomla!

1. In-depth guide to programming Joomla!

2. Design and build secure and robust components, modules and plugins

3. Includes a comprehensive reference to the major areas of the Joomla! framework

Please check **www.PacktPub.com** for information on our titles

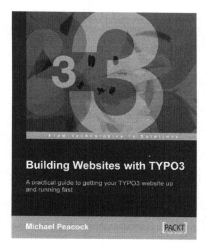

Building Websites with TYPO3

ISBN: 978-1-847191-11-3   Paperback: 250 pages

A practical guide to getting your TYPO3 website up and running fast

1. A practical step-by-step tutorial to creating your TYPO3 website

2. Install and configure TYPO3

3. Master all the important aspects of TYPO3, including the backend, the frontend, content management, and templates

4. Gain hands-on experience by developing an example site through the book

Mastering TypoScript: TYPO3 Website, Template, and Extension Development

ISBN: 1-904811-97-3   Paperback: 400 pages

A complete guide to understanding and using TypoScript, TYPO3's powerful configuration language.

1. Powerful control and customization using TypoScript

2. Covers templates, extensions, admin, interface, menus, and database control

3. You don't need to be an experienced PHP developer to use the power of TypoScript

Please check **www.PacktPub.com** for information on our titles

Made in the USA